A Guide to the Listing, Assessment, and Taxation of Property in North Carolina

A GUIDE TO THE

Listing, Assessment, and Taxation of Property

IN NORTH CAROLINA

Shea Riggsbee Denning

UNC
SCHOOL OF
GOVERNMENT

The School of Government at the University of North Carolina at Chapel Hill works to improve the lives of North Carolinians by engaging in practical scholarship that helps public officials and citizens understand and improve state and local government. Established in 1931 as the Institute of Government, the School provides educational, advisory, and research services for state and local governments. The School of Government is also home to a nationally ranked graduate program in public administration and specialized centers focused on information technology, environmental finance, and civic education for youth.

As the largest university-based local government training, advisory, and research organization in the United States, the School of Government offers up to 200 courses, seminars, and specialized conferences for more than 12,000 public officials each year. In addition, faculty members annually publish approximately fifty books, book chapters, bulletins, and other reference works related to state and local government. Each day that the General Assembly is in session, the School produces the Daily Bulletin, which reports on the day's activities for members of the legislature and others who need to follow the course of legislation.

The Master of Public Administration Program is a full-time, two-year program that serves up to sixty students annually. It consistently ranks among the best public administration graduate programs in the country, particularly in city management. With courses ranging from public policy analysis to ethics and management, the program educates leaders for local, state, and federal governments and nonprofit organizations.

Operating support for the School of Government's programs and activities comes from many sources, including state appropriations, local government membership dues, private contributions, publication sales, course fees, and service contracts. Visit www.sog.unc.edu or call 919.966.5381 for more information on the School's courses, publications, programs, and services.

Printed in the United States of America

13 12 11 10 09   1 2 3 4 5

ISBN 978-1-56011-602-8

♾ This publication is printed on permanent, acid-free paper in compliance with the North Carolina General Statutes.

♻ Printed on recycled paper

Acknowledgments

The author expresses her appreciation to Professor Joseph S. Ferrell, who has served as a faculty member of the School of Government for more than forty years and who is currently serving as secretary to the faculty of the University. Professor Ferrell's previous work and writings in this field provided the foundation for and are reflected in this publication.

Contents

1 History and Characteristics of Property Taxation in North Carolina and the Machinery Act 1

1.1 History of Property Taxation in North Carolina 4

1.2 Constitutional Provisions Governing Taxation 8

1.3 The Machinery Act 11

1.4 Nature of the Property Tax 12

2 Administration of the Property Tax 19

2.1 Terms and Qualifications of the County Tax Assessor 22

2.2 The Property Tax Calendar 24

2.3 Setting the Tax Rate 27

3 The Listing of Property for Taxation 35

3.1 Categories of Property: Real and Personal 37

3.2 The Mechanics of Listing 41

3.3. Listing Personal Property 47

3.4 What the Abstract Must Contain 52

3.5 Listing Aids 54

3.6 Due Process Requirements 57

3.7 Listing Period 59

3.8 Place for Listing 61

3.9 Special Situs Rules 62

3.10 Applications for Exemption, Exclusion, or Other Special Tax Status 66

3.11 Discovery of Unlisted Property 67

3.12 Public Records Law 70

4 Appraisal and Assessment of Property 89

4.1 Appraising Real Property 92

4.2 Appraising Personal Property 98

4.3 Assessment of Public Service Company Property 100

5 Review and Appeal 111

5.1 Notification regarding Applications for Exemption or Exclusion 113

5.2 Notification of the Assessed Value of Property 114

5.3 Review of Assessments 114

5.4 Changes to the Value of Real Property in a Nonreappraisal Year 136

6 Classified Motor Vehicles 145

6.1 Classified Motor Vehicles 148

6.2 Listing and Assessment of Registered Classified Motor Vehicles 149

6.3 Amended Article 22A, Effective 2011 159

7 Exemptions and Exclusions 165

7.1 Exemptions 167

7.2 Exclusions 187

7.3 Applying for Special Tax Treatment 194

7.4 Discovery of Property Entitled to Exemption or Exclusion 198

7.5 Special Rules for Classified Motor Vehicles 198

7.6 Review of Exempt Property 199

7.7 Assessment at Present-Use Value 200

8 Release and Refund 225

8.1 Action by the Governing Board 227

8.2 Procedures for Requesting a Refund or Release 231

Appendix An Outline of Property Tax Exemptions and Exclusions 233

Index 275

A Guide to the Listing, Assessment, and Taxation of Property in North Carolina

1 History and Characteristics of Property Taxation in North Carolina and the Machinery Act

1.1 History of Property Taxation in North Carolina 4

1.2 Constitutional Provisions Governing Taxation 8

1.2.1 Taxation for Public Purposes Only 8

1.2.2 The Power to Exempt and Classify 9

1.2.3 Uniform Rule Requirement and Service Districts 10

1.3 The Machinery Act 11

1.4 Nature of the Property Tax 12

1 History and Characteristics of Property Taxation in North Carolina and the Machinery Act

Property taxes are one of the oldest forms of taxation in the United States and have been central among revenue sources in North Carolina since the early days of statehood.[1] Before 1931, property taxes were levied by the state as well as by local governments. Now, such taxes are levied only by cities, counties, and special districts. While reliance on the property tax has declined dramatically since local governments were first authorized to levy local retail sales taxes in 1971,[2] property taxes remain an important revenue source for cities and counties, comprising about 20 percent of total city revenues and 40 percent of county revenues.[3] Indeed, property taxes comprise the single largest source of revenue for counties in North Carolina. For municipalities, property taxes are the largest source of revenue other than fees for utility services. Unlike revenues generated from utilities such as water and sewer, which generally pay only for the service provided, property taxes paid to local governments subsidize all types of government functions and services, from schools to health departments to jails to trash disposal.

Both real and personal property are subject to taxation in North Carolina. Real property includes land, buildings, and permanent fixtures, as well as rights and privileges pertaining to land, such as mineral or forestry rights. Personal property includes all other property, both tangible and intangible, that is not permanently affixed to land, although most types of intangible personal property are exempt from property taxation in North Carolina

Property taxes are said to be *in rem*, from the Latin phrase meaning "on the thing," because they are levied upon the property itself, unlike *in personam* taxes, such as income taxes, which are levied "on the person." Notwithstanding the in rem nature of the property tax, however, property owners who fail to pay property taxes are personally liable for the amount of the taxes.

1.1 History of Property Taxation in North Carolina[4]

While property taxes were an important revenue source for many northern colonies during the colonial period, capitation taxes imposed on citizens based on an established amount per citizen, known as poll taxes, provided the major source of revenue for colonial and county governments in North Carolina.[5] Two explanations have been offered for the state's reliance on the poll tax: First, the eastern landowners who controlled North Carolina's colonial assembly opposed a system of property taxes that would have placed upon them the lion's share of the tax burden. Because the poll tax was levied on every male of a certain age, the large landowners' share of the tax burden was considerably less than it would have been under a property tax regime. Second, the Crown's unpopular and poorly administered system of levying quit-rents, an annual charge per acre of land, may have rendered the levy of property taxes a practical and political impossibility.

While the eastern landowners retained control under the state government established by the North Carolina Constitution of 1776, their power waned during the Revolutionary War, when common citizens were called upon to fight for independence. In 1777 the General Assembly enacted a tax system in which a property tax levied on nearly every type of property became the principal tax, and the poll tax was relegated to secondary status. This new system of taxation did not survive the war. Within a few years, intangible property, such as stocks, bonds, and bank accounts, was taxed at a fraction of its value. Subsequently, livestock and improvements to real property were exempted from the tax base.

The Revenue Act of 1784 further eroded the property tax base by providing for the taxation of all rural land at a set amount per acre, while town lots were taxed based on value. The act also exempted personal property from taxation. As a result, by 1812, the poll tax produced twice as much revenue as the property tax.

The North Carolina Constitution of 1835 ushered in a new system of taxation based upon ability to pay. Ad valorem taxes on real property and poll taxes were supplemented by taxes on income, inheritance, luxuries, and capital of merchants and corporations, as well as numerous license taxes imposed for the privilege of engaging in business. By 1854, the income tax produced more revenue than property taxes on real property.

During the Civil War, the General Assembly enacted legislation taxing most forms of property according to value, including improvements to land, household furniture and other personal property, and intangible personal property. This comported with the nationwide movement toward uniform and universal taxation. The state constitution adopted in 1868, after the Civil War, provided for a poll tax on males between the ages of twenty-one and fifty to be levied at the state and local level and required that 75 percent of poll tax revenues be used for education and 25 percent for care of the poor. The rate of the poll tax was set at the equivalent of the tax on $300 in property, not to exceed $2. The state constitution also mandated uniform and universal taxation of property. Local governments, however, were permitted to levy taxes without voter approval only for necessary expenses. The provision equalizing and limiting the rate for poll taxes based upon the rate of the property tax effectively limited the combined rate at which state and county property taxes could be levied to 66 $^2/_3$ cents per $100 of value, or, stated in terms of the poll tax, $2 per $300.

Notwithstanding the stated rate limitation, by 1914, the property tax rate in nearly every county exceeded 66 $^2/_3$ cents per hundred.[6] This is so because the North Carolina Supreme Court interpreted the equation and limitation clause to apply only to the levy of taxes for general purposes and not to taxes levied for a special purpose.

The 1868 constitution also required the General Assembly to provide a general and uniform system of schools for four months of the year. Counties were required to levy poll and property taxes sufficient to produce revenues that would, when combined with state revenues, support the newly mandated school terms.

The mandate for school funding became more difficult for counties to satisfy after state courts ruled that schools were not a "necessary expense."[7] Thus, for a time, counties could not levy property taxes to fund schools without first obtaining voter approval. Convincing voters to vote to increase their own tax burden was then, as it is now, a difficult feat. In 1927 the North Carolina Supreme Court changed its view on the matter, holding that counties, acting as administrative agencies of the state, could levy taxes necessary to maintain schools for the constitutionally required term without seeking voter approval.[8]

Between 1900 and 1921, taxpayers were required to list property and income with township list takers every four years. List takers, who were appointed every four years to record property for purposes of state and local taxation, primarily relied upon taxpayers' honesty in reporting the nature and extent of property owned and its value. List takers worked separately from one another and followed no uniform guides for estimating value. Though their work was reviewed by the county, that review was largely a formality. Neither list takers nor any other county officials were charged with the duty of inspecting property to determine the accuracy of the information reported. The honor system predictably led to the underreporting and undervaluation of taxable property. The low assessments that resulted required localities to increase the rate of property taxes in order to obtain additional funds. Due to the constitutional rate limitation on property taxes, local officials were required to obtain voter approval to levy taxes at a higher rate. The average countywide property tax rate in 1919 was $1.51. By way of contrast, the average countywide tax rate in the 2006–07 fiscal year was 65 cents.[9] The high rates in the early twentieth century exacerbated taxpayers' undervaluation of property and their omission of property from tax lists.

In 1919, at the urging of then-Governor Thomas W. Bickett, the General Assembly passed the Revaluation Act, which mandated a statewide revaluation of all property. The State Tax Commission, which had been created in 1901, was charged with supervising the revaluation. The state commission appointed a tax supervisor in each county to coordinate and oversee the work of list takers in preparation for the 1920 revaluation. The assessed value of property tripled in the revaluation of 1919–20, and more than one million acres of land were added to the tax lists. The tax supervisor ultimately gained a permanent role in the state's system of ad valorem taxation. While the duties and powers of the supervisor expanded, the importance of the list taker declined. The position of tax supervisor evolved into the modern-day office of tax assessor.

In 1921 the General Assembly enacted a state-administered corporate and personal income tax and abandoned the property tax to local governments. Except for a brief period during the Great Depression, property taxes have remained strictly a source of local, rather than state, revenue. The state's abandonment of property tax revenues in 1921 marked an important and lasting shift in the financing model for state and local governments in North Carolina: revenues from the property tax fund local government functions, while statewide sources of revenue, such as the income tax, gasoline tax, and state retail sales tax, are used to pay for state programs.

Another significant change in North Carolina government financing took place in the early 1930s, when the state assumed responsibility for financing schools, roads, and prisons—three central governmental functions that had previously been relegated to counties. The state funded these programs by levying a 3 percent state retail sales tax, as well as a tax on alcoholic beverages, and by increasing franchise and income tax rates. North Carolina's prescient shift to a centralized model of funding based upon income and sales tax revenue rather than on property taxes enabled the state to meet demands for increased public services through reliance on rising revenues from the income tax, without having to dramatically increase tax rates or impose additional taxes.

Along with the constitutional mandate for a general property tax, the egalitarian principle of uniform and universal taxation of property reflected in the 1868 constitution was effectively abandoned in 1936 upon the enactment of a constitutional amendment permitting the General Assembly to classify property for assessment at a reduced rate or for exclusion from the tax base. A 1961 amendment ended the practice of classifying property for exclusion or reduced taxation through local acts that applied only to a particular city or county by requiring that the classification power be exercised only on a statewide basis. The General Assembly has exercised its power to classify property on numerous occasions. The classification with the largest financial impact permits the taxation of certain agricultural property based upon its rental value as agricultural property rather than its market value based upon its highest and best use.

The 1971 amendments to the North Carolina Constitution eliminated the constitutional limitation on the tax rate and gave the General Assembly authority to decide when voter approval would be required for property tax levies.

The history of the property tax undoubtedly influences both taxpayer aversion to and local government reliance upon this significant revenue source. In recent years, local officials sensitive to voters' negative views of the property tax have sought authorization from the General Assembly to raise revenue from other sources, including sales taxes, fees imposed upon users of particular services, availability fees levied at a flat rate upon all occupied dwellings, land transfer taxes, occupancy taxes, taxes on prepared meals, impact taxes, and motor vehicle fees. At the same time, property owners have lobbied the General Assembly for exclusion or reduced taxation of business inventory, intangible property, residences owned by elderly persons, agricultural property, and other special categories of property. Beginning in the 1980s and continuing to the present day, the legislature has responded to constituent concerns by excluding from the tax base or providing reduced taxation of numerous categories of property. The granting of such exemptions and the lowering of tax burdens on certain types of property has eroded the constitutional mandate of uniformity—and thus equity—in taxation.

1.2 Constitutional Provisions Governing Taxation

1.2.1 Taxation for Public Purposes Only

Article V of the North Carolina Constitution establishes the ground rules for the levying of any state or local tax, and a review of its provisions is a logical starting point for a discussion of the levy of property taxes by local governments. The constitution permits the power of taxation to be used "for public purposes only."[10] Thus a city or county wishing to pay for a program, function, or activity with property tax revenues must ensure that the program, function, or activity serves a public purpose. This analysis requires more than simply determining whether the expenditure somehow benefits more than a limited segment of the community. A public benefit that is merely incidental to a principal benefit for a private party does not satisfy the public-purpose test. Conversely, the levying of a tax primarily intended to benefit the community at large by bestowing a benefit upon a private party does not render the tax unconstitutional. The North Carolina Supreme Court has considered both types of expenditures.

In 1947 the state supreme court struck down as unconstitutional a local act that permitted the Town of Tarboro to issue bonds and levy taxes to construct a hotel that the town planned to own and maintain.[11] While recognizing that the proposed hotel would promote business in Tarboro and enhance property values, the court held that such benefits were too incidental to justify the expenditure of public funds for what was essentially a private business. Because the cost of constructing the hotel was not a public purpose, the court concluded that the General Assembly exceeded its authority in authorizing the expenditure of tax revenues for the construction of a municipal hotel. In reaching its conclusion, the court listed many types of expenditures that fell within the definition of public purposes, including streets, sidewalks, bridges, water, light and sewerage plants, municipal buildings, auditoriums, hospitals, playgrounds, parks, railroads, armories, fairs, and airports.

Consideration of the Town of Tarboro case in the modern era of economic incentive grants raises the question of whether tax revenues may be expended in incentive payments to private businesses, which are designed to lure the businesses to locate or expand in a particular jurisdiction. Are such incentive payments for a public purpose? The state supreme court answered this question affirmatively in a 1996 case resulting from a lawsuit filed by a private citizen, William Maready, against the City of Winston-Salem and Forsyth County.[12] Maready alleged that a state statute authorizing local governments to make economic development incentive grants to private businesses was unconstitutional because it violated the constitutional requirement that the power of taxation be used only for public purposes. Maready challenged twenty-four economic development incentive projects entered into by the city or county at a cost of $13 million, most of which was generated from property taxes. The city and county estimated that these programs resulted in a $240-million increase in the tax base and the creation of 5,500 new jobs.

The state supreme court sided with the city and county, determining that the incentive payments were made to spur economic development, which had long been recognized as a proper governmental function, in order to further the general economic welfare of city and county residents. In distinguishing a 1968 opinion in which it struck down a statute that authorized the issuance of industrial revenue bonds to finance the construction of facilities for private industry, the supreme court explained the incongruity of preventing cities and counties that expend large sums on humanitarian and social programs "from promoting the provision of jobs for the unemployed, an increase in the tax base, and the prevention of economic stagnation."[13]

1.2.2 The Power to Exempt and Classify

A constitutional provision dating from Article V, Section 2(3), of the North Carolina Constitution of 1868 exempts from taxation property belonging to the state, counties, and municipal corporations. The provision further authorizes the General Assembly to exempt from taxation cemeteries; property held for educational, scientific, literary, cultural, charitable, or religious purposes; personal property valued at no more than $300; and $1,000 in property held and used as the place of residence of the owner. As previously noted, the constitution was subsequently amended to require that every such exemption apply statewide and be made by general law uniformly applicable in every county, city, or special district. Only the General Assembly may grant exemptions. Statutes enacted pursuant to the General Assembly's power to exempt property are codified in the Machinery Act at Sections 105-278.1 through 105-278.8 of the North Carolina General Statutes.[14]

The General Assembly gained the exclusive power to classify property for taxation in a provision added to the state constitution in 1936. The constitution requires that all such classifications be made by general law uniformly applicable in every county, city, town, and other unit of local government and that each class must be taxed by uniform rule.

The granting, in 1936, of the power to classify property rendered largely meaningless the permissible exemptions clause dating from 1868. This is because the General Assembly may enact a general law designating a certain type of property as a special class and then exclude that class from taxation.

1.2.3 Uniform Rule Requirement and Service Districts

The uniform rule requirement mandates uniformity in the tax rate as well as in the mode of assessment. This uniformity must be coextensive with the territory to which it applies. Thus a local tax, such as the property tax, must be based upon rates and standards of assessment that apply uniformly throughout the city, county, or special or service district in which the tax is levied.[15] As a practical matter, the General Assembly has enacted legislation requiring that all property, other than certain public service company property and property located in a development financing district, be assessed for taxation at its true value or use value (in the case of certain agricultural, horticultural, or forestland property).[16] Moreover, the Machinery Act provides that the county assessor's assessment of all property other than public service company system property, which is assessed by the state Department of Revenue, applies to all cities and all special and service districts within the county.[17] An exception applies to property located in a city that straddles two or more counties. The governing board for such a city may appoint a city assessor to appraise and assess city property.[18]

Given the constitutional requirement that the mode of assessment and rate of taxation be uniform throughout a taxing district, it would be necessary, absent specific constitutional authorization, to establish a special district—a separate unit of local government—in order to levy taxes at increased rates in defined territorial areas within a particular taxing unit. A provision added to the state constitution in 1973, however, permits the General Assembly to enact laws authorizing the governing body of a taxing unit to define such a territorial area and to levy additional taxes within the area to provide for additional or greater services, facilities, or functions in the defined area.[19] The same year the constitution was so amended, the General Assembly enacted county and municipal service district acts, authorizing cities and counties to define territorial areas in which increased taxes may be levied to fund watershed improvement projects, beach erosion control, sewage systems, and other services.[20]

1.3 The Machinery Act

The Machinery Act, codified at Subchapter II of Chapter 105 of the General Statutes, sets forth the procedures for assessing and collecting property taxes. The title of the act dates from the time of a state-levied property tax. Before 1931, the General Assembly passed each session a Revenue Act, which levied the property tax, and a Machinery Act, which set forth the procedures for levying and collecting the tax.[21] A permanent Machinery Act, governing the assessment and collection of local property taxes, was enacted in 1939.[22] The 1939 version of the Machinery Act was overhauled in 1971. The 1971 Machinery Act, as modified by subsequent enactments of the General Assembly, remains in effect today. Because the Machinery Act has not been substantially amended in more than thirty years, and because technology, the World Wide Web, and the Internet have dramatically changed the way in which all business, including government business, is transacted and the way in which records are maintained, it is difficult to square all modern tax office operations with certain provisions of the Machinery Act.

All property, real and personal, within the jurisdiction of the state, is subject to taxation unless exempted from taxation by the state constitution or the General Assembly or unless classified by the General Assembly as a special class of property to be excluded from the tax base.[23] The Machinery Act divides property into two general types: *real* and *personal*. Land, buildings, improvements, permanent fixtures, and all rights belonging to land, along with residential manufactured homes situated on land owned by the owner of the manufactured home, are considered to be real property.[24] Property that does not satisfy the statutory definition of real property is classified as personal property.[25] Personal property is further subdivided into tangible property, such as motor vehicles, boats, and machinery, and intangible property, such as bank accounts, stocks, and bonds. All real and personal property is taxable unless specifically exempted or excluded from taxation. Thus taxation is the rule and exemption or exclusion the exception.[26] As previously noted, very little intangible property is subject to ad valorem taxation today. All one hundred counties and most cities levy property taxes. In fiscal year 2006–07, the average tax rate was 65 cents per $100 in value for counties and 44 cents per $100 for cities.[27] County tax rates ranged from 26 cents to $1.10 per $100, while city rates ranged from 2 to 82 cents per $100.[28]

1.4 Nature of the Property Tax

Neither the longevity of the taxation scheme nor its critical role in the financing of local government has been sufficient to insulate the tax from frequent and vociferous criticism.[29] And while taxes in general do not enjoy widespread popularity, property taxes in particular command disdain from the public and politicians in ways that many other state and local taxes do not.[30] Such criticism often increases in step with property values in a reappraisal year and with rates in a year in which those rates are increased.[31] However, in contrast with the flogging property taxes generally receive in the press and among the populace, they remain favored by many economists and other experts in public finance.[32]

Numerous reasons underlie the disconnect between the populace's and the professionals' perception of the tax. Undoubtedly, local government reliance on the property tax, combined with the tax's inherent ability to interfere with, and in some cases, jeopardize, the right to possess property—particularly residential property—have contributed to its unpopularity. Joan Youngman, senior fellow at the Lincoln Institute of Land Policy in Cambridge, Massachusetts, explored some of the reasons why property taxes are viewed as unfair in a 2002 article.[33] Youngman states that property taxes themselves are sometimes criticized as unfair when the fairness debate actually centers around the expenditure of tax proceeds, noting as an example the availability of greater property tax revenues in wealthier school districts.[34] In addition, Youngman opines that the relative simplicity of the tax may hurt its popularity, as the populace's exposure to the tax and ability to readily calculate its impact render the tax subject to increased scrutiny.[35] In contrast, sales taxes, which are collected in small amounts spread over hundreds, if not thousands, of transactions in a given year, are far less visible or readily calculated and thus often are a "politically palatable" replacement for the property tax.[36]

Youngman explores the long-running debate among economists as to whether property taxes are regressive, proportional, or progressive.[37] A tax is regressive if it consumes a larger percentage of the income of lower-income taxpayers than of those who earn a higher income.[38] A proportional tax consumes a constant percentage of income across different income levels, while a progressive tax consumes a higher percentage of income as income rises.[39] A large part of the debate hinges upon whether income is defined as long-term or permanent income or as annual income.[40] Youngman notes that because home purchases and housing decisions are long-term in nature and arguably reflect income or prospects for income over many years, this debate becomes particularly important when considering the economic impact of property taxes on residential property.[41]

Youngman separates economists' views of the economic impact of property taxes into three categories:[42]

1. The "old view," which considers taxes on land to be progressive based on the assumption that landholdings are concentrated among higher-income taxpayers and taxes on residential property to be regressive because housing expenditures are not thought to rise as rapidly as income
2. The "new view," which considers property taxes to be a part of a nationwide tax on wealth and capital that is progressive because capital is concentrated among high income households
3. The "benefit view," which considers property taxes to be the price paid for a bundle of local services (under this view, the economic burden can be determined only by comparing the tax paid to the benefit received)[43]

Youngman notes, however, that for the most part, the public debate about tax fairness does not employ technical economic terms.[44] Instead, public and political perception of the tax is influenced by factors such as the tax rate, the integrity of the assessment and collection processes, the ability to appeal tax assessment and collection determinations to an impartial body, and the way in which the tax base is defined.[45] The extent to which the tax levying scheme incorporates social values—for example, by exempting property owned by community, religious, and civic organizations or by affording special provisions of relief to certain classes of citizens, such as the elderly and disabled—also, in Youngman's view, affects the public's perception of its fairness.[46]

On the professional side of the debate, property taxes are popular because they "provide[] 'fiscal empowerment' to local governments," along with a stable source of revenue from one year to the next that keeps pace with the economy.[47] Moreover, substitute sources of funding, such as sales taxes and user charges, are less stable, more regressive, and less transparent.[48] Reductions in local services also may accompany property tax limits.[49]

It may not be possible to reconcile the economics with the politics. Professors Cornia and Walters, of the Romney Institute of Public Management at Brigham Young University, may have said it best:

> The reality . . . is that although the property tax is viewed positively by legal experts and economists, it has virtually no political traction. Policies to increase the property tax have taken a backseat to the more popular political issue of limiting the property tax. No one gets elected on the promise of using more property tax, but on promising to limit or reduce property tax.

Notes

1. Charles D. Liner, *The Evolution of North Carolina's State and Local Tax System, in* State and Local Government Relations in North Carolina 52, 53 (2d ed. 1995) (hereinafter *Evolution of North Carolina's Tax System*).

2. *Evolution of North Carolina's Tax System* at 62 (reporting that property taxes comprised 96.4 percent of local government revenue in 1970 but only 71.2 percent in 1992).

3. North Carolina Department of State Treasurer Memorandum No. 1098 (May 2008), *available at* www.treasurer.state.nc.us/lgc/LGCMemos/Memo1098.pdf (last visited Dec. 8, 2008) (hereinafter Memorandum No. 1098). The statewide summary information is available at www.nctreasurer.com/lgc/units/D_E.htm#ALLGROUP (counties) and www.nctreasurer.com/lgc/units/D_AG.htm (cities).

4. This section draws heavily on Charles D. Liner, *The Origins and Development of the North Carolina System of Taxation*, Popular Government, Summer 1979, at 41, and Liner's previously cited chapter, *Evolution of North Carolina's Tax System*.

5. S. Ry. Co. v. Bd. of Comm'rs of Buncombe County, 148 N.C. 248, 251–54, 61 S.E. 700, 701–02 (1908) (Clark, J. concurring) (discussing history and nature of poll taxes).

6. Moose v. Bd. of Comm'rs of Alexander County, 172 N.C. 419, 422, 90 S.E. 441, 446 (1916).

7. *See, e.g.*, Stephens Co. v. City of Charlotte, 172 N.C. 564, 90 S.E. 588 (1916).

8. Frazier v. Bd. of Comm'rs of Guilford County, 194 N.C. 49, 62, 138 S.E. 433, 439 (1927).

9. Memorandum No. 1098.

10. N.C. Const. art. V, § 2.

11. Nash v. Town of Tarboro, 227 N.C. 283, 42 S.E.2d 209 (1947).

12. Maready v. City of Winston-Salem, 342 N.C. 708, 467 S.E.2d 615 (1996).

13. *Id.* at 722, 467 S.E.2d at 624.

14. N.C. Gen. Stat. § 105-278.6A (hereinafter G.S.) is an exercise of the General Assembly's authority to *exclude*, rather than *exempt*, property from taxation.

15. Hajoca Corp. v. Clayton, 277 N.C. 560, 569, 178 S.E.2d 481, 487 (1971).

16. G.S. 105-284.

17. G.S. 105-284, -327, -328.

18. G.S. 105-328.

19. N.C. Const. art. V, § 2(4). *See also* David M. Lawrence, Local Government Finance in North Carolina § 1600, at 283–84 (2d ed. 1990) (discussing uniformity provision and constitutional provision authorizing creation of service districts).

20. G.S. 153A-301; 160A-536.

21. Joseph S. Ferrell, *A Taxpayer's Guide to Property Tax Revaluation,* Popular Government, Winter 1982, at 35.

22. N.C. Pub. Laws 1939, ch. 310.

23. G.S. 105-274.

24. G.S. 105-273(13).

25. G.S. 105-273(8), (14) (defining intangible and tangible personal property).

26. Albert Coates, *The Battle of Exemptions*, 19 N.C. L. Rev. 154, 165 (1940).

27. Memorandum No. 1098 at 4; North Carolina Department of State Treasurer Memorandum No. 1099 at 4 (May 19, 2008), *available at* www.nctreasurer.com/lgc/LGCMemos/Memo1099.pdf (last visited Dec. 8, 2008) (hereinafter Memorandum No. 1099).

28. Memorandum No. 1098 at 10; Memorandum No. 1099 at 31.

29. *See* Joan Youngman, *Enlarging the Property Tax Debate—Regressivity and Fairness*, 26 St. Tax Notes 45 (Oct. 7, 2002) (hereinafter *Enlarging the Property Tax Debate*) (citing articles and commentary published in various U.S. newspapers and other publications characterizing property taxes as regressive and noting that in many cases use of the term " 'regressive' " is simply a dramatic way of calling the tax unfair); *see also* Jon Shure, *Tax cut? OK, now let's get serious; Income tax is much more closely tied than property tax to ability to pay. Raising a fair tax to lower an unfair tax is a good idea*, Philadelphia Inquirer, March 1, 2007, at B2.

30. *See* Shea Riggsbee Denning & Gary A. Wagner, *The Property Tax*, *in* County and Municipal Government in North Carolina (David M. Lawrence ed., UNC School of Government 2007), *available at* www.sog.unc.edu (citing results of national surveys conducted annually by the U.S. Advisory Commission on Intergovernmental Relations from 1972 to 1994 in which local property taxes were perceived by the general public to be the "least fair" of the selected taxes in seven of the surveys and the second "least fair" tax (trailing only the federal income tax) in all other surveys).

31. *See Enlarging the Property Tax Debate* at 50 (noting the "actions that promote progressivity and accuracy in taxation, such as long-delayed revaluations, may be considered unfair when they upset settled expectations of property owners).

32. A 1994 survey of National Tax Association members repeated a 1934 Tax Policy League survey of senior American public finance professors. One question asked, "Should there be a retention of property tax as a major source of local revenue?" In 1934, 86 percent of respondents agreed. In 1994, 85 percent agreed. *Enlarging the Property Tax Debate* at 50.

33. *Enlarging the Property Tax Debate* at 45–52.

34. *Id.* at 50.

35. *Id.*

36. *Id.*

37. *Id.* at 47–49.

38. *Enlarging the Property Tax Debate* at 46.

39. *Id.*

40. *Id.* at 47.

41. *Id.*

42. *Id.* at 47–48.

43. *Id.* at 48.

44. *Enlarging the Property Tax Debate* at 49.

45. *Id.*

46. *Id.*

47. J. Fred Giertz, *The Property Tax Bound*, 59:3 NAT'L TAX J. 695, 700, 703 (2006) (finding that when compared to the corporate income tax, individual income tax, and sales tax based upon 25 years of data in Illinois, the property tax base had the highest growth rate and the lowest standard deviation in growth rates); see also Gary C. Cornia & Lawrence C. Walters, *Full Disclosure: Controlling Property Tax Increases During Periods of Increasing Housing Values*, 59:3 NAT'L TAX J. 735, 736 (2006) (hereinafter *Full Disclosure*) (opining that the property tax has a number of attributes that make efforts to retain and strengthen it worthwhile; the property tax provides state and local governments with fiscal stability and fiscal autonomy).

48. *Full Disclosure* at 738 (citing research that "lower property taxes appear to result in more revenue from narrow excise taxes and user charges and that such sources of funding are potentially less stable, more regressive, and less transparent"); *Enlarging the Property Tax Debate* at 46, 50 (characterizing sales tax as "much less visible than property or income taxes" and explaining that "a flat-rate general sales tax will be regressive if low-income consumers spend a greater percentage of their incomes on taxable purchases than do wealthier households able to save and invest more").

49. Thomas A. Downs & David N. Figlio, *Do Tax and Expenditure Limits Provide a Free Lunch? Evidence on the Link Between Limits and Public Sector Quality*, 52:1 NAT'L TAX J. 113, 124–25 (1999) (summarizing research on the relationship between tax and expenditure limits on the performance of public school students).

2 Administration of the Property Tax

2.1 Terms and Qualifications of the County Tax Assessor 22

2.2 The Property Tax Calendar 24

2.2.1 Real Estate Transfers, Prorations, and Annexation 26

2.3 Setting the Tax Rate 27

2.3.1 Actual versus Effective Tax Rates 28

2.3.2 Revenue-Neutral Rate 29

2 Administration of the Property Tax

The Machinery Act, Subchapter II of Chapter 105 of the North Carolina General Statutes (hereinafter G.S.), prescribes the administrative structure for listing, assessing, and collecting property taxes. The county assessor and the county and city tax collector are central to this structure. The county commissioners appoint, pay, assist, and supervise the county assessor and collector. The city council does the same by appointing a city tax collector or by entering into an agreement with the county that provides for the county collection of city taxes. The county assessor also is supervised at the state level by the Department of Revenue and the Property Tax Commission.

Traditionally, the county board of commissioners appointed separate individuals to serve in the roles of county assessor and tax collector. The assessor and tax collector headed separate departments and reported to the board of commissioners and the county manager independently of each other. Some counties still follow the traditional model, while others have combined the assessing and collecting functions in a single tax department under one department head. Some counties accomplish this by appointing the same person assessor and tax collector. The Machinery Act permits the office of assessor to be held concurrently with any other appointive or elective office except that of county commissioner.[1] Other counties appoint a tax administrator who heads a combined tax department. A tax assessor may serve as administrator as well as collector without violating the prohibition on holding more than two appointive or elective offices because the third position—tax administrator—is an administrative and not an appointed or elected position.

The work of the county assessor is subject to review by the county board of equalization and review. The principal function of this board is to hear and decide taxpayer appeals. In many counties, the board of equalization and review is made up of the county commissioners, who sit for that purpose for a limited time each year. In other counties, special boards of equalization and review are appointed by the county commissioners. Some of these special boards have been created by local acts of the General Assembly. Others have been created by resolution of the board of county commissioners pursuant to general enabling legislation.

At the state level, the Department of Revenue is charged with supervising the valuation and taxation of property by local units of government and, in limited cases, with appraising property for local taxation. The Property Tax Commission is a statewide administrative appeals board that has the power to review and change listing and valuation decisions made by local officials or the Department of Revenue.

2.1 Terms and Qualifications of the County Tax Assessor

As noted above, unlike assessors in most jurisdictions across the United States,[2] county assessors in North Carolina are appointed rather than elected. And unlike most county employees, tax assessors are appointed by the county board of commissioners rather than by the county manager.[3] The term of office is two years, beginning on July 1 of odd-numbered years.[4] Appointment in an odd-numbered year insulates the assessor in some measure from even-year election pressures and politics. An assessor who has completed a two-year term and has been certified by the Department of Revenue may be reappointed for a four-year term at the discretion of the board. During his or her appointed term, an assessor is not an at-will employee whose employment may be terminated at any time. Instead, an assessor may only be removed from office for "good cause;" that is, for a reason that affects the assessor's performance of the duties of the office, that is substantial, and that directly affects the public interest.[5] Before an assessor is removed from office for such a reason, the board of commissioners must provide the assessor notice in writing of the reasons for his or her impending dismissal and must permit the assessor an opportunity to appear and be heard at a public session of the board.

Persons appointed as assessor must be at least twenty-one years old as of the date of employment and must have a high school diploma or certificate of equivalency or, in the alternative, five years employment experience in a vocation reasonably related to the duties of a county assessor.[6] Within two years of the date of appointment, an assessor must achieve a passing score in courses approved by the Department of Revenue covering the following topics: (1) state law governing the listing, appraisal, and assessment of property for taxation; (2) the theory and practice of estimating the fair market value of real property for ad valorem tax purposes; (3) the theory and practice of estimating the fair market value of personal property for ad valorem tax purposes; and (4) property tax assessment administration.[7] As a practical matter, the requirements are satisfied by an assessor's having completed and passed the examination in the following courses: (1) Property Tax Listing and Assessing in North Carolina, a course co-sponsored by the UNC School of Government and the Department of Revenue; (2) Real Property Appraisal, International Association of Assessing Officers (IAAO) Course 101; (3) Personal Property Appraisal, a Department of Revenue course; and (4) Assessment Administration, IAAO Course 400. After completing and passing these four courses and exams, the assessor must pass a comprehensive examination in property tax administration conducted by the Department of Revenue. Until an assessor completes these requirements, the assessor is deemed to serve in an "acting capacity."[8] Once an assessor meets the requirements, the assessor is certified by the Department of Revenue. An acting assessor who fails to qualify for certification within two years of appointment may not be reappointed until all of the certification requirements are met.[9]

Once certified, to retain the position of county assessor an assessor must complete at least thirty hours of instruction every two years in the appraisal or assessment of property to remain eligible for reappointment.

Upon his or her appointment, an assessor must take the oath constitutionally required of all persons elected or appointed to office but also must promise not to allow his or her "actions as assessor to be influenced by personal or political friendships or obligations."[10] This additional oath requirement emphasizes the necessity of impartiality on the part of the assessor.

The assessor cannot, of course, single-handedly carry out the duties of the office. The assessor accordingly is authorized "within budgeted appropriations" to "employ listers, appraisers, and clerical assistants necessary to carry out the listing, appraisal, assessing, and billing functions required by law."[11] Each person employed by an assessor as a real property appraiser or as a personal property appraiser must, during his or her first year of employment and every other year thereafter, attend a course of instruction in his or her area of work.[12] In addition, at the end of the appraiser's first year of employment, he or she must pass a comprehensive examination in property tax administration conducted by the Department of Revenue.

Boards of commissioners also are authorized, upon recommendation of the assessor, to appoint one or more assistant assessors.[13] Boards seldom exercise this authority. Boards also may, and frequently do, employ appraisal firms, mapping firms, and other outside contractors to assist appraisers in performing their duties. The most common situation in which such outside contractors are employed is during a year in which a county reappraises its real property. Any person employed by an appraisal firm whose duties include the appraisal of property for the county must pass a comprehensive exam administered by the Department of Revenue.[14] In hiring an appraisal firm, a board of commissioners must give primary consideration to firms registered with the Department of Revenue.

2.2 The Property Tax Calendar

Many citizens and local government officials are surprised to learn that property taxes are levied for a *fiscal year* that opens on July 1 and closes on the following June 30.[15] This confusion is likely caused by several factors. First, North Carolina real estate attorneys routinely prorate taxes between buyers and sellers in real estate closings on a calendar year basis. Second, the January 1 date of assessment and the January 6 delinquency date the following year roughly follow a calendar year cycle. In addition, property taxes levied for the 2008–09 year generally are referred to simply as "2008 taxes."[16] Anyone familiar with local government finance and budgeting will recognize, however, that property taxes, which are the bread and butter of local government finance, could be levied on nothing other than a fiscal year basis. After all, county commissioners and city council members adopt their budgets and set the property tax rate by July 1 of each year.[17] Bills for property taxes, which supply the revenue for budgeted expenditures, are then mailed to taxpayers as soon as possible after July 1. Taxes are due September 1 (a date that is widely ignored by taxpayers in all taxing jurisdictions that do not offer a discount for early payment of taxes) and are payable without interest at any time through the following January 5. Most taxpayers, and all mortgage companies paying on behalf of homeowners, pay property taxes before January 1 so that the amount paid may be deducted from the property owner's income tax return for the current calendar year. Thus, midway through the fiscal year, the local government unit receives most of its revenues from current fiscal year property taxes.

In order to estimate the probable revenues from property taxes levied at a given rate, the local governing board must know the total assessed value of property subject to taxation in its jurisdiction, as well as the jurisdiction's collection percentage in the current year. In order for the board to determine the assessed value, the Machinery Act requires that all appeals of the taxation or assessment of real property (in years in which there is no countywide reappraisal of real property) be filed by July 1—the date by which the tax levy must be established. In reappraisal years, such appeals must be filed no later than December 1.

To tax property according to value in the correct taxing jurisdiction and bill the taxes to the proper owner, the taxing authorities must know where the property is located, its value, who owns the property, and whether it is subject to taxation. Because these characteristics may change over time, the Machinery Act sets January 1 as the date for determining the *situs* (location for purposes of taxation), value, ownership, and taxability of property. Situs, taxability, and ownership of real and personal property (other than registered motor vehicles) are determined annually as of the January 1 that precedes the fiscal year for which taxes are to be levied. Situs, taxability, and ownership of registered motor vehicles are determined as of the date of vehicle registration. The value of real property is determined as of January 1 of the year in which property is reappraised. Counties must conduct a countywide reappraisal at least every eight years. Personal property other than registered motor vehicles is valued annually as of January 1. Registered motor vehicles are valued as of January 1 of the year in which the taxes become due.

The information needed to determine situs, taxability, ownership, and value is compiled each year during the listing period, which begins in January and normally runs for about thirty days. During this time, taxpayers must submit to the county assessor a list of their taxable personal property other than registered motor vehicles and must report any improvements they have made to their real property. While taxpayers formerly were required to list real as well as personal property, every county now has a permanent listing system for real property, under which the assessor lists all real property. The form on which taxable property is declared is called the *abstract*. The abstract for real property is typically referred to more specifically as a *property record card*. The listing period also is the time for property owners who want to claim the benefit of exemption or other special tax treatment to submit their applications.

After the listing period closes, the county assessor determines the appraised and assessed value of each taxable item and compiles the *scroll*, which is a tentative list of taxable property showing the owner's name and address and the assessed value of his or her taxable property, and a *tax book*, which shows the amount of taxes due.[18] The Machinery Act permits these documents to be prepared separately or to be prepared as a *combined record*, a somewhat archaic requirement given that this data now exists in a computerized data base where it can be readily printed as a combined or separate list. Together, the scroll, tax book, and combined record are termed *tax records*. The scroll must be submitted to the board of equalization and review for approval.[19] The board is authorized to add to and change the scroll on its own initiative but, in practice, virtually all of the changes made by a board result from appeals by property owners.

After the board of equalization and review has completed its work and the tax rate has been set in the city's or county's budget ordinance, which must be adopted by July 1,[20] the tax office computes the amount of taxes due for each property. Tax receipts prepared from information in the tax book—which might more accurately be termed the *tax database*—double as billing notices to taxpayers.

2.2.1 Real Estate Transfers, Prorations, and Annexation

In nearly every real estate transfer, property taxes are prorated between the buyer and seller. A portion of the property taxes attributable to the period of the seller's ownership is deducted from the seller's proceeds and credited to the buyer. Unfortunately, the proration of taxes upon the transfer of real property leads to confusion because of the manner in which such prorations are calculated. Though property taxes are levied on a fiscal year basis, real estate attorneys generally prorate them based upon a calendar year.[21] Pursuant to the calendar year method of proration, if property is sold on July 1, 2008, one-half of the 2008 property taxes is deducted from the seller's proceeds—even though the seller did not own the property during the period for which the 2008 taxes were levied (July 1, 2008, through June 30, 2009).

The practice of prorating fiscal year taxes on a calendar year basis can create considerable confusion upon the sale of a newly annexed property. Newly annexed areas are subject to property taxes in proportion to the period of time that the area is within the city during the current tax year.[22] For example, suppose a city annexes property on August 15, 2007. Property owners in the annexed area are responsible for city taxes for the number of months remaining after the annexation in the current fiscal year. These property owners will thus be responsible for ten months of 2007 taxes. These taxes are for the period September 1, 2007, through June 30, 2008. Suppose that one of the property owners whose property recently has been annexed sells the property on June 30, 2008. At closing, the 2008 taxes are prorated on a calendar year basis, and six months of taxes are deducted from the seller's proceeds. The seller, having just learned in the annexation process that taxes are levied on a fiscal year basis, believes that the closing agreement does not fairly represent his share of the taxes since he paid city and county taxes on December 31, 2007, for the tax year concluding June 30, 2008. The seller is, of course, correct. Nonetheless, it is important to note that the city and county in this example are not being paid double. Instead, by virtue of the closing agreement, the seller has simply subsidized the buyer's portion of 2008 taxes.

Property taxes are not billed based on a partial fiscal year, however, when territory is added to fire districts, sanitary districts, and other special taxing districts after July 1. If property is not located within a tax district on July 1, it cannot be taxed by the district for the current fiscal year. There are special statutes that require cities annexing portions of fire tax districts to make partial refunds of fire district taxes to property owners in the annexed area.[23] Otherwise, the statute requiring payment of municipal taxes for the number of months remaining after annexation in the fiscal year would result in property owners paying twice for fire protection in the same fiscal year.

2.3 Setting the Tax Rate

The tax rate is determined by dividing the budgeted revenue by the total value of assessed property (in other words, the tax base).[24] If budgeted property tax revenue is B, total assessed value is V, and the tax rate is R, this may be stated as the following formula: $R = B / V$. This is, of course, an overly simplified formula given that no taxing unit collects 100 percent of the property taxes levied. Thus, in setting the rate, the Budget and Fiscal Control Act prohibits the taxing unit from estimating a percentage of collection of property taxes greater than the percentage collection for the preceding fiscal year.[25] The rate derived from the above calculation (R) must be divided by the appropriate collection percentage to arrive at the actual tax rate, R_1.

An example may help illustrate the manner in which this calculation is made. Suppose that the total assessed value of all taxable property (V)

in Carolina County for the 2008–09 fiscal year is $3,000,000,000, and Carolina County has budgeted revenues of $19,500,000 (*B*) from property taxes. Applying the simple formula stated above, R = B [19,500,000] / V [3,000,000,000], the tax rate (*R*) equals 0.0065. Yet Carolina County's collection percentage for 2007–08 is 97 percent, and the county cannot assume a higher rate of collection for 2008–09. If the county levies a tax at the rate of 0.0065, it must presume that it will not receive *B* [19,500,000] but instead will receive no more than 97 percent of *B*, or no more than $18,915,000. If the tax rate is set at 0.0065, the county may experience a shortfall of $585,000 (or more, if the collection rate falls below 97 percent). The collection percentage may be factored into the tax rate calculation in one of two ways. First, *B* [19,500,000] may be divided by the collection percentage [.97], resulting in B_1 [20,103,092.78]. The resulting formula is R_1 [.006701] = B_1 [20,103,092.78] / *V* [3,000,000,00]. The tax rate, rounded to the nearest ten thousandth, is .0067. Multiplying R_1 [.0067] by *V* [3,000,000,000] and multiplying the result by .97 results in budgeted revenue *B* [$19,500,000]. Another way to reach the same result is to divide the rate *R* [.0065] resulting from the simple formula by the collection percentage, 0.97. The quotient is R_1 [.006701].

The tax rate stated in Carolina County's budget will be $.67 or 67 cents, rather than 0.0067. This is so because, in North Carolina, property tax rates are stated in terms of dollars per hundred. Thus the calculated rate of 0.0067 per dollar equals a rate of 0.67 per hundred dollars. A taxpayer in Carolina County with property assessed at $100,000 in value will owe $670 in taxes at this rate. This figure may be derived by multiplying $100,000 by 0.0067 or by dividing $100,000 by 100 and multiplying the result by 0.67.[26]

2.3.1 Actual versus Effective Tax Rates

In its annual report on city and county management of cash and taxes, the Department of the State Treasurer lists actual and effective tax rates for each city and county. Obviously, the actual tax rate is the rate set by the governing body of a taxing unit for a particular year. Effective tax rates, in contrast to actual tax rates, illustrate the manner in which increases in property values lower the stated tax rate applicable to a parcel of property. For example, a tax rate of 50 cents applied to a tax base of $10 billion results in a tax levy of $50 million. If the market value of taxable property increases to $12 billion but the assessed value remains $10 billion, the effective tax rate is approximately 42 cents. This is so because the taxing unit is imposing $50 million in property taxes on a tax base of $12 billion. The property tax paid divided by the actual market value of the property equals 42 cents—the effective tax rate. Because taxing units reappraise property on differing schedules and experience different levels of economic growth, the publication of an effective tax rate helps local officials compare the tax rate imposed by one governmental unit to those imposed by other governmental units.

2.3.2 Revenue-Neutral Rate

A new term was introduced into the tax lexicon in 2005: the *revenue-neutral tax rate*. Unlike the effective tax rate, which facilitates comparison of the tax rates set by different jurisdictions, the revenue-neutral rate provides a comparison of the tax burden borne by property owners within a particular taxing unit before and after reappraisal. The revenue-neutral rate is the rate for the fiscal year after reappraisal that, taking into account expected rates of growth in the tax base and excluding increases in market value recognized by the reappraisal, would produce revenue that equals the current year's tax levy. The expected rate of growth in the reappraisal year is based upon an average of increases or decreases in the assessed value since the last reappraisal. This growth or decline is based upon additions to or reductions in a taxing unit's base of taxable property rather than on the increases and decreases in market value that are accounted for by the effective tax rate but are not recouped by the taxing unit in nonreappraisal years. Changes to the real property tax base in nonreappraisal years result from construction of new homes and businesses, improvements to existing structures, divisions and conveyances of land, rezoning, and other occurrences unrelated to the economic conditions affecting the taxing unit in general. Changes in the personal property tax base occur each year because personal property is valued on an annual basis; moreover, personal property generally depreciates, or decreases in value, from one year to the next. G.S. 159-11(e) provides that the growth factor used in calculating the revenue-neutral rate must be based upon the average increase in the tax base "due to improvements since the last general reappraisal."[27] The term *improvements*, in this context, includes not only real property improvements but also all additions and reductions in the tax base recognized in nonrevaluation years.

Adoption of a revenue-neutral rate in the year of a reappraisal will not, however, prevent taxes assessed against real property from increasing.[28] This is so because, in a reappraisal year, a realignment occurs in the tax burden imposed upon real and personal property.[29] In a reappraisal year, the assessed value of real property equals its market value as of January 1 of that year.

In each subsequent year, the assessed value of real property (other than new construction) remains constant, though its market value typically increases. Personal property, in contrast, is valued at its market value every year. Because real property is assessed at *less than* its current market value in the years subsequent to a reappraisal and the assessed value of personal property *equals* its market value in those years, personal property bears a greater portion of the overall tax burden in relation to its true value. That imbalance is corrected in a reappraisal year, when real property again shares equitably in the tax burden imposed. This realignment almost always results in real property comprising a larger percentage of the overall tax base in a reappraisal year. Thus, even under a revenue-neutral rate, a larger portion of revenue is generated from real property in a reappraisal year than from personal property. As a result, many individual real property owners receive increased tax bills in such a year.

A sample calculation may assist in illustrating the point. Assume that Carolina County has a $3 billion tax base and a tax rate of $.70 in the 2007–08 fiscal year. Seventy-eight percent of this base value ($2,340,000,000) is derived from the assessed value of taxable real property; 10 percent ($300,000,000) is derived from the valuation of personal property other than registered motor vehicles; 10 percent is derived from the valuation of registered motor vehicles ($300,000,000); and 2 percent ($60,000,000) is derived from the valuation of public service company system property. The 2007–08 tax levy totals $21,000,000 ($3,000,000,000 * $.0070). Also assume that 2008 is a reappraisal year and that the rate of growth in the tax base in each year since Carolina County's last revaluation averages 3 percent. If the tax base after reappraisal increases by 15 percent, to $3.45 billion, the revenue-neutral rate for 2008–09 will be $.63.[30] If the value of all personal property and public service company property increases by 3 percent in the reappraisal year, real property values as a percentage of the total tax base will increase from 78 to 80.3 percent. Thus taxes assessed on real property at the revenue-neutral tax rate will increase from $16,380,000 in 2007–08 to $17,367,949.57 in 2008–09. Taxes assessed on personal property, registered motor vehicles, and public service company system property will decrease from $4,620,000 to $4,262,050.43. The impact upon individual tax assessments will depend upon the rate at which the property has appreciated or depreciated. These calculations are set forth in table 2.1.

Table 2.1 Calculation of Revenue-Neutral Tax Rate

Calculation of Revenue-Neutral Tax Rate	**2007–08**	**2008–09**
Tax Base	3,000,000,000	3,450,000,000
Overall Growth in Reappraisal Year		15%
Increase in Personal Property Value in Reappraisal Year		3%
Real Property Assessed Value	2,340,000,000	2,770,200,000
Personal Property Assessed Value	300,000,000.00	309,000,000.00
Registered Motor Vehicle Assessed Value	300,000,000.00	309,000,000.00
Public Service Company System Property	60,000,000.00	61,800,000.00
Tax Rate in 2007–08	0.70	
Tax Levy in 2007–08	21,000,000.00	
Rate Necessary to Produce 2007–08 Revenue in 2008–09		0.61
Average Annual Increase in Tax Base Since Last Revaluation		3%
Revenue-Neutral Rate for 2008–09		0.63
Tax Levy in Reappraisal Year at Revenue-Neutral Rate		21,630,000.00
Change in Personal Property Levy		-7.75%
Change in Real Property Tax Levy		6.03%
Tax Base	2007–08	2008–09
Real Property	78%	80.30%
Personal Property	10%	8.96%
Registered Motor Vehicles	10%	8.96%
Public Service Company System Property	2%	1.79%
Tax Levy by Property Type	2007–08	2008–09
Real Property	16,380,000.00	17,367,949.57
Personal Property	2,100,000.00	1,937,295.65
Registered Motor Vehicles	2,100,000.00	1,937,295.65
Public Service Company System Property	420,000.00	387,459.13

Notes

1. N.C. Gen. Stat. § 105-294(f) (hereinafter G.S.). Article VI, Section 9, of the North Carolina Constitution provides that "[n]o person shall hold concurrently any two or more appointive offices . . . except as the General Assembly shall provide by general law."

2. *See* Gary C. Cornia & Lawrence C. Walters, *Full Disclosure: Controlling Property Tax Increases During Periods of Increasing Housing Values*, 59:3 Nat'l Tax J., 736 (2006).

3. *See* G.S. 153A-82 (providing that the county manager shall appoint all employees except those who are elected or whose appointment is otherwise provided by law). The county tax collector, county attorney, county manager, and county clerk, like the county assessor, are appointed by the board of commissioners. *See* G.S. 105-349 (county tax collector); G.S. 153A-114 (county attorney); G.S. 153A-81 (county manager); G.S. 153A-111 (county clerk).

4. G.S. 105-294(a). Assessors must, on occasion, be appointed during even-numbered years if there is a vacancy in the office. Given that the Machinery Act sets forth a reappointment schedule based upon odd-numbered-year reappointments, boards of commissioners appointing assessors in even-numbered years should make these appointments effective through June 30 of the next odd-numbered year. The board may then resume the Machinery Act schedule of appointments July 1 of the odd numbered year.

5. 63C Am. Jur. 2d *Public Officers and Employees* § 183 (2005).

6. G.S. 105-294(b).

7. G.S. 105-294(b)(3).

8. G.S. 105-294(c).

9. *Id.*

10. G.S. 105-295.

11. G.S. 105-296(b).

12. *Id.*

13. G.S. 105-297.

14. G.S. 105-297. This exam differs from the comprehensive exam for county appraisers. If an appraiser for an appraisal firm passes the UNC School of Government and Department of Revenue Property Tax Listing and Assessing in North Carolina course along with either IAAO 101, for real property appraisers, or the Department of Revenue's business personal property course, for personal property appraisers, the comprehensive exam requirement is waived.

15. *See* G.S. 105-285(d).

16. This differs from the department of state treasurer's convention of referring to fiscal years by the year in which they end. Thus "2008 taxes" are levied for the 2009 fiscal year in the nomenclature of the state treasurer.

17. G.S. 159-13(a).

18. G.S. 105-319(a).

19. G.S. 105-319(d).

20. G.S. 159-13(a).

21. Indeed, the General Assembly specifically endorsed this method of proration

in 2006 by enacting new G.S. 39-60, which states that the calendar-year basis is the presumptive manner of prorating property taxes upon the sale of real property.

22. G.S. 160A-58.10.

23. G.S. 69-25.15 (setting out the tax refund required for voted fire tax districts that have been annexed by the municipality); G.S. 153A-304.1 (setting out the tax refund required for county fire service districts that have been annexed by the municipality).

24. *See, e.g.,* Nathan B. Anderson, *Property Tax Limitations: An Interpretive Review,* 59:3 Nat'l Tax J. 685, 686 (2006).

25. G.S. 159-13(b)(6).

26. Some other states express property tax rates as mills per dollar. There are 1,000 mills in a dollar (10 mills to a penny). A decimal rate tax of 0.0067 would be expressed as 6.7 mills per $1 (.0067 x 1,000).

27. For a detailed discussion of the method for calculating a revenue-neutral tax rate, see Shea Riggsbee Denning and William C. Rivenbark, *Statement of Revenue-Neutral Tax Rate and Provision for Mid-Year Property Tax Rate Change,* Loc. Fin. Bull. No. 32 at 2 (UNC School of Government, November 2004).

28. *See Technical Discussion—Revenue Neutral Tax Rate, available at* www.co.forsyth.nc.us/Tax/reval.pdf (last visited July 5, 2008).

29. *See id.*

30. This revenue-neutral rate is calculated by first determining the rate that must be imposed upon the reappraised tax base to produce revenues equal to those for the current fiscal year. The new tax base is $3.45 billion. The current year's levy is $21 million. Thus a tax rate of $.61 per hundred would have to be imposed to produce revenues equaling those of the current year [($3,450,000,000/100)/$21,000,000 = $.61]. This rate is then increased by 3 percent, the average annual percentage increase in the tax base due to improvements since the last general reappraisal [$.61 x 1.03]. The resulting rate is 0.6283, rounded to $.63. The resulting tax levy is $21,630,000.

3 The Listing of Property for Taxation

3.1 Categories of Property: Real and Personal 37

3.1.1 Real Property Defined 37

3.1.2 Personal Property Defined 39

3.2 The Mechanics of Listing 41

3.2.1 Listing Real Property 42

3.2.2 Rules for Listing Real Property 44

3.2.3 Public Records Reflecting a Transfer of Interest in Real Property 46

3.3. Listing Personal Property 47

3.3.1 Listing of Property Owned in Connection with Various Business Enterprises 49

3.3.2 Multiple Owners 50

3.3.3 Unknown Owner 50

3.3.4 Listing of Time-Share Property 51

3.3.5 Ownership of Motor Vehicles 51

3.3.6 Reports of Property Held by Others 51

3.4 What the Abstract Must Contain 52

3.4.1 Signed Affirmation 53

3.5 Listing Aids 54

3.5.1 Subpoena Power 54

3.5.2 Information from the Department of Revenue 55

3.5.3 Report of Property by Multicounty Business 55

3.5.4 Other Assessment Information 56

3.6 Due Process Requirements 57

3.7 Listing Period 59

3.8 Place for Listing 61

3.9 Special Situs Rules 62

3.9.1 Tax Situs of Property of Decedents and Fiduciaries 65

3.9.2 Servicemembers Civil Relief Act 66

3.10 Applications for Exemption, Exclusion, or Other Special Tax Status 66

3.11 Discovery of Unlisted Property 67

3.12 Public Records Law 70

3.12.1 Custody 71

3.12.2 Public Access 71

3.12.3 Geographic Information System Records 72

3.12.4 Confidential Information 73

3.12.5 Retention 78

3 The Listing of Property for Taxation

As discussed in Chapter 2, each county assessor must maintain a scroll of all property within the county subject to taxation. This chapter addresses the manner for determining what property is included, or listed, on the scroll and the laws governing how—and where—such property should be listed.

The chapter begins with a discussion of the legal characterization of certain types of property and then addresses legal forms of ownership. Next follows a discussion of the rules for listing such property and the mechanisms for determining that listings are accurate. The chapter then addresses laws governing the determination of which jurisdictions may tax certain property. It also describes the process for adding unlisted property to the tax scrolls—known as *discovery*. The chapter concludes by discussing public records laws pertaining to tax listing records.

3.1 Categories of Property: Real and Personal

The Machinery Act divides property into two main categories: real and personal. Because significant differences exist in the rules governing taxation of these types of property, it is critical that tax assessors and other tax office personnel involved in the listing of property for taxation be able to distinguish between the two.

3.1.1 Real Property Defined

Real property is defined as real estate, land, buildings, structures, improvements, and permanent fixtures on the land, and all rights and privileges belonging or appertaining to the property.[1] While the first several components of this definition—real estate, land, buildings, and structures—are words commonly used and understood, improvements, permanent fixtures, and rights and privileges are terms of art that merit some additional explanation.

3.1.1.1. Improvements. *Improvements* are additions to property that add to its intrinsic value. The term includes items such as roads, as well as buildings and other structures.[2]

3.1.1.2. Fixtures. *Fixtures* are articles of property originally considered personal property that are annexed to or become inseparable from land and thus are considered part of the real property.[3] Thus, for example, a chairlift system at an amusement park that is attached to the poured concrete foundations might properly be considered a fixture, notwithstanding that certain component parts of the chairlift system are moveable.[4] Items such as underground storage tanks, manufactured homes, or commercial structures could be considered either fixtures or personal property, depending upon the manner in which the items are attached to real property, the nature of the items, the purpose for which they are attached, and the intentions of the parties involved.[5]

The person or entity making the improvement also is an important factor for consideration. When an owner makes an addition to the land, the presumption is that the addition is made to enhance the value of the land, and the article of personal property becomes part of the land.[6] When a tenant or someone else who does not own the land makes such an improvement, the law recognizes that the tenant likely intends to remove any additions upon termination of the tenant's interest in the land.[7]

3.1.1.3 Rights and Privileges. The term *rights and privileges belonging or appertaining to property* includes entitlements ranging from the right to harvest water, minerals, or standing timber from land, to the right to obtain membership in a country club or community center by virtue of property ownership, to the right to use common property titled to a homeowners association. It also conceivably could include the right to use the air above a certain parcel of real estate, perhaps for purposes of advertising. Because almost no intangible personal property is subject to ad valorem taxation, these intangible—but clearly valuable—rights would escape taxation were they not expressly defined as real property. Moreover, because they are all clearly associated with an identifiable parcel of property, their taxation as an interest in real property comports with the general understanding of real property ownership as consisting of a bundle of rights.

3.1.1.4 Manufactured Homes. *Manufactured homes* are structures designed to be used as dwellings that are built on a permanent chassis and can be moved in one or more sections. Manufactured homes must be at least 8 feet wide or 40 feet long or, when erected on-site, must be at least 320 square feet.[8]

A manufactured home is considered real property if it meets the following four conditions. First, it must be residential. Second, the moving hitch, wheels, and axles must be removed. Third, it must be on a permanent foundation. Finally, to be considered real property, a manufactured home must be situated upon land owned by the owner of the manufactured home or on land in which the owner of the manufactured home has a leasehold interest pursuant to a lease with a primary term of at least twenty years; moreover, any such qualifying lease must expressly provide for disposition of the manufactured home upon termination of the lease. A manufactured home that does not meet all of these conditions is considered tangible personal property.

For many years, assessors routinely listed double-wide manufactured homes as "leasehold improvements," a type of real property, regardless of whether the homes met the requirements set forth in Section 105-273(13) of the North Carolina General Statutes (hereinafter G.S.). This practice ended in 2001 when G.S. 105-273(13) was amended to specify that manufactured homes that *did not* meet the subsection's specific definition were "considered tangible personal property." The current version of G.S. 105-273(13) makes clear that the distinction between single-wide and double-wide is not relevant for purposes of determining whether a manufactured home is real or personal property.

3.1.2 Personal Property Defined

The Machinery Act defines *personal property* as all property other than real property, and it divides personal property into two subcategories: intangible and tangible personal property. *Intangible personal property* is defined as "patents, copyrights, secret processes, formulae, good will, trademarks, trade brands, franchises, stocks, bonds, cash, bank deposits, notes, evidences of debt, leasehold interests in exempted real property, bills and accounts receivable, and other like property."[9] All other personal property is considered *tangible*.[10]

Because the Machinery Act excludes from taxation all intangible personal property other than leasehold interests in exempted real property and software not otherwise excluded from taxation, these subcategories of intangible personal property are the most important to explore in more detail.

3.1.2.1 Leasehold Interests in Exempted Real Property. As mentioned in Chapter 1, the North Carolina Constitution exempts property owned by governmental units from taxation. Such property is exempt regardless of the purpose for which it is used. For example, suppose that the City of Tarheelville owns a ten-story office building that it rents to a privately owned bank for the bank's commercial use. The use of the building for commercial purposes does not render it taxable, because property owned by the state is exempt regardless of the purpose for which it is used.[11] Thus it is clear that the city's interest in the building and underlying land is not taxable. Suppose, however, that the City of Tarheelville entered into a thirty-year lease of the building to the private bank in 1985 at the rate of $10,000 per month and that in the current market, office space of this size and quality commands a monthly lease payment of $50,000. The bank would then have a valuable, and taxable, interest in this property, which it could—theoretically and perhaps practically, depending upon the terms of the lease—sublease for far more than it is required to pay to the city each month. The difference between the amount the bank must pay pursuant to its lease and the market rate for leasing similar property comprises the taxable leasehold interest in this otherwise exempt property.[12]

3.1.2.2 Software. Certain computer software is specifically excluded from taxation. All other software, in contrast, is subject to taxation. Therefore, to understand what software is taxable, it is necessary to learn what software has been exempted from taxation.

3.1.2.2.1. Software Excluded from Taxation. Computer software and any documentation related to the computer software are excluded from taxation. *Computer software* is defined as any program or routine used to cause a computer to perform a specific task or set of tasks. The term includes system and application programs and database storage and management programs. The exclusion from taxation does not, however, extend to two types of computer software: embedded software and software purchased from an unrelated entity that is capitalized on the taxpayer's books. Software falling in either of these two specific categories is taxable.

3.1.2.2.2 Taxable Software. *Embedded software* is defined as computer instructions, or microcode, that resides permanently in the internal memory of a computer system or other equipment and is not intended to be removed without terminating the operation of the computer system or equipment and removing a computer chip, a circuit, or another mechanical device. Embedded software is taxable. By providing for the taxation of software inextricably linked with computer hardware, the Machinery Act permits assessors to value computer equipment as a whole without requiring them to apportion value among a device's hardware and software components.[13]

Software purchased or licensed from a person unrelated to the taxpayer and capitalized on the taxpayer's books along with other long-term assets according to generally accepted accounting principles also is taxable. A person is considered to be unrelated to the taxpayer if the taxpayer and the person are not subject to any common ownership and neither has an ownership interest in the other. This exception to the general exemption for computer software distinguishes between software owned by the software engineers who developed it, such as IBM and SAS Institute, and software purchased and held by a taxpayer as a capital asset.[14] The former is exempt, in the same way that inventory of a manufacturer of tangible goods is exempt, while the latter, like other business personal property, is taxable.[15]

3.2 The Mechanics of Listing

All real property and all taxable personal property must be listed for taxation on an abstract, which commonly is referred to as a *property record card* when the property listed thereon is real property. The processes by which real and personal property are listed differ significantly, since all one hundred counties in North Carolina now have a permanent listing system for real property and in most circumstances owners of real property have no duty to list real property with the city or county. Taxpayers continue to be responsible, however, for listing taxable personal property (other than most registered motor vehicles) on an annual basis. This section explains the tax records associated with listing, the types of ownership interests that must be reflected on a property record card for real property, the place for listing real and personal property, and the process for discovering property not listed with the taxing unit.

3.2.1 Listing Real Property

3.2.1.1 Abstracts and Property Record Cards. The county assessor is responsible for creating an abstract or property record card for all real property in the county.[16] This process is referred to as a *permanent listing system* and its implementation in the 1990s and early twenty-first century marked a departure from traditional listing methodology in which the duty to list property subject to taxation was borne by the owner of real as well as personal property.[17] Even in a permanent listing system, however, owners of real property remain responsible for listing buildings and other improvements valued at more than $100 that have been acquired, begun, erected, damaged, or destroyed since the time of the last appraisal.[18] The listing abstract or property record card reflects the owner of record as of the listing date, which is January 1, for all property other than exempt property transferred after January 1 but before July 1.[19] The term *owner of record* denotes ownership as reflected in a document of public record; that is, a deed, judgment, probated will, or other document reflecting ownership filed in the official record maintained by the clerk of superior court or register of deeds.

3.2.1.2 Forms of Ownership of Real Property. Determining the ownership of real property requires some understanding of the types of ownership interests one can have in real property. Ownership interests can vary from absolute ownership of property to the mere right to possess the property, or some portion of it, for a defined term.[20] The term *property* refers not only to land itself but to the right to possess, use, enjoy, and dispose of it and to the corresponding right to exclude others from its use.[21]

3.2.1.2.1 Estates in Land. Ownership interests in real property are traditionally described as *estates in land*.[22] A *fee simple estate in land* is the most extensive—or, put another way, the least restricted—form of ownership. The owner of such an estate has the full right to use and dispose of the property.[23] Other lesser estates may entitle the owner to possess the property for the term of the life of a natural person, referred to as a *life estate*, or to use and dispose of minerals, timber, or game from the property.[24]

3.2.1.2.2 Tenancy. In addition to encompassing different rights to use, enjoy, and dispose of real property, estates in land can be owned in different ways. The legal relationship between or among joint owners of property is typically described as a type of *tenancy*.[25] Property jointly owned by more than one person may be owned by those persons as *joint tenants* or as *tenants by the entireties.*

Estates in land owned by a husband and wife may be owned by them as tenants by the entireties, which means that the couple does not own the land in shares, but instead the two share unified ownership and are considered one person under the law.[26] Estates in land owned by two or more persons who are not married may be owned by those persons as *joint tenants* with right of survivorship or as *tenants in common.*[27] In a joint tenancy, ownership, though shared by more than one person, is single and unified as though the joint tenants were a single legal entity.[28] Upon the death of one joint tenant, the other is vested with an undivided interest in the property.[29] Tenants in common, in contrast, share equally in the land, but each has a separately defined ownership interest.[30] Each tenant in common has a right to enter upon the land and enjoy it jointly with the other.[31] Each co-tenant is entitled to his or her share of rents and profits, and one co-tenant is entitled to an accounting for rents collected by the other co-tenant.[32]

Real property is valued and assessed under the Machinery Act based upon its true, or market, value in its highest and best use. Thus, while encumbrances such as easements or dedications of property to a particular use affect the valuation of property for tax purposes, fractional ownership interests do not. Property is valued as though one owner owned the entire interest in the property; personal encumbrances, such as deeds of trust, do not affect the market value of property and are not considered for assessment purposes.[33] However, because the ownership interests must be reflected on the property record card pursuant to G.S. 105-302 and because they determine the personal property subject to enforced collection remedies for nonpayment, they remain important.

3.2.1.2.3 Easements. An easement is a right to use land belonging to another. An easement may be characterized as *appurtenant* or *in gross.* An appurtenant easement attaches to and passes with the benefited property (referred to as the *dominant tenement*) as an associated right of ownership. An easement in gross, in contrast, is not associated with any particular estate in land. Instead, an easement in gross is an individual right to use land belonging to someone else and usually terminates with the death of the individual who possesses the right.[34]

3.2.2 Rules for Listing Real Property

When more than one party has an ownership interest in a given parcel of real property, G.S. 105-302 specifies in whose name the property is to be listed. The listing rules applicable to specific situations are set forth below.

3.2.2.1 Property Subject to a Mortgage or Deed of Trust. Real property, particularly residential real property, commonly is subject to a deed of trust, in which legal title to a parcel is held by a trustee. The person who granted the deed of trust or mortgage is considered the owner of the equity of redemption, meaning that the person has a right to pay the debt and thereby cancel the security interest that the lender holds against his or her property. In everyday parlance, the owner of the equity of redemption is thought of as the owner of the property; it would be unusual to refer to the trustee as the owner. The Machinery Act comports with this understanding by requiring that property be listed in the name of the owner of the equity of redemption.

3.2.2.2 Real Property Owned by a Corporation, Association, or Partnership. Real property owned by a corporation, an unincorporated association, or a partnership must be listed in the name of the entity that owns the property.

3.2.2.3 Real Property Owned in Connection with a Sole Proprietorship. Real property owned in connection with a sole proprietorship must be listed in the name of the owner, with the name of the proprietorship noted on the abstract. Thus, for example, property owned by John Jones in connection with Jones Supply, a sole proprietorship, should be listed in the name of John Jones d/b/a Jones Supply.

3.2.2.4 Listing Real Property When Last Known Owner Is Deceased. If a person dies in possession of real property, and the property is not in the control of an executor or administrator, the property must be listed in the names of the heirs or devisees once the assessor has been given notice of those persons' names and the division of the estate. If the assessor has not yet received such notice and does not know the identities of the persons who inherited the property, the property may be listed as property of "the heirs of [the decedent]" if there is no will, or "the devisees of [the decedent]" if there is a will. On the rare occasions in which an executor or administrator has control of real property on January 1, the property must be listed in the name of the fiduciary, noting his fiduciary capacity. The rule is the same for other property held by a fiduciary such as a trustee or guardian; such property likewise must be listed in the name of the fiduciary in his or her fiduciary capacity.

3.2.2.5 Real Property Subject to a Life Estate. If ownership of a parcel is shared between a life tenant and a remainderman, the life tenant is considered the owner and is the person in whose name the property must be listed. The assessor must note on the abstract that the owner is a life tenant or tenant for the life of another, which means that the tenant has a life estate measured by the life of someone other than the tenant.

3.2.2.6 Real Property Owned by Tenants in Common. Real property owned by tenants in common is generally listed on one abstract in the names of all of the owners. Assessors may, upon request, permit tenants in common who are not co-partners to list their respective undivided interests on separate abstracts but, in practice, assessors seldom, if ever, allow tenants in common to list their interests separately.

3.2.2.7 Real Property Owned by Husband and Wife as Tenants by the Entirety. Real property owned by husband and wife as tenants by the entirety must be listed on a single abstract in the names of both the husband and wife, and their tenancy by the entirety ownership must be noted on the abstract.

3.2.2.8 Separate Ownership of Improvements. When land is owned by one party and improvements on the property or other rights to the property (such as mineral, timber, quarry, waterpower, or similar rights) are owned by another party, the interests of the owner of the land must be listed separately from the interests of the owner of improvements or other rights. The assessor may list the property in the name of the land owner if the owners have so agreed by contract.

3.2.2.9 Unknown Owner. If title to real property that is occupied is disputed or the assessor cannot determine who owns the property, the assessor must list the property in the name of the occupant. If title to unoccupied property is in dispute or the owner cannot be determined, the property must be listed in the name of "unknown owner." Once the owner's identity is determined, the assessor must list the property in the name of that owner. The corrected listing has the same force and effect as if the property had been listed in the owner's name all along. The listing of property in the name of "unknown owner" does not affect the validity of the tax lien.

An assessor must furnish to the state, upon request, a report of all properties in the assessor's jurisdiction that are listed in the name of "unknown owner."[35]

3.2.2.10 Real Property Owned under a Time-Sharing Arrangement. Assessors must list real property owned under a time-sharing arrangement but managed by a homeowners association or other managing entity in the name of the managing entity.

3.2.3 Public Records Reflecting a Transfer of Interest in Real Property

Several types of public records may evidence a transfer of interest in real property. Title to real property may transfer by will or intestate succession upon the death of the owner, by deed, or by judgment or order of a court. Documents transferring title to property from one owner to the next are referred to collectively as the *chain of title.*

The most common public record operating to transfer record title to property is a deed recorded with the register of deeds. Outside the context of special judicial or legal proceedings, property is generally transferred by *warranty* or *quitclaim deed.*[36] Warranty deeds are conveyances in which the grantor (the person or entity transferring the property to a new owner) guarantees the title conveyed to the grantee.[37] Quitclaim deeds convey only the grantor's current interest, if any, in the property.[38] The grantor makes no promises or guarantees with respect to the title. It is important to note, however, that a quitclaim deed is as effective as any other deed in conveying whatever interest the grantor has in the property.[39] Quitclaim deeds traditionally were used to release or abandon some previously asserted claim or interest in land,[40] thereby removing clouds from the title to property.[41] However, they can also properly be used to convey property when a grantor does not wish to guarantee title. Unfortunately, quitclaim deeds from grantors who appear nowhere in the chain of title occasionally are recorded in an attempt to cloud title to property. Tax assessors sometimes question whether the recording of such a deed requires property affected by such a deed to be listed to an "unknown owner" on the basis that title to the property is disputed. In the author's opinion, there is no requirement that the assessor change listing records to acknowledge a deed from a grantor that indisputably falls outside the chain of title for such property.[42] Changing records to recognize such documents could result in the name of the true owner of the property being removed from the abstract, which, in turn, might mean that the new owner would not be notified of property taxes owed.[43]

When property is transferred by will, the clerk will enter a certificate of probate filed along with the will in the office of the clerk of superior court in the county where the will is probated. While a copy of a probated will may be filed with the clerk of superior court in the county where the land is situated if that is different from the one where the will is probated, there is no requirement that this be done.[44] When the owner of real property dies without a will, the final accounting by the personal representative for the estate (assuming an estate is opened), which is approved by the clerk and filed in the estate file, will indicate the disposition of the decedent's real property.[45] Title to real property vests in heirs at the time of death rather than at the time of the final accounting.[46] Thus the date of death is the date of the change in record ownership, though the identity of these record owners may not be ascertained until a later date.

3.3. Listing Personal Property

Owners of taxable personal property (other than classified registered motor vehicles) are charged with the duty to annually list such property, which involves preparing and filing a listing form, or abstract, itemizing the property in the detail prescribed by an abstract form approved by the Department of Revenue.[47] The model personal property listing form issued by the Department of Revenue provides for the listing of personal property in one of eight categories: (1) machinery and equipment, (2) construction in progress, (3) computer equipment, (4) office furniture and fixtures, (5) leasehold improvements, (6) supplies, (7) expensed items, and (8) other property. Taxpayers also must list unregistered motor vehicles, watercraft, and aircraft and must include historical cost information for all property listed.

Determining the ownership of personal property can be difficult, since frequently there are no documents of record that definitively establish title. Under the common law, possession of personal property was considered the "strongest evidence of ownership," which gave rise to a presumption that the possessor had title to, and thus was the owner of, the property.[48] This presumption could be rebutted by demonstrating that one other than the possessor had title to the property.[49] The common law also recognized property owners' ability to entrust their property to the possession of others without effecting a transfer of title, noting that if the law were otherwise "no man could safely leave his watch with a watchmaker for repairs."[50] While it is clear that the watchmaker does not own the watch left with him for purposes of making repairs, other business agreements related to personal property may render it difficult to determine the party that owns the property.

An example may help illustrate a common situation in which questions arise regarding the ownership of business personal property. Suppose that Adam Able sells to Zeta Zade a specialized printing machine that he owns. Suppose as well that the sales agreement specifies that Able retains title to and the right to repossess the printing machine upon Zade's failure to make timely monthly payments of $1,000 over a period of thirty-six months. The agreement further states that upon full payment of the purchase price, legal title transfers to Zade and Able's security interest is terminated. Who is the owner for listing purposes? Able, who has legal title? Or Zade, who has possession of the property and the right to title upon full payment of the purchase price?

The Machinery Act identifies Zade as the owner who has the duty to list. G.S. 105-309 provides that where a seller, or vendor, retains title to personal property under a conditional bill of sale or other contract to secure payment of the purchase price, the property must be listed by and in the name of the buyer, or vendee, of the personal property if the buyer has possession of or the right to use the property. Able is the vendor, Zade the vendee; thus the equipment must be listed in Zade's name, and it is her duty to list it.

However, what if the agreement between Able and Zade were worded differently? Suppose that the agreement provides that Able assigns to Zade his right to occupy the premises at 101 Printer's Lane and that Zade agrees to make all lease payments required for the premises for a three-year period. Assume that the agreement further provides that Zade may use the printing machine located in the leased premises and that Able will transfer the printing machine to Zade at the end of the three-year period if Zade complies with all obligations under the lease for the full three-year period. Suppose further that the printing machine is seven years old and has a ten-year useful life. Who has the duty to list the machine in this circumstance? Zade is no longer the vendee of the personal property under a conditional bill of sale. Able has title to the printing machine, regardless of his agreement to transfer the equipment at the end of the lease period. Thus Able is the owner responsible for listing the machine.[51]

Let us consider another scenario in which it may be difficult to identify the owner of personal property. Betty Brown is a farmer in Eastern North Carolina and is experiencing significant financial difficulties due to a seven-month drought that destroyed most of her soybean crop. Brown needs cash to begin planting for next year. Clyde Conniver agrees to buy several valuable plows and other tractor attachments from Brown for $5,000. The market value of this equipment is approximately $20,000. The bill of sale signed by Conniver and Brown on December 15, 2008, provides that Brown may repurchase the equipment from Conniver for a purchase price of $6,000 any time before May 1, 2009. After that date, Conniver may dispose of the equipment as he sees fit. Who is the owner with the duty to list the equipment for taxation in 2009?

The Machinery Act requires Brown to list the property in her name. G.S. 105-306(c)(1) provides for the listing of personal property that is subject to a "chattel mortgage" in the name of the owner of the equity of redemption. A *chattel mortgage* is a conditional sale of personal property made to provide security for the payment of a debt or the performance of some other obligation.[52] A bill of sale, like the one signed by Conniver and Brown, that gives the seller an option to repurchase the property or a bill of sale providing that the purchaser will re-convey the property when a debt is timely repaid is a chattel mortgage.[53] The Machinery Act requires that such property be listed in the name of the seller who has the right to redeem or repurchase the property.

3.3.1 Listing of Property Owned in Connection with Various Business Enterprises

The Machinery Act also specifies how property owned by or held in connection with certain business enterprises must be listed.

Personal property owned by a corporation, partnership, or unincorporated association must be listed in the name of the owning entity.[54] For example, restaurant equipment owned by Best Burgers in Town Inc. must be listed on an abstract in the name of Best Burgers in Town Inc.

Property held in connection with a sole proprietorship must be listed in the name of the owner, with the name and address of the proprietorship noted on the abstract.[55] For example, if Tom Brown owns and operates a restaurant named Pancakes All Day as a sole proprietorship, restaurant equipment situated in Pancakes All Day and owned by Brown must be listed in the name of Tom Brown d/b/a Pancakes All Day.

G.S. 105-306(c)(5) specifies the manner for listing property most recently owned by an individual who dies in possession of the property. If the property is under the control of an executor or administrator, that person must list the property in his or her fiduciary capacity. Likewise, other property in which legal title resides in a trustee, guardian, or fiduciary must be listed by that person in his or her capacity as trustee, guardian, or fiduciary. If the property is not under an executor's or administrator's control, the property is to be listed in the names of the next of kin or legatees once those persons are identified; until that time, the property may be listed as property of the "next of kin of [the decedent]" or "the legatees of [the decedent]." The next of kin or legatees are responsible for notifying the assessor of their names and the division of the estate and, as new owners, are responsible for listing the property.

3.3.2 Multiple Owners

The Machinery Act provides that personal property owned by two or more persons jointly must be separately listed by each owner and the abstract must state the value of each individual owner's interest. Personal property owned jointly by a husband and wife may, however, be listed on one abstract in both names.

3.3.3 Unknown Owner

On occasion, the tax assessor will not be able to identify the owner of taxable personal property. This inability to identify the owner may result from an ownership dispute among parties claiming the property or, since liability for payment of taxes accompanies ownership, a dispute in which potential owners *disclaim* ownership of the property. A tax assessor may also be unable to identify the owner of discovered property for which no abstract was filed during the listing period. The Machinery Act requires that personal property for which no owner can be identified or for which ownership is in dispute be listed in the name of the person who has possession of the property. If the property is not in anyone's possession, the Machinery Act directs that the property be listed in the name of "unknown owner."

3.3.4 Listing of Time-Share Property

The Machinery Act requires that personal property owned under a time-sharing arrangement but managed by a homeowners association or other managing entity be listed in the name of the managing entity.

3.3.5 Ownership of Motor Vehicles

Special rules govern the determination of ownership of *motor vehicles*, which are defined as "[e]very vehicle which is self-propelled and every vehicle designed to run upon the highways which is pulled by a self-propelled vehicle [but not mopeds]."[56] Manufactured homes are classified as motor vehicles for purposes of interpreting the application of motor vehicle laws to manufactured homes. G.S. 20-72(b) provides that no title to a motor vehicle shall pass until the transferor executes an assignment and warranty of title on the reverse of the certificate of title and delivers the motor vehicle to the transferee. While the North Carolina Court of Appeals has considered a manufactured home affixed to land as capable of being transferred by deed,[57] the general rule for manufactured homes classified as personal property is that legal title is transferred by assignment and warranty of certificate of title. Manufactured homes may also be converted to real property and removed from the Division of Motor Vehicles (DMV) titling system by surrender of title pursuant to the provisions of G.S. 20-109.2. Pursuant to G.S. 105-306(a), taxable personal property is to be listed in the name of the owner. In the case of manufactured homes and other motor vehicles, the owner in whose name the property must be listed is the person or persons whose name appears on the certificate of title.

3.3.6 Reports of Property Held by Others

Though only the owner of personal property is required to list the property for taxation, persons who possess certain taxable items of personal property owned by others are required to report those holdings to the county each year. Operators of manufactured-home parks, marinas, and aircraft hangers must furnish to the county assessor by January 15 of each year the name of the owner and a description of the property in their possession.[58] In addition, any other person in possession of another's taxable, tangible personal property for any business purpose is required to provide the owner's name and a description of the property to the assessor annually by January 15.[59]

As previously mentioned, the ownership of personal property is determined annually as of the January 1 preceding the tax year that opens the following July 1. The value and situs—the property's location for tax purposes—also are determined annually as of January 1.

3.4 What the Abstract Must Contain

The Machinery Act sets forth numerous specific requirements for information that must be provided on an abstract.[60]

All abstracts must show the taxpayer's name, residence address, and, if required by the assessor, business address. An abstract listing property for an individual trading under a firm name must show the individual's name and address and the name and address of the business firm. An abstract for property owned by an unincorporated association must contain the name and address of the principal officers of the association as well as the name and address of the association. Similarly, an abstract for partnership property must contain the names and addresses of the full partners in addition to the name and address of the partnership.

The requirements for abstracts listing real property differ depending upon whether the real property is divided into lots. For tracts of real property not divided into lots, the property record card must describe the real property by stating the following:[61]

1. The township in which the property is located
2. The number of acres in the tract or, if smaller than an acre, the dimensions of the parcel
3. The tract name (if any), the names of at least two adjoining landowners, a reference to the tract's designation on any map maintained in the office of the assessor or on file in the office of the register of deeds, or some other description sufficient to identify and locate the parcel
4. If applicable, the number of acres of cleared land, woodland, land containing mineral or quarry deposits, land that could be developed for waterpower, and wasteland

For real property divided into lots, the abstract must specify:[62]

1. The township in which the property is located
2. The dimensions of the lot
3. The location of the lot (including its street number, if any)

4. The lot's designation on a map maintained in the assessor's office or on file with the register of deeds or some other description sufficient to identify and locate the property

Abstracts for all real property, both tracts and lots, must specify the portion of the tract or parcel located within municipal boundaries and must contain a short description of any buildings and other improvements thereon having a value in excess of $100.[63] In addition, if improvements or separate rights to property, such as mineral rights, are owned by someone other than the owner of the tract of land, the abstract for the land must include the name and address of the separate owner and must specify the rights owned by that person. An owner of the buildings, improvements, or rights in the land may list that ownership interest separately, in which case the tract, parcel, or lot on which the buildings or other improvements are situated and its owner must be identified. Alternatively, the land owner and the owner of the improvements or separate rights may agree to list the property in the name of the owner of the land.[64]

Abstracts for personal property must indicate the township and municipality, if any, in which the property is taxable.[65] Property must be itemized in the detail required on the county's abstract form, which must be approved by the Department of Revenue. The abstract form for personal property must indicate which property, if any, is subject to a tax credit under G.S. 105-151.21, which provides an income tax credit for property taxes paid by farmers on farm machinery.[66]

3.4.1 Signed Affirmation

The following signed affirmation must be affixed to each abstract on which a taxpayer lists personal property:

> Under penalties prescribed by law, I hereby affirm that to the best of my knowledge and belief this listing, including any accompanying statements, inventories, schedules, and other information, is true and complete.[67]

The affirmation must be signed by the person whose duty it is to list the property, except in certain situations. If an individual taxpayer is unable to list his or her property, a guardian, authorized agent, or other person with knowledge of and charged with the care of the person and property of the taxpayer must sign the required affirmation, noting the capacity in which he or she has signed.[68] In such a case, the person who signs the affirmation must affirm that he or she is familiar with the extent and true value of all the taxpayer's property subject to taxation in the county and that the affirmation is based on all the information he or she knows.[69]

Abstracts listing property owned by a corporation, partnership, or unincorporated association must be accompanied by an affirmation signed by a principal officer of the taxpayer or by a full-time employee officially empowered by a principal officer of the taxpayer to list the property and sign the affirmation annexed to the abstract.[70] A certified public accountant or tax preparer *may not* sign the affirmation on behalf of the corporation unless that person also is a principal officer or full-time employee of the corporation.

Finally, abstracts for real and personal property must contain, or be distributed with, a notice informing taxpayers of tax relief available under the homestead property tax exclusion provided for in G.S. 105-277.1 and the property tax homestead circuit breaker provided for in G.S. 105-277.1B.[71] These homestead relief benefits are discussed in greater detail in Chapter 7, "Exemptions and Exclusions."

3.5 Listing Aids

The assessor or others working in the business personal property section of the tax office may sometimes wish to obtain additional information to verify the accuracy and completeness of a listing form submitted by a taxpayer. The assessor may, after receiving and carefully reviewing a personal property abstract submitted by a taxpayer operating as a business enterprise, require the taxpayer to submit a detailed inventory, statement of assets and liabilities, or other similar information pertinent to the discovery or appraisal of property in the county.[72] Additional information provided to the assessor beyond what is required to be shown on the abstract itself is not a public record open to inspection.[73] Any assessor or other official or employee who discloses such additional information, except as is necessary for listing or appraising property in the performance of official duties or in administrative or judicial proceedings relating to his or her official duties, is guilty of a Class 3 misdemeanor and punishable by a fine not exceeding $50.

3.5.1 Subpoena Power

The assessor is authorized to subpoena persons and documents whenever he or she has reasonable grounds for believing that such a person has knowledge or that such documents contain information pertinent to the discovery or valuation of property subject to taxation in the county. The assessor also may subpoena persons or documents to obtain information necessary for compliance with the requirements as to what the tax list shall contain.[74] A subpoena from the tax assessor must be signed by the chairperson of the board of equalization and review if that board is in session or by the chairperson of the board of county commissioners and must be served by an officer qualified to serve subpoenas. Any person who willfully fails or refuses to appear, produce subpoenaed documents, or testify is guilty of a Class 1 misdemeanor.

3.5.2 Information from the Department of Revenue

The Department of Revenue may furnish to a tax official information contained in a report to it or any other state department (such as a state income tax return) and any information the department may have in its possession that may assist a local tax official in securing complete tax listings, appraising or assessing taxable property, collecting taxes, or presenting information in administrative or judicial proceedings involving the listing, appraisal, or assessment of property.[75] Local officials, employees, and agents may not reveal these documents or the information contained therein to the public, except as required in judicial or administrative proceedings under the provisions of the Machinery Act. Improperly using or disclosing such information constitutes a Class 1 misdemeanor pursuant to G.S. 153A-148.1 (applicable to county officials) and G.S. 160A-208.1 (applicable to city officials). A person convicted under either provision must be dismissed from public office or employment and may not hold public office or employment in North Carolina for five years after the violation. Copies of depreciation schedules from a taxpayer's income tax returns obtained from the Department of Revenue are an example of records that are not open to public inspection under this provision.

3.5.3 Report of Property by Multicounty Business

A taxpayer who is engaged in business in more than one North Carolina county and who owns real or tangible personal property in connection with the multicounty business must, upon the request of the Department of Revenue or the assessor of the county in which part of the business property is situated, file a report with the Department of Revenue stating the following information as of the date for listing property:

1. The counties in the state in which the taxpayer's business personal property is located

2. The taxpayer's county-by-county investment in business property situated in North Carolina
3. The taxpayer's total investment in business property situated in North Carolina[76]

The report must be sworn to by the owner of the property.[77] If the owner is a corporation, partnership, or unincorporated association, the report must be sworn to by a principal officer of the owner who has knowledge of the facts contained in the report.[78]

3.5.4 Other Assessment Information

3.5.4.1 Information from the Register of Deeds. To facilitate the accurate listing of real property for taxation, the board of county commissioners may require the register of deeds, upon the recording of a conveyance of real property (other than a deed of trust or mortgage), to certify to the assessor the name of the person conveying the property, the name and address of the person to whom the property is conveyed, a description of the property sufficient to locate and identify it, and a statement as to whether the parcel is conveyed in whole or part.[79] Alternatively, the board of county commissioners may require the register of deeds to refuse to record a conveyance of real property unless the deed has been presented to the assessor and the assessor has noted thereon that he or she has obtained the desired information from the conveyance and from the person recording it.[80] Under this system of pre-recordation review, the assessor can assign a parcel identification number to the resulting parcel before the conveyance is recorded. Regardless of whether a county imposes either review requirement upon its register of deeds, it obviously is essential to the accurate listing of real property that the county assessor or one of his or her employees promptly review all conveyances recorded with the register of deeds in order to ensure that tax records and maps are current and accurate.

3.5.4.2 Review of Building Permits. North Carolina law requires that a building permit be obtained before any construction or repair work may be performed on any commercial building and before any such work costing $5,000 or more may be performed on a single-family residence or farm building.[81] Because building permits are required for most substantial construction or improvement projects, all counties now routinely obtain and review building permits for use in listing and assessing improvements to real property. Even under today's permanent listing system for real property, property owners are required to annually list buildings and other improvements valued at more than $100 acquired, begun, erected, damaged, or destroyed since the time of the last appraisal.[82] Such improvements include renovations or additions to existing structures, paving, and construction of decks or patios but do not include betterments for which no reappraisal can occur in a reappraisal year, such as painting and landscaping.[83] Because few taxpayers comply with—or are even aware of—the requirement to list improvements to real property, a tax assessor can accomplish two objectives by listing and reappraising property based upon building permits. First, the assessor can immediately add the value of the improvements to the tax rolls, and second, the assessor can avoid discovering the improvements and assessing a penalty at some later date. No system is foolproof, however, and if a tax assessor fails to list an improvement for which a building permit was obtained, the existence of the building permit will not prevent the assessor from discovering the improvement.

3.6 Due Process Requirements

Local governments may only tax property that is subject to the jurisdiction of the state on the assessment date, which, for real and personal property other than registered motor vehicles, is January 1.[84] Property may constitutionally be subject to state or local property taxes only if there is a minimum connection between the state and the property it seeks to tax.[85] That is, the taxing power exerted by the state or local government must have a "'fiscal relation to protection, opportunities and benefits given by the state. The simple but controlling question is whether the state has given anything for which it can ask in return.'"[86] Taxation without such a connection violates the due process clause of the Fourteenth Amendment of the United States Constitution.[87]

The North Carolina Supreme Court considered in *Billings Transfer Corp. v. County of Davidson* whether the entire value of the truck fleet of a North Carolina–based trucking company was taxable by Davidson County for the years 1963 and 1964 or whether, as the trucking company contended, the county was obligated to apportion the taxes based on the ratio of miles traveled in North Carolina to total miles traveled. Then, as now, the Machinery Act provided that a corporation's tangible personal property was taxable at the place at which its principal North Carolina office was located, which, for Billings Transfer Corporation (Billings), was Davidson County. Billings argued that a portion of its rolling stock was taxable in the other states through which it regularly transported goods. The state supreme court noted that a state of domicile could not tax tangible personal property of its citizens that is permanently located in another state and agreed with Billings that Davidson County could tax only the portion of Billings's property that had not acquired a tax situs elsewhere. The court cited United States Supreme Court decisions holding that tax situs for vehicles operated in a state other than the state where the owner resides is established if vehicles are operated along fixed routes on regular schedules or the vehicles are habitually situated and employed within the other state throughout the tax year. That sort of continuous presence supports the imposition of an ad valorem tax based on the average number of vehicles that are continuously present in the nondomiciliary state. Such taxation by apportionment precludes taxation of *all* of the property by the state of residence. However, a mere general showing of the continuous use of tangible movable property in another state is *not* sufficient to prevent the domiciliary state from imposing a tax on the property. The taxpayer bears the burden of demonstrating that taxation by the state of domicile is improper because the taxpayer's property has acquired a tax situs elsewhere. It was on this last point that the state supreme court determined that Billings failed to meet its burden. The court held that it could not determine from Billings's evidence that a defined portion of its property had acquired a tax situs in a nondomiciliary state during the years in question.

A corollary to the principles articulated in *Billings Transfer* is that taxable tangible property belonging to a nonresident is subject to local property taxes in North Carolina if it has acquired a more or less permanent location in the state as distinguished from a transient or temporary presence.[88] Tangible personal property of a nonresident passing through North Carolina for temporary purposes only is not subject to property taxation by a city or county within the state. Personal property belonging to a nonresident must be in the state for an indefinite time or some considerable definite time and must be used in North Carolina in much the same manner as other property used in the state to be taxable in North Carolina.[89]

3.7 Listing Period

The listing period is the month of January, though the county board of commissioners may extend the general listing period for up to thirty additional days in a nonreappraisal year and up to sixty additional days in a reappraisal year.[90] At least ten days before the date as of which property is to be listed, the assessor must advertise in a newspaper having general circulation in the county and post in at least five public places in each township in the county a notice specifying the following: (1) the date as of which property is to be listed; (2) the date on which listing will begin; (3) the date on which listing will end; (4) the times between these dates during which lists will be accepted; (5) the place or places at which lists will be accepted; and (6) a statement that all persons who, on the date that property is to be listed, own property that is subject to taxation must list such property within the period set forth in the notice and that any person who fails to do so will be subject to the penalties prescribed by law.[91] If the county extends the listing period, the assessor must advertise that extension in the same way that he or she advertised the initial listing period.

The board also may, upon written request and good cause shown, grant individual listing extensions up to April 15. Many taxpayers request such an extension in order to base the information for personal property listing upon the schedules they prepare for income tax reporting purposes. A county that provides for the electronic listing of business personal property may extend up to June 1 the period for listing such property.

The Machinery Act requires that property be listed in any city or town in which it is subject to taxation in addition to being listed in the county where it is subject to being taxed. In lieu of requiring property owners to separately list property with a city or town, the Machinery Act permits a municipality to obtain from the county or counties in which it is located lists of property subject to taxation by the municipality. While cities and towns retain the authority to require separate listing,[92] no municipality in North Carolina today requires that taxpayers submit a separate listing form.

The Machinery Act is written as though all abstracts are filed in person and provides that the assessor may exercise discretion to allow for the filing of abstracts by mail. In practice, most abstracts are submitted by mail. Counties also may allow the electronic filing of abstracts. Pursuant to G.S. 105-311(b), abstracts filed by mail are considered filed as of the date shown on the postmark affixed by the United States Postal Service. If no date is shown or the postmark is affixed by a private party rather than the United States Postal Service, the abstract is considered filed when received in the office of the assessor. If a dispute arises regarding the timely filing of an abstract, the taxpayer bears the burden of demonstrating timely filing.

Timeliness of filing can only be determined under G.S. 105-311(b) when an envelope is available for examination.[93] In *Winston-Salem Joint Venture v. City of Winston-Salem*,[94] the city and county alleged that they never received a listing form for business personal property located in Hanes Mall in Winston-Salem. The taxpayer's accountant contended that he filed and mailed a listing form on February 24, 1978, before the listing period concluded on March 2, 1978. The city and county discovered the unlisted property and assessed a penalty of more than $22,000. The taxpayer paid the penalty under protest and filed an action in Forsyth County Superior Court to recover the penalty. The trial court granted judgment for the city and county based on its determination that no listing form was ever received and dismissed the taxpayer's suit. The taxpayer appealed, and the court of appeals held that for G.S. 105-311 to apply "there must be conclusive evidence of the existence of an envelope." To conclude otherwise would enlarge the scope of the statute and allow a city or county, by denying receipt of an abstract, to foreclose the taxpayer from proving timely receipt. The court of appeals held that when "there was no conclusive evidence of the existence of an envelope," the "common law"—in other words, the holdings of courts in previous cases—rather than G.S. 105-311 controlled resolution of the issue of receipt. The court then cited the common law principle that evidence of the deposit in the mail of a letter, properly stamped and addressed, warranted a finding that it was received in due course by the addressee. The city and county's evidence in *Winston-Salem Joint Venture* that the mailing was never received raised a factual conflict as to whether the taxpayer mailed the listing form in time for the city and county to receive it before the listing deadline expired. The case was remanded to the trial court, and the taxpayer prevailed at trial by persuading the jury that it timely listed its real property.[95]

Taxing units may consider the court's holding in *Winston-Salem Joint Venture* as instructive on two points. First, taxing units should keep copies of the envelopes accompanying late-mailed abstracts, in the event a dispute arises over the date of receipt. Adoption of this practice presumably would not have changed the outcome in *Winston-Salem Joint Venture*, however, since Forsyth County alleged that it never received the listing form. The second point for which the court's analysis is useful is that it provides taxing units, and their attorneys, with some direction in evaluating whether a listing form that it never received might be deemed timely filed.

3.8 Place for Listing

All taxable real property other than public service company system property must be listed in the county where it is located.[96] If any portion of the real property is situated within the boundaries of a city, that information must appear on the abstract. With the exception of property situated at the borders of a city or county, the proper listing place for real property generally is easy to determine, given the permanent, affixed nature of such property.

As previously noted, personal property is divided into two types under the Machinery Act: tangible and intangible. *Intangible property* is defined as "patents, copyrights, secret processes, formulae, good will, trademarks, trade brands, franchises, stocks, bonds, cash, bank deposits, notes, evidences of debt, leasehold interests in exempted real property, bills and accounts receivable, and other like property."[97] *Tangible property* is defined as "all personal property that is not intangible and that is not permanently affixed to real property."[98] The general rule governing the listing of taxable personal property requires that it be listed in the county in which the place of taxation is located under the rules set forth in the Machinery Act.[99] Tangible personal property generally is taxable at the residence of the owner.[100] Personal property within the state that belongs to owners who have no fixed residence in North Carolina is taxable at the place at which it is situated.[101]

The residence of an individual person who has two or more places in the state at which he occasionally dwells is the place at which the person dwelt for the longest period of time during the calendar year immediately preceding the date as of which the property is to be listed for taxation.[102] The residence of a domestic or foreign taxpayer other than an individual person is the place at which its principal North Carolina place of business is located.[103]

3.9 Special Situs Rules

There are several exceptions to the general rule that personal property is taxable at the residence of the owner. First, tangible personal property situated at or commonly used at a temporary or seasonal dwelling owned or leased by the owner of the personal property is taxable at the place at which the temporary or seasonal dwelling is situated, rather than the owner's residence.[104] The term *situated* means "more or less permanently located." Under this rule, a boat kept at an owner's seasonal beach residence is taxable in the jurisdiction where the seasonal residence is located rather than in the jurisdiction where the individual lives.

The second exception applies to tangible personal property situated at or commonly used in connection with a business premises used by the owner of the personal property or by an agent or employee of the owner. Such property is taxable at the place at which the business premises are situated.[105] Thus cash registers owned by a company with its principal offices in Mecklenburg County but located in a store in Carteret County are subject to taxation by Carteret County, not Mecklenburg County. This rule also governs the taxation of tangible personal property that may be used by the general public, such as vending machines, rendering such property taxable by the taxing unit in which the property is situated rather than by the taxing unit in which the owner of the property resides.

The third exception applies to property situated at or commonly used in connection with a premise owned, hired, occupied, or used by a person who is in possession of the personal property under a business agreement with the owner of the property. Such personal property is taxable at the place of the possessor's premises. The term *business agreement* is defined as a commercial lease, bailment for hire, consignment, or similar business arrangement. Thus computer equipment leased by a company with its principal office in Durham County to a business for use in its Wake County office building is taxable in Wake County, not Durham County.

Moreover, while G.S. 105-304(f)(4) provides that the presence of property in one of the locations specified in the exceptions on January 1 is prima facie evidence that it is situated at or commonly used in connection with that location, the temporary absence of tangible personal property on January 1 from the place at which it is taxable under the three exceptions outlined above does not defeat application of the rules. The temporary absence rule and the corollary definition of situated were applied in *In re Bassett Furniture Industries, Inc.*, to uphold Rockingham County's taxation of an airplane owned by a furniture company with its principal office and place of business in Bassett, Virginia.[106] Bassett Furniture Industries (Bassett) purchased a jet in May 1983. Before that time, Bassett, which had no principal place of business in North Carolina, stored all of its aircraft at the Blue Ridge Airport in Spencer, Virginia, where it had constructed a permanent hangar. The Blue Ridge Airport did not, however, have a runway long enough for taking off and landing Basset's jet. As a result, in June 1983, Bassett entered into a month-to-month lease for hangar space with an operator at the Shiloh Airport in Rockingham County, located about thirty-five miles from its headquarters. Bassett began using the Shiloh Airport for its jet in July 1983.

That same summer, Bassett negotiated with Blue Ridge Airport authorities to lengthen the runway at Blue Ridge. These negotiations culminated in an August 1983 contract to lengthen the runway in a project scheduled to be completed in September 1984.

In the meantime, Bassett hangared the jet at Shiloh from July 1983 until June 1984. During that time, Bassett occasionally used the jet at Blue Ridge. Indeed, on January 1, 1984, the jet was located at the Blue Ridge Airport. However, from January 4, 1984, until June 1984, Bassett used the jet solely at the Shiloh Airport. Virginia law required that sales tax be paid on the jet when it became based in Virginia; Basset did not pay the sales tax until August 1984.

Bassett argued that the jet was not within the jurisdiction of North Carolina on January 1, 1984, and that it was therefore not subject to taxation by Rockingham County. Bassett argued that the taxation of the jet deprived the company of its property and denied it equal protection under the law in violation of the due process and equal protection clauses of the Fourteenth Amendment as the jet had no tax situs in North Carolina.

The North Carolina Court of Appeals disagreed. Citing G.S. 105-274(b) for the proposition that "[n]o provision of [the Machinery Act] shall be construed to exempt from taxation any property situated in this State belonging to any foreign corporation unless the context of the provision clearly indicates a legislative intent to grant such an exemption" and the provision of G.S. 105-304 that "[t]angible personal property owned by a domestic or foreign taxpayer . . . that has no principal office in this State shall be taxable at the place in this State at which the property is situated," the court concluded that the airplane was situated in North Carolina within the meaning of the Machinery Act. The court noted that *situated* was defined as "more or less permanently located."

The court of appeals looked to the state supreme court's interpretation of "more or less permanently located" in *In re Appeal of Finishing Touch Co.*,[107] a case in which the state supreme court adopted the following analysis regarding the taxation of tangible personal property:

> Before tangible personal property may be taxed in a state other than the domicil of the owner, it must have acquired a more or less permanent location in that state, and not merely a transient or temporary one. Generally, chattels merely temporarily or transiently within the limits of a state are not subject to its property taxes. Tangible personal property passing through or in the state for temporary purposes only, if it belongs to a nonresident, is not subject to taxation under a statute providing that all real and personal property in the state shall be assessed and taxed. . . . A criterion is whether the property is there for an indefinite time or some considerable definite time, and whether it is used or exists there to be used in much the same manner as other property is used in that community. . . . Permanency in the sense of permanency of real estate is not essential to the establishment of a taxable situs for tangible personal property. It means a more or less permanent location for the time being. The ownership and uses for which the property is designed, and the circumstances of its being in the state, are so various that the question is often more a question of fact than of law. In the final analysis, the test perhaps is whether or not property is within the state solely for use and profit there . . . .[108]

The court of appeals reasoned that in order to be taxable in a particular jurisdiction, personal property had to "be associated with the general mass of property in the state, as contrasted with a transient status [that is, the] likelihood of being in one state today and in another tomorrow." The court determined that, regardless of its absence from Rockingham County on January 1, 1984, the jet was situated or more or less permanently located in Rockingham County on that date and therefore had a tax situs in Rockingham County for the 1984 tax year.

Figure 3.1 sets forth the general rule and the exceptions for determining the tax situs of personal property.

Figure 3.1—Tax Situs of Personal Property

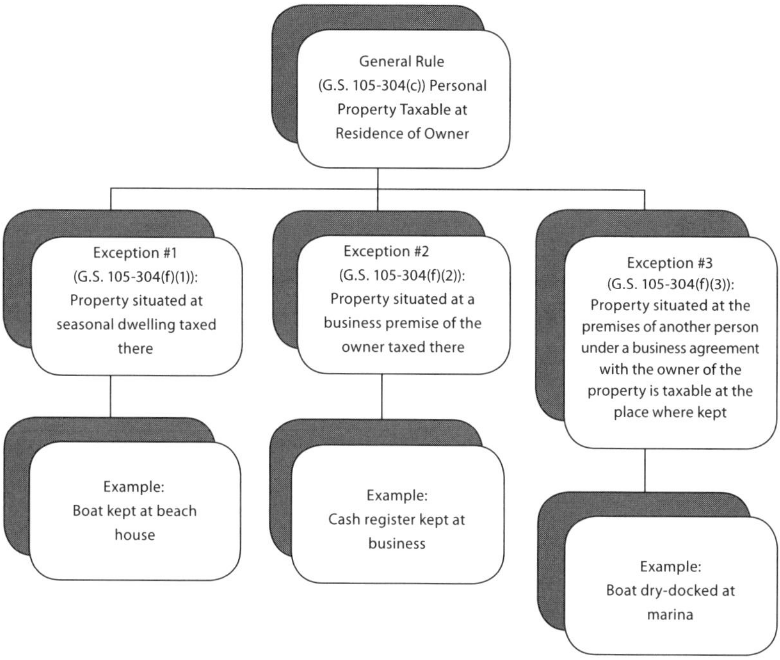

3.9.1 Tax Situs of Property of Decedents and Fiduciaries

When a person dies in possession of personal property, the estate often may not be settled by the following January 1. In such circumstances, the decedent's tangible personal property is taxable at the place it would be taxable if the decedent were still alive and still residing at the place where the decedent resided at the time he or she died.

The tax location, or situs, of tangible personal property within the state that is held by a fiduciary for the benefit of another depends upon whether any beneficiary is a resident of North Carolina. If any beneficiary is a resident of the state, an amount representing that beneficiary's portion of the property is taxable at the place where it would be taxable if the beneficiary owned that portion outright. Any portion attributable to a nonresident beneficiary is taxable at the place at which it would be taxable if the fiduciary were the beneficial owner of the property.

Given that taxpayers will only list property they consider to be located for tax purposes in a particular taxing unit, appeals regarding disputes over the proper tax situs of property arise in the context of property listed by the assessor in a discovery procedure, which is discussed below.[109]

3.9.2 Servicemembers Civil Relief Act

The Servicemembers Civil Relief Act[110] provides that a "servicemember shall neither lose nor acquire a residence or domicile for purposes of taxation with respect to the person, personal property, or income of the servicemember by reason of being absent or present in any tax jurisdiction of the United States solely in compliance with military orders" and that "the personal property of a servicemember shall not be deemed to be located or present in, or to have a situs for taxation in, the tax jurisdiction in which the servicemember is serving in compliance with military orders." Thus the personal property of a member of the uniformed services[111] who is present in a North Carolina county solely because of military orders (that is, the servicemember's permanent residence or domicile, indicated as his or her "home of record" on the Leave and Earnings statement, is elsewhere) is not subject to ad valorem taxation.[112] This rule "does not prevent taxation by a tax jurisdiction with respect to personal property used in or arising from a trade or business, if it has jurisdiction."[113] Moreover, it does not bar taxation of property owned by the spouse of a deployed servicemember if that property has a tax situs in a taxing unit in North Carolina. Finally, if the servicemember's home of record is North Carolina, the property is fully taxable by the taxing unit or units where it is situated. For example, a car owned by a servicemember whose permanent residence is in Mitchell County, North Carolina, but who is stationed on active duty at Fort Bragg in Cumberland County, North Carolina, is taxable by Mitchell County rather than Cumberland County.

3.10 Applications for Exemption, Exclusion, or Other Special Tax Status

Most applications requesting the exemption or exclusion of property from taxation or the taxation of property based upon its present-use value must be filed with the county during the regular listing period. The taxpayer must indicate any municipality in which the property is located on the application filed with the county. Most applications for exemption or exclusion need only be filed once, with subsequent applications required only for disqualifying changes in circumstances. The governing board of a county or city may grant late-filed applications for exemption or exclusion within the calendar year in which the original exemption application was filed upon the taxpayer's demonstration of good cause for the late filing.[114]

3.11 Discovery of Unlisted Property

The county assessor or municipal official charged with discovery of unlisted property at the city level is responsible for ensuring that all property not properly listed during the regular listing period be listed, assessed, and taxed.[115] To *discover* property means to determine that it has not been timely listed; that a taxpayer made a substantial understatement of listed property; or that the property was granted an exemption or exclusion for which it did not qualify.[116] Discovered property is listed in the name of the person who should have listed the property or in whose name the county was required to list the property under its permanent listing system.[117] A discovery is made on the date the property is listed or the existing listing is corrected.[118] The assessor must, in addition to listing the property, make a tentative appraisal of the discovered property.[119] The assessor then must mail a notice of the discovery to the person in whose name the discovered property is listed.[120] The notice must contain the person's name and address, a description of the property, a tentative appraisal of the property, and a statement that the listing and appraisal will become final unless the taxpayer files a written appeal with the assessor within thirty days from the date of the notice.[121]

If the taxpayer files a timely written appeal of the discovery with the assessor, the assessor must set up a conference with the taxpayer, during which the taxpayer may present evidence or argument regarding the discovery.[122] Within fifteen days after the conference, the assessor must give the taxpayer written notice of his or her final decision, unless the taxpayer has signed an agreement accepting the listing and appraisal.[123] The taxpayer has fifteen days from the date of the notice from the assessor to request review of the assessor's decision by the board of equalization and review or, if that board is not in session, by the board of county commissioners.[124] Unless the taxpayer requests review by the county board at the conference, the taxpayer must make the request in writing to the assessor.[125]

Taxpayers sometimes contend that they may challenge in a discovery appeal all assessments of property for the year at issue, including the assessment of property that was not a part of the discovery. The argument, in essence, is that the taxpayer may have overpaid taxes on other assets in the years in question and that it would be inequitable to require the taxpayer to pay additional taxes without taking into account the earlier over-assessment and resulting overpayment. Acceptance of this argument would enable taxpayers whose property was discovered to challenge assessments from previous years that otherwise could not be challenged. This interpretation does not square with the time limits for appealing valuations for a particular year and the Machinery Act's clear preference for stability in the tax base. Upon taxpayer challenge, assessors should consider only the valuation of property that is the subject of a discovery.

When property is discovered and listed to a taxpayer in a given year, a presumption arises that it should have been listed for the previous five years unless the taxpayer demonstrates that the property did not exist in those years, that it actually was listed, or that it was not the taxpayer's duty to list the property during the years in question.[126] If someone other than the taxpayer in whose name the discovery is made was charged with the duty to list the property during one or more years of the discovery, the property must be listed in the name of that taxpayer.[127] The discovery is still deemed to be made for all years as of the date the assessor first listed the property.[128]

When property is discovered, it is taxed for the year in which it is discovered and for any of the preceding five years during which it was not taxed.[129] The tax amount for each year is based upon the assessed value the property should have been assigned in each year and the tax rate in effect for that year.[130] If the discovery is based on an understatement of value or quantity of property, the tax included in the discovery is based upon the additional valuation.[131]

A penalty of 10 percent of the amount of the tax resulting from the discovery, plus an additional 10 percent of the same amount for each subsequent listing period that elapsed before the property was discovered, applies to each year of the discovery.[132] The penalty is computed separately for each year in which the property was not timely listed.[133] The year, the amount of tax for the year, and the total of penalties for failure to list in that year are shown separately on the tax records.[134] The taxes and penalties for all years then are totaled on a single tax receipt.[135] These penalties apply even if the property is actually listed by the taxpayer during the calendar year in which the fiscal year opens but is not timely listed. While such penalties are commonly termed *late-listing penalties*, they are imposed pursuant to G.S. 105-312 and are technically *discovery penalties*. A sample discovery calculation is set forth in table 3.1.

Table 3.1 Sample Discovery Calculation

The business personal property section of the Knapp County Assessor's Office determined in March 2009 that ABC Corporation failed to list any of its taxable machinery and equipment for the past ten years. The maximum allowable tax and penalty that will be due upon a 2009 discovery of the property are set forth below. Taxes resulting from a 2009 discovery are treated as 2009–10 taxes and are due September 1, 2009. They are last payable at par (without interest) on January 5, 2010.

Year	Value	Tax Rate	Taxes	Penalty	Penalty Amount	Total
2009	$300,000	$0.50	$1,500.00	10%	$150.00	$1,650.00
2008	$250,000	$0.60	$1,500.00	20%	$300.00	$1,800.00
2007	$275,000	$0.70	$1,925.00	30%	$577.50	$2,502.50
2006	$315,000	$0.50	$1,575.00	40%	$630.00	$2,205.00
2005	$325,000	$0.55	$1,787.50	50%	$893.75	$2,681.25
2004	$375,000	$0.55	$2,062.50	60%	$1237.50	$3,300.00
Total	$1,840,000		$10,350.00		$3,788.75	$14,138.75

Discovery penalties are imposed based upon a taxpayer's failure to properly and timely list taxable property. As previously discussed, in a permanent listing system, the duty to list real property (other than new improvements) is borne by the assessor rather than the taxpayer. The Machinery Act thus specifically provides that no penalty applies to the failure to list real property, though such property may be the subject of a discovery.[136] Discovery penalties *do* apply to discoveries resulting from the taxpayer's failure to report the construction or acquisition of improvements on and separate rights in real property.

The governing board of a city or county is authorized, upon petition of the taxpayer, to compromise, settle, or adjust a city's or county's claim for taxes arising from a discovery after a receipt for the discovery has been charged to the tax collector and before the taxes have been paid.[137] The board of county commissioners may, by resolution, delegate its authority to compromise discovered amounts to the board of equalization and review. The Machinery Act provides no guidance on the standards for compromising discovered amounts[138] and allows any portion (or all) of the discovered taxes, as well as penalties, to be forgiven upon petition by the taxpayer. Cities may delegate their compromise authority to the county or may reserve to their own governing boards the right to grant or deny discovery appeals.

The Machinery Act does not specify whether a taxpayer may appeal the city's or county's denial of a petition to compromise taxes pursuant to G.S. 105-312(k) to the Property Tax Commission, and no North Carolina courts have addressed the issue. As a practical matter, the Property Tax Commission has accepted and ruled upon at least one appeal of a board's compromise decision under G.S. 105-312. In a 1990 order, the commission upheld the Onslow County Board of Equalization and Review's denial of a request to release a late-listing penalty imposed upon the taxpayer's listing of property two days after the conclusion of the regular listing period.[139] Noting that "[t]he decision as to whether to compromise pursuant to G.S. 105-312(k) is a purely discretionary matter," the commission held that "where the county board acts in good faith, its decision must stand."[140]

Property exempted upon application of the taxpayer may be subject to discovery for failure to notify the assessor of change or disqualifying circumstances. If unlisted property for which no exemption or exclusion application has been filed is discovered, the property owner must be afforded the opportunity upon appeal to demonstrate that the property is eligible for exemption or exclusion. If the owner carries this burden, then the board may approve the exemption or exclusion.[141]

3.12 Public Records Law

Most of the records maintained by the tax assessor are public records that may be viewed by any person upon request. *Public records* are broadly defined to include "all documents, papers, letters, maps, books, photographs, films, sound recordings, magnetic or other tapes, electronic data-processing records, artifacts, or other documentary material, regardless of physical form or characteristics, made or received pursuant to law or ordinance in connection with the transaction of public business by any agency of North Carolina government or its subdivisions."[142] North Carolina law provides that "public records and public information compiled by the agencies of North Carolina government or its subdivisions are the property of the people."[143] It is, therefore, "the policy of this State that the people may obtain copies of their public records and public information free or at minimal cost unless otherwise specifically provided by law."[144] The term *minimal cost* means the actual cost of reproducing the public record or public information.[145]

3.12.1 Custody

The Machinery Act requires that county tax records be filed in the office of the assessor unless the board of county commissioners requires them to be filed in some other public office.[146] The public official in charge of an office where public records are housed is the legal custodian of the records.[147] Thus the county assessor is the legal custodian of all county tax records.[148] Municipal tax records must be filed in the public office of the municipality designated by the governing body. Most municipalities designate the office of the tax collector as the place for the filing of tax records, thereby rendering the tax collector the legal custodian of municipal tax records.[149]

The custodian of a public record may not destroy, sell, lend, or otherwise dispose of it except in accordance with legally established procedures.[150] Any person who unlawfully removes a public record from the office where it is usually kept or who alters, defaces, or destroys a public record is guilty of a Class 3 misdemeanor.[151] An offense of this class subjects an offender with no prior convictions to a possible sentence of up to ten days and a fine of up to $500.[152] The assessor is required to deliver to his or her successor all public records in his or her custody.[153] Failure to deliver the records is a Class 1 misdemeanor.[154] An offense of this class subjects an offender with no prior convictions to a possible sentence of up to forty-five days and a fine in the court's discretion.[155] The assessor is entitled to the custody of all public records for which he or she is responsible and may make a formal demand for them from anyone having unlawful possession of them.[156] Any person in unlawful possession of public records who refuses or neglects to return them to their custodian on demand is also guilty of a Class 1 misdemeanor.[157] There is also a civil procedure for regaining custody of public records from someone not entitled to have them.[158]

3.12.2 Public Access

Every person has the right to inspect and copy any public record unless there is a statute that specifically makes the record confidential.[159] The person desiring to view or obtain a public record does not have to disclose the reason for the request.[160] The custodian must permit inspection of such records "at reasonable times and under reasonable supervision" and must provide copies of records "as promptly as possible" upon payment of any required fees.[161]

Persons requesting copies of public records may obtain them "in any and all media in which the public agency is capable of providing them."[162] The choice of medium is the citizen's; the custodian is not allowed to dictate that choice but may charge different fees for different media.[163] Unless another law specifies the fee to be charged for copies, or a certified copy is requested, the custodian of a public record may charge no more than the actual cost of making the requested copies.[164] *Actual cost* is limited to "direct, chargeable costs related to the reproduction of a public record" and does not include costs that the agency would have incurred anyway.[165] Thus a tax assessor may not impose a charge based upon the salary or hourly wages of an employee who produces the copies or based upon the fixed cost of depreciation of the equipment used to make the copy.[166] There is a special exception for requests that require extensive use of information technology or extensive clerical or supervisory assistance from tax office personnel.[167] Occasionally, local tax officials receive requests for reports, lists, or other compilations of data that do not exist. Cities and counties are not required to create computer databases that they have not otherwise created or that are not otherwise required to be created in order to respond to such requests.[168]

3.12.3 Geographic Information System Records

The duty to create and maintain county tax maps and geographic information system (GIS) databases commonly is charged to the office of the tax assessor. Thus the assessor must respond to requests for access to and copies of GIS records. G.S. 132-10 provides that GIS databases and data files developed and operated by counties and cities are public records and requires counties and cities to provide public access to such systems by public access terminals or other devices.[169] In addition, a county or city must furnish, at reasonable cost, copies of its GIS databases and files, in documentary or electronic form, to anyone requesting them. While the statute does not define the term *reasonable cost*, it likely includes charges that cannot be included in actual cost, such as personnel costs associated with producing the copy and copy equipment depreciation.[170] Cities and counties probably cannot attempt to recoup the costs of developing the GIS database through charges for copies of GIS records.[171]

As a condition of furnishing an electronic copy of its GIS records, a county or city may require that the person obtaining the copy agree in writing that the copy will not be resold or otherwise used for trade or commercial purposes. If the person refuses to so agree, the county or city may refuse to supply the record.[172] Publication or broadcast by the news media, real estate trade associations, or multiple listing services operated by real estate trade associations are not considered use for a commercial purpose. Likewise, resale at cost by a real estate trade association or a multiple listing service operated by a real estate trade association is not a resale or use of the data for a trade or commercial purpose.

If a city or county so wishes, it may provide a copy of its GIS database to a person who desires to use the records for a commercial purpose. In such a case, the city or county is not bound by the reasonable cost limitation and may set whatever price it wishes as a condition of providing the database.[173]

3.12.4 Confidential Information

Several categories of public records are not open to public inspection. For some of them, the law provides simply that the custodian is under no legal obligation to allow public access. For others, the law goes further and makes it a crime to permit public access.

3.12.4.1 Security Features of Information Systems. No governmental agency is required to disclose security features of its electronic data processing systems, information technology systems, telecommunications networks, or electronic security systems.[174]

3.12.4.2 Information about a Taxpayer's Income or Receipts. Local tax records that contain information about a taxpayer's income or receipts are not open to public inspection.[175] A tax assessor or appraiser may obtain such information, for example, in connection with an appraisal of income-producing property. Current or former officials or employees who have or had access to information of this nature may disclose it only as necessary to administer a tax, to comply with a law or court order, to the state attorney general, or to a regional public transportation authority or the Department of Revenue, for limited purposes. Unlawful disclosure of this information is a Class 1 misdemeanor. An offense of this class subjects an offender with no prior convictions to a possible sentence of up to forty-five days and a fine in the court's discretion.[176] If the offender is currently a public officer or employee, he or she must be dismissed and may not hold any other public office or employment in North Carolina for five years thereafter.

Tax officials and employees may, however, include on a property tax receipt the amount of property taxes due and the amount of property taxes deferred on a residence entitled to tax relief under the circuit breaker tax relief program,[177] notwithstanding that inclusion of this amount on a tax receipt, which is a public record, provides information from which the taxpayer's income may be calculated.[178]

3.12.4.3 Supplemental Financial Information. There is no right of public access to information not required to appear on the abstract that a taxpayer has supplied at the request of the assessor in order to enable the assessor to properly list and assess the property.[179] Examples of this kind of information include financial statements, rent schedules, copies of lease agreements, acquisition cost of fixed assets, and depreciation schedules supplied by the taxpayer. Unlawful disclosure of this information is a Class 3 misdemeanor, punishable only by a fine not exceeding $50.[180]

3.12.4.4 Written Communications from Legal Counsel. The public records law allows any public agency to withhold from public access for up to three years any written communication that falls within the attorney–client privilege and is related to any litigation involving the agency.[181] In the context of the assessor's office, this exception would cover any correspondence between the tax office and an attorney representing the county in a property tax appeal. There is no penalty for disclosing information of this type.

3.12.4.5 Personnel Records. Personnel files of public employees, former employees, or applicants for employment are not open to public inspection,[182] but certain information about each current county employee is a matter of public record. This information includes name, age, date of original employment, current position title, current salary, date and amount of the most recent increase or decrease in salary, date of the most recent change in position classification, and the office to which the employee is currently assigned. A public official who knowingly, willingly, and with malice allows access to a personnel file is guilty of a Class 3 misdemeanor punishable only by a fine up to $500.[183] Any person not authorized to have access to a confidential personnel file also commits a Class 3 misdemeanor punishable only by a fine up to $500 by knowingly and willfully examining the file or removing or copying any portion of it.[184]

3.12.4.6 Identifying Information. County assessors frequently request that taxpayers provide their Social Security or tax identification numbers. Listing forms mailed to taxpayers often request that such identifying information be noted on the form returned to the tax office. This information is useful to the county tax collector if enforced collection measures, such as attachment of bank accounts or the setoff of state income tax refunds owed to taxpayers, become necessary to enforce the payment of taxes.

The Identity Theft Protection Act of 2005 contains several provisions that govern the collection and dissemination of such identifying information. G.S. 132-1.10(b)(1) prohibits governmental units and their agents and employees from collecting a Social Security number from an individual unless the governmental unit is authorized by law to collect the number or collection of the number is "otherwise imperative for the performance of [the] agency's duties and responsibilities." A governmental unit or agency that collects Social Security numbers pursuant to either exception must segregate the number on a separate page from other records or take other appropriate measures so that it may easily be redacted pursuant to a public records request.[185] The governmental unit must also provide an individual with a statement of the purpose for which the number is collected and used.[186] The number may be used only for the stated purpose.[187]

State and local governments may, under federal law, require an individual to provide his or her Social Security number as part of the administration of a state or local tax.[188] Thus taxing units may continue to collect Social Security numbers pursuant to the administration of the property tax but must ensure that such numbers are stored in a manner to adequately protect them from disclosure. Taxing units also must ensure that requests for Social Security numbers comport with the requirements of the State Privacy Act, enacted in 2001. The State Privacy Act, codified at G.S. 143-64.6, requires a local government requesting disclosure of a Social Security number to inform the individual whether the disclosure is mandatory or voluntary, by what authority the number is solicited, and what uses will be made of the number.

Many taxing units use commercial databases to obtain taxpayer information, including Social Security numbers. Social Security numbers gathered from third parties must, like numbers gathered from individuals, be safeguarded from public disclosure. G.S. 132-1.10(b)(5) bars governmental units from intentionally communicating or making available to the general public a person's Social Security number or other *identifying information*, defined as a tax identification number, driver's license number, checking or savings account number, credit or debit card number, PIN code for a financial transaction card, digital signature, biometric data, fingerprints, or password, or a number or information that could be used to access a person's financial resources (other than an e-mail name or address, Internet account number, or Internet identification name). A separate provision of Chapter 132 defines *person* as an individual, corporation, government, governmental subdivision or agency, business trust, estate, trust, partnership, association, joint venture, or any other legal or commercial entity. Thus taxing units may not disclose identifying information, including tax identification numbers, for either businesses or individuals.

As of July 1, 2007, governmental units may no longer print an individual's Social Security number on materials mailed to the individual, unless state or federal law requires that the number appear on the document or unless the number is redacted.[189] If state or federal law requires that the Social Security number appear on a mailed document, no portion of the number may be printed on a postcard or be visible on the outside of an envelope.[190] Because there is no requirement that listing forms contain a taxpayer's Social Security number, that number should not appear on a listing form mailed to the taxpayer. In addition, because most listing forms from previous years contain Social Security numbers, tax assessors must ensure that those numbers are redacted before abstracts are disclosed to the public.

3.12.4.7 Division of Motor Vehicles Records. The federal Driver's Privacy Protection Act (DPPA) prohibits the release of personal, identifying information about an individual obtained from the Division of Motor Vehicles.[191] The federal act does not prohibit the release of information that identifies a particular car, such as make, model, tag, or vehicle identification number (VIN) number, nor does it prohibit the release of documents that the county generates documenting its action on taxpayer requests for refunds of motor vehicle taxes.[192]

While the plain language of the federal law prohibits a taxing unit from releasing an individual's name, address, or driver's license number obtained from the Division of Motor Vehicles, in 2005 the Chief Deputy Attorney General issued an advisory opinion letter to George Tatum, then Commissioner of DMV, opining that "[m]otor vehicle registration information provided by DMV to local taxing authorities should also be provided upon request in accordance with the Public Records Act."[193] Although acknowledging that "a literal reading of the DPPA's definition of 'personal information,' . . . can be interpreted to preclude the release of information connecting a particular vehicle to a[n] individual name and address," the attorney general letter opined that "the better interpretation . . . allows a local taxing authority to release vehicle tax information in accordance with North Carolina's Public Records Act."[194] The attorney general's opinion leaves counties in somewhat of a predicament given that it appears, at least in the view of this author, to contradict federal law. County assessors should, at a minimum, seek advice from legal counsel before disclosing personally identifying information obtained from DMV.

3.12.4.8 Address Confidentiality Program. The Address Confidentiality Program is a program of the state attorney general's office that protects the confidentiality of the address of a relocated victim of domestic violence, sexual offense, stalking, or human trafficking to prevent assailants from finding the victim through public records.[195] Participants in the program are issued address confidentiality program authorization cards.[196] Program participants then must request that state and local agencies use the address designated by the attorney general as their substitute address.[197] The Attorney General acts as the agent of the program participant for purposes of service of process and receiving and forwarding first-class mail or certified or registered mail.[198] The substitute address is *not* used for purposes of listing, appraising, assessing, or collecting property taxes. Thus property owned by a program participant remains taxable in the jurisdiction in which it is taxable pursuant to the situs provisions of the Machinery Act. Nonetheless, a program participant's actual address and telephone number are *not* public record and must not be revealed by the taxing unit.[199]

For purposes of levying and collecting property taxes on motor vehicles, the Attorney General must provide the county or city tax assessor or collector a list of names and actual addresses of program participants who reside in the county or city.[200] The list may be used only for listing, appraising, assessing, and collecting taxes on motor vehicles in the county or city to which the list is provided.[201] No current or former officer, employee, or agent of a county or city may disclose the information to any other person.[202]

Any person who knowingly and intentionally obtains or discloses information in violation of G.S. Chapter 15C shall be guilty of a Class 1 misdemeanor and assessed a fine not to exceed $2,500.[203]

3.12.5 Retention

The Department of Cultural Resources is the state's official archival agency and no records may be destroyed without its consent.[204] The department has adopted a series of Records Retention and Disposition Schedules for almost all forms of records held by local governments.[205] In order to be able to dispose of records pursuant to one of these schedules, a city's or county's governing board must sign an agreement with the department promising to comply with the schedule.[206] When a city or county so agrees and subsequently destroys a record pursuant to an agreement, it must do so by burning the record, shredding the record, placing the record in an acid vat, burying the record, or selling the record as waste paper.[207]

Notes

1. N.C. Gen. Stat. § 105-273(13) (hereinafter G.S.).

2. Pritchard v. Williams, 181 N.C. 46, 106 S.E. 144 (1921).

3. Hughes v. Young, 115 N.C. App. 325, 328, 444 S.E.2d 248, 250 (1994).

4. Little v. Nat'l Serv. Indus., Inc., 79 N.C. App. 688, 340 S.E.2d 510 (1986).

5. *See Little*, 79 N.C. App. at 692, 340 S.E.2d at 513 (setting forth tests for determining whether property is a fixture and concluding that chairlift system is a fixture); *see also* Moore's Ferry Dev. Corp. v. City of Hickory, 166 N.C. App. 441, 447, 601 S.E.2d 900, 904 (2004) (applying the *Little* test and concluding that visitors center is personal property); *Hughes*, 115 N.C. App. at 329, 444 S.E.2d at 250–51 (applying *Little* test and concluding that mobile home is real property); Wilson v. McLeod Oil Co., Inc., 327 N.C. 491, 515–18, 398 S.E.2d 586, 598–600 (1990) (applying *Little* test and concluding that certain underground gasoline storage tanks are personal property, while others may be considered improvements to real property).

6. *Little*, 79 N.C. App. at 692, 340 S.E.2d at 513.

7. *Id.* at 693; 340 S.E.2d at 513.

8. G.S. 105-273(13) (incorporating definition of manufactured home in G.S. 143-143.9(6)). Questions may arise regarding whether the term *manufactured home* includes structures referred to as mobile homes. The term *mobile home* is defined in G.S. 105-316.7 (for purposes of the statutes governing the issuance of moving permits) as "a structure that (i) is designed, constructed, and intended for use as a dwelling house, office, place of business, or similar place of habitation and (ii) is capable of being transported from place to place on wheels attached to its frame. It also means a manufactured home as described in G.S. 105-273(13)." Thus manufactured homes appear to be a subset of the structures referred to as mobile homes.

9. G.S. 105-273(8).

10. G.S. 105-273(13).

11. *In re* University of North Carolina, 300 N.C. 563, 268 S.E.2d 472 (1980).

12. *See* Marks v. Comm'r of Internal Revenue, T.C.M. 1985-179 (explaining that "[a] leasehold interest has value when the contract rent which the tenant is obligated to pay is less than the fair market rent which the leased property could command in a competitive real estate market").

13. William A. Campbell and Joseph S. Ferrell, *Local Taxes and Tax Collection, in* North Carolina Legislation 1993 119, 120 (Joseph S. Ferrell ed., 1993).

14. *Id.* at 119–20.

15. *Id.*

16. G.S. 105-303(b)(1).

17. *See, e.g.*, Tores v. Justices of the County Court of Rowan, 6 N.C. 167 (1812) (discussing taxpayer listing of billiard table).

18. G.S. 105-303(b)(2); 105-309(c)(3),(4).

19. G.S. 105-285.

20. *See* Shoemaker (Moye) v. Coates, 218 NC 251, 256, 10 S.E.2d 810, 814 (1940).

21. Kaplan v. Prolife Action League of Greensboro, 123 N.C. App. 720, 726, 475 S.E.2d 247, 252 (1996).

22. Vann v. Edwards, 135 N.C. 661, 47 S.E.2d 784.

23. Christmas v. Winston, 152 N.C. 48, 67 S.E. 58 (1910); *see also* Marks v. Comm'r of Internal Revenue, T.C.M. 1985-179 (describing fee simple absolute interest in property as including "all property rights that an owner can have in property, exclusive of governmental restrictions on the property, such as the powers of taxation, condemnation, and eminent domain.")

24. *See In re Lee*, 85 N.C. App. 302, 304, 354 S.E.2d 759, 761 (1987).

25. *See* Bernatavicius v. Bernatavicius, 156 N.E. 685 (Mass. 1927).

26. *See* Olive v. Biggs, 276 N.C. 445, 457, 173 S.E.2d 301, 309 (1970); Young v. Young, 43 N.C. App. 419, 426, 259 S.E.2d 348, 352 (1979).

27. *See* Hollowell v. Hollowell, 333 N.C. 706, 713, 430 S.E.2d 235, 240 (1993); Hagler v. Hagler, 319 N.C. 287, 292, 354 S.E.2d 228, 233 (1987); *Young*, 43 N.C. App. at 426–27.

28. *Hollowell*, 333 N.C. at 713 (citing THOMAS F. BERGIN and PAUL G. HASKELL, *Preface* to ESTATES IN LAND AND FUTURE INTERESTS at 54–55 (2d ed. 1984)).

29. *Hollowell,* 333 N.C. at 709; 430 S.E.2d at 238.

30. Dearman v. Bruns, 11 N.C. App. 564, 566, 181 S.E.2d 809, 811 (1971).

31. *Id.*

32. *Id.*

33. *In re* Belk-Broome Co., 119 N.C. App. 470, 478, 458 S.E.2d 921, 926 (1995).

34. J.A. Shingleton v. State, 260 N.C. 451 (1963).

35. G.S. 105-302.1.

36. 1 PATRICK K. HETRICK and JAMES B. MCLAUGHLIN, JR., WEBSTER'S REAL ESTATE LAW IN NORTH CAROLINA § 10-2 (5th ed. 1999) (hereinafter WEBSTER'S REAL ESTATE LAW).

37. WEBSTER'S REAL ESTATE LAW § 10-3. Warranty deeds generally contain covenants of title, seisen, and warranty. A *covenant of title* is a promise by the grantor that he or she has a fee simple estate in the property. *See, e.g.*, Hawks v. Brindle, 51 N.C. App. 19, 23, 275 S.E.2d 277, 280 (1981) (reciting language of warranty deed providing that "the grantor covenants that he is seized of said premises in fee"). A *covenant of seisen* is a promise by the grantor that he or she has title to the land conveyed at the time the deed is delivered. Riddle v. Nelson, 84 N.C. App. 656, 353 S.E.2d 866 (1987); *see also Hawks*, 51 N.C. App. at 23, 275 S.E.2d at 280 (reciting language from deed that grantor covenants that he "has the right to convey the same in fee simple"). A *covenant of warranty* is a promise to defend the title against the claims of others. *Hawks*, 51 N.C. App. at 23, 275 S.E.2d at 280 (reciting language that grantor covenants to "warrant and defend the said title to the same against the lawful claims of all persons whomsoever").

38. WEBSTER'S REAL ESTATE LAW § 10-4.

39. Hayes v. Ricard, 245 N.C. 691, 692, 97 S.E.2d 105, 109 (1957).

40. *Id.*

41. WEBSTER'S REAL ESTATE LAW § 10-4.

42. The recording of such quitclaim deeds generally is part of a scheme based on the fallacy that a person may obtain title to property by having it listed in his or her name and by paying taxes on the property. The tax office does not establish record title to property; instead, its documents reflect sources of record title derived from deeds or other legal

instruments. Moreover, a person with no interest in a parcel of property does not acquire an interest in the property by paying the taxes assessed thereon. The only statutory provisions linking the payment of taxes with an interest in property are G.S. 105-363, 105-386, and 1-38(b), (c). The first of these statutes, G.S. 105-363, provides that a co-tenant or joint owner of property may pay the entire amount of taxes constituting a lien on property and thereby acquire a lien on the shares of co-tenants. The second, G.S. 105-386, provides that a lienholder may pay taxes that constitute a lien on the property and thereby acquire a lien upon the property. Finally, G.S. 1-38(b), (c) provides that the marking of boundaries and the recording of a map prepared from a survey combined with the listing and payment of taxes on property constitutes prima facie evidence of possession of real property by a person who claims adverse possession under color of title. Because, however, the grantee of a deed does not have color of title if he or she knows the deed is fraudulent, WEBSTER'S REAL ESTATE LAW § 14-11, at 656–57, this last provision does not apply to the sorts of schemes described above.

43. Failure to notify the owner that taxes are owed does not invalidate the taxes owed, since all interested persons are charged with notice of taxes, but it would, nonetheless, be an undesirable outcome. *See* G.S. 105-348.

44. G.S. 31-20.

45. G.S. 28A-21-2; 28A-23-1.

46. G.S. 28A-15-2(b).

47. G.S. 105-306; 105-309. The willful failure or refusal to timely list taxable personal property is a Class 2 misdemeanor. G.S. 105-308. In addition, any person who willfully attempts or willfully aids and abets any person to attempt, in any manner, to evade or defeat the taxes imposed under this Subchapter, by removing or concealing the property or by other means, is guilty of a Class 2 misdemeanor. G.S. 105-308.

48. Boyce v. Williams, 84 N.C. 275, 275, 37 Am. Rep. 618, 618 (1881).

49. *Id.*

50. American Exchange Nat. Bank v. Winder, 198 N.C. 18, 21, 150 S.E. 489, 491 (1929).

51. *See, e.g.*, Szabo Food Service, Inc. v. Balentines, Inc., 285 N.C. 452, 206 S.E.2d 242 (1974) (holding that lessor of cafeteria equipment was owner and required to list property, notwithstanding lessor's agreement to convey equipment to lessee upon termination of sublease and at the end of equipment's useful life).

52. Beard v. Newsome, 76 N.C. App. 476, 333 S.E.2d 527 (1985).

53. *Id.*; *see also* G.S. 25-1-203 (prescribing factors for consideration in determining whether a transaction in the form of a lease creates a lease or security interest under the Uniform Commercial Code).

54. G.S. 105-306(c)(3).

55. G.S. 105-306(c)(4).

56. G.S. 20-4.01(23).

57. *See* Hughes v. Young, 115 N.C. App. 325, 444 S.E.2d 248 (1994).

58. G.S. 105-316.

59. G.S. 105-315.

60. G.S. 105-309.

61. G.S. 105-309(c)(1).
62. G.S. 105-309(c)(2).
63. G.S. 105-309.
64. G.S. 105-309(c)(5)(b) (citing G.S. 105-302(c)(11)).
65. G.S. 105-309(d).
66. *Id.*
67. G.S. 105-310.
68. G.S. 105-311(a)(1).
69. G.S. 105-310.
70. G.S. 105-311(a)(2).
71. G.S. 105-309(f).
72. G.S. 105-296(h) (presumably these specific criteria must be satisfied with respect to business entity taxpayers before an assessor may require a taxpayer to submit additional information to support the listing and valuation of personal property under the more general terms of G.S. 105-309(d)).
73. G.S. 105-309(h). The assessor must, however, make such documents available for inspection, upon request, by the Department of Revenue or the Employment Security Commission.
74. G.S. 105-296(g).
75. G.S. 105-289(e).
76. G.S. 105-313.
77. *Id.*
78. *Id.*
79. G.S. 105-303(a)(1).
80. G.S. 105-303(a)(2).
81. G.S. 153A-357; 160A-417.
82. G.S. 105-309(c)(4), which pre-dates the permanent listing of real property, requires a listing of all improvements erected "since the time of the last appraisal." If construed literally, this provision would require the taxpayer to file an abstract listing new construction every year until the county's next revaluation. Under today's permanent listing system, this provision may best be interpreted to require the taxpayer to list the improvement during the first listing period of its existence but not every year thereafter. Once the taxpayer lists the improvement, it then becomes part of the permanent listing.
83. G.S. 105-287(b)(3) (listing betterments for which no change in value may be recognized in a non-revaluation year).
84. Billings Transfer Corp. v. County of Davidson, 276 N.C. 19, 170 S.E.2d 873 (1969).
85. Quill Corp. v. N.D., 504 U.S. 298, 306 (1992).
86. *Billings Transfer Corp.*, 276 N.C. at 24–25 (quoting Wis. v. J.C. Penney Co., 311 U.S. 435 (1940)).
87. *Id.*
88. *In re* Hanes Dye and Finishing Co., 285 NC 598, 207 S.E.2d 729 (1974).
89. *Id.*; *see also In re* Bassett Furniture Indus., Inc., 79 NC App. 258, 339 S.E.2d 16 (1986).

90. G.S. 105-307(a), (b).

91. G.S. 105-296.

92. G.S. 105-326(a).

93. Winston-Salem Joint Venture v. City of Winston-Salem, 54 N.C. App. 202, 282 S.E.2d 509 (1981), *rev. denied*, 304 N.C. 728, 288 S.E.2d 803 (1982), *appeal after remand*, Winston-Salem Joint Venture v. City of Winston-Salem, 65 N.C. App. 532, 310 S.E.2d 58 (1983).

94. 54 N.C. App. 202, 282 S.E.2d 509 (1981).

95. *See* Winston-Salem Joint Venture v. City of Winston-Salem, 65 N.C. App. 532, 310 S.E.2d 58 (1983).

96. G.S. 105-301.

97. G.S. 105-273(8).

98. G.S. 105-273(14).

99. G.S. 105-304. Cities can require separate listing under G.S. 105-326 but in practice seldom exercise this authority.

100. G.S. 105-304(c). Almost no intangible personal property is subject to property taxation. G.S. 105-275(31). Leasehold interests in exempt real property are an exception; the Machinery Act provides that such interests are taxable where the real property is located.

101. G.S. 105-304(d).

102. G.S. 105-304(c)(1).

103. G.S. 105-304(c)(2).

104. G.S. 105-304(f)(1).

105. G.S. 105-304(f)(2).

106. 79 N.C. App. 258, 339 S.E.2d 16 (1986).

107. *In re* Hanes Dye and Finishing Co., 285 N.C. at 611, 207 S.E.2d at 737.

108. *Id.* at 611, 207 S.E.2d at 737 (quoting 71 Am. Jur. 2d, *State and Local Taxation* §§ 660 & 661 (internal quotations omitted)).

109. *See, e.g.*, *In re* McLean Trucking Co., 283 N.C. 650 (1973).

110. Pub. L. No. 108-189, 117 Stat. 2835 (codified at 50 App. U.S.C. § 501–596.

111. *Uniformed services* refers to the armed forces (the Army, Navy, Air Force, Marine Corps, and Coast Guard), the commissioned corps of the National Oceanic and Atmospheric Administration, and the commissioned corps of the Public Health Service. 50 App. U.S.C. § 511(b) (incorporating definition of uniformed services from 10 U.S.C. § 101(a)(5)).

112. 50 App. U.S.C. § 571.

113. *Id.*

114. G.S. 105-282.1(a1).

115. G.S. 105-312; 105-326.

116. G.S. 105-273(6b).

117. G.S. 105-312(d).

118. *Id.*

119. *Id.*

120. *Id.*
121. *Id.*
122. *Id.*
123. G.S. 105-312(d).
124. *Id.*
125. *Id.*
126. G.S. 105-312(f).
127. *Id.*
128. *Id.*
129. G.S. 105-312(g).
130. *Id.*
131. *Id.*
132. G.S. 105-312(h).
133. *Id.*
134. *Id.*
135. *Id.*
136. G.S. 105-303(b)(3).
137. G.S. 105-312(k), (l); *see also* WILLIAM A. CAMPBELL, PROPERTY TAX COLLECTION IN NORTH CAROLINA 114 (4th ed. 1998) (noting that the "power to settle or adjust the claim can be exercised only before the taxpayer pays the bill").
138. The state supreme court, in *Stoneville v. Commissioners of Stoneville*, refused to compel the board of commissioners of the town of Stoneville to list and assess property located within the town on the basis that the plaintiff citizens failed to demonstrate that the board of commissioners acted in bad faith or abused its power or discretion in compromising the taxes resulting from the discovery. 210 N.C. 226, 186 S.E.2d 342 (1936). If this same deferential standard of review applies to challenges of boards' exercise of authority under current G.S. 105-312, it appears that governing boards have wide latitude in considering such matters.
139. *In re* Popkin Brothers Enters., Inc., 90 P.T.C. 82 (August 23, 1991).
140. *Id.*
141. G.S. 105-282.1(c). This statutory provision results in an inequity, which was demonstrated in *In re Wesleyan Education Center*. 68 N.C. App. 742, 316 S.E.2d 87 (1984). In that case, the Wesleyan Education Center, a nonprofit corporation, listed its property during the 1982 listing period but did not apply for tax exempt status until June 30, 1982, four months after the listing period had ended and after being notified by the Forsyth County Tax Assessor that the property was no longer exempt. The taxpayer appeared before the board of equalization and review to appeal the denial of tax exempt status. The board denied exemption on the grounds that the taxpayer had not filed an application during the listing period. At that time, there was no provision permitting the board to approve late-filed applications. The Property Tax Commission agreed with the board that the Machinery Act did not permit the tax assessor or board of equalization and review to grant an exemption for property that the owner listed but for which the owner failed to file an application for exemption. The taxpayer appealed to the court of

appeals, arguing that the provision in G.S. 105-282.1(c) permitting a property owner to demonstrate that discovered property met the conditions for exemption permitted the late-filed application. The taxpayer pointed out the inequity of interpreting the Machinery Act to permit a review of the exempt status of property owned by a taxpayer who failed to list the property but denying a hearing to a taxpayer who listed property and did not file an application for exemption until after the listing period. The court of appeals rejected the taxpayer's argument, concluding that the statutory language was clear and, moreover, the result was justifiable because granting an exemption to property that was not listed and therefore not included in the tax base upon which the county's budget was based did not jeopardize the county's budget as might the removal of property included in the tax base.

142. G.S. 132-1(a).

143. G.S. 132-1(b).

144. *Id.*

145. *Id.*

146. G.S. 105-321(a).

147. G.S. 132-2.

148. G.S. 105-321(a).

149. *Id.*

150. G.S. 132-3(a).

151. *Id.*

152. *Id.*

153. G.S. 132-4.

154. *Id.*

155. G.S. 15A-1340.23.

156. G.S. 132-5.

157. *Id.*

158. G.S. 132-5.1.

159. David M. Lawrence, Public Records Law for North Carolina Local Governments 30 (1997) (hereinafter Public Records Law) (noting that the rights of inspection and copying extend to "'any person' and there is no reason to think the quoted words are limited in any way" and further commenting that the rights extend to citizens and noncitizens as well as corporations and other groups).

160. G.S. 132-6(b).

161. *Id.*

162. G.S. 132-6.2(a).

163. *Id.*

164. G.S. 132-6.2(b).

165. *Id.*

166. Public Records Law at 44.

167. *Id.*

168. G.S. 132-6.1(c).

169. *Id.*

170. Public Records Law at 181.

171. *Id.*

172. David M. Lawrence, Public Records Law For North Carolina Local Governments 49–50 (Supp. 1997–2003).

173. Public Records Law at 181–82.

174. G.S. 132-6.1(c).

175. G.S. 132-1.1(b); 153A-148.1; 160A-208.1.

176. G.S. 15A-1340.23.

177. G.S. 153A-148.1(a)(6) (applicable to county officers, employees, and agents); 160A-208.1(a)(4) (applicable to city officers, employees, and agents); *cf.* G.S. 15A-1340.23 (providing for a fine of up to $200 for Class 3 misdemeanor and imprisonment for up to twenty days).

178. A taxpayer's income may be determined from the amount of the tax bill for a taxpayer who receives relief under the circuit breaker program since the tax bill may not exceed a specified percentage of the taxpayer's income (4 or 5 percent, depending upon the taxpayer's level of income). *See* G.S. 105-277.1B(f).

179. G.S. 105-296(h); 105-309(d).

180. The Machinery Act specifically provides a less severe penalty for this offense than is generally the case for Class 3 misdemeanors.

181. G.S. 132-1.1(a).

182. G.S. 153A-98.

183. G.S. 153A-98(e).

184. G.S. 153A-98(f).

185. G.S. 132-1.10(b)(3).

186. *Id.*

187. G.S. 132-1.10(b)(4).

188. 42 U.S.C. § 405(c)(2)(C)(i).

189. G.S. 132-1.10(b)(9). The term *redacted* is not defined in the Identity Theft Protection Act and it is unclear as to whether the inclusion of only the last four digits of a Social Security number meets the definition. The term *redacted* is defined in the State Privacy Act, codified at G.S. Chapter 143, to encompass the exclusion of all but the last four digits of a Social Security number. David Lawrence, *Public Records, in* North Carolina Legislation 2005 223, 224 (Martha H. Harris ed., 2005).

190. G.S. 132-1.10(b)(9).

191. 18 U.S.C. § 2721.

192. Even though the original motor vehicle bill was generated from information provided by the Division of Motor Vehicles (DMV), the documentation of requests for refunds of taxes and actions thereon are based upon a request from a taxpayer. Such a request severs the DMV connection by reoffering the information for consideration by the tax office.

193. Letter from Chief Deputy Attorney General Grayson Kelley to George Tatum, Commissioner, North Carolina Division of Motor Vehicles (February 9, 2005).

194. *Id.*

195. G.S. 15C-3.

196. G.S. 15C-4(d).
197. G.S. 15C-8.
198. G.S. 15C-3.
199. G.S. 15C-8(g).
200. G.S. 15C-8(f).
201. *Id.*
202. *Id.*
203. G.S. 15C-9(f).
204. G.S. 121-5(a), (b).
205. PUBLIC RECORDS LAW at 51.
206. *Id.*
207. *Id.* at 51–52 (citing N.C. ADMIN. CODE tit. 7, ch. 4M, § .0510 (June 1989)).

4 Appraisal and Assessment of Property

4.1 Appraising Real Property 92

4.1.1 Reappraisal Cycle for Real Property 92

4.1.2 Valuation Standard for Real Property 95

4.1.3 Schedule of Values 96

4.2 Appraising Personal Property 98

4.3 Assessment of Public Service Company Property 100

4.3.1 Sales Assessment Ratios and the Assessment of Public Service Company Property 102

4.3.2 Assessment of Railroad Property 104

4 Appraisal and Assessment of Property

The next step in the process of imposing an ad valorem tax on property, following the identification, characterization, and listing of the property, is determining its value. This chapter discusses the statutory framework under which that determination is made, including the timeline and legal requirements governing the appraisal and assessment of property by North Carolina counties.

These days, any discussion of the process of reappraising land, homes, and other buildings for tax purposes—particularly if the property is residential and is located at the coast, on a lake, or in the mountains—is likely to include the term "sticker shock."[1] Unfortunately, such discussions also frequently include taxpayers' expressions of frustration, confusion, and mistrust of the assessment process. More than half of the counties in North Carolina reappraise land, homes, buildings, and other structures, defined as *real property*, only once every eight years, and many taxpayers have limited knowledge of the laws and procedures governing the valuation and assessment of such property for taxation by local governments.[2] Eight-year reappraisals in high-growth areas have resulted in values that double, triple, or even quadruple from one reappraisal to the next. In contrast, business personal property and motor vehicles are assessed for taxation every year by counties in North Carolina, and that process generally attracts little notice, let alone sticker shock. The differences in taxpayer sentiment may be attributed to several factors, among them the differing ways in which real and personal property are added to the tax rolls (the former by the tax assessor and the latter generally by the taxpayer), the shorter cycle for reappraisal of personal property as compared to real property, and the depreciation of personal property over time as contrasted with the typical appreciation of real property. Taxpayers also may view taxes on personal property used to produce income as a cost of doing business, whereas real property taxes may be considered an unavoidable, burdensome obligation imposed upon a citizen's home. The uniform standard governing the county assessor's appraisal of all property, real and personal, is that property be *appraised* at its market value; that is, the price at which it would change hands between a willing and financially able buyer and a willing seller, neither being under any compulsion to buy or sell and both having reasonable knowledge of all the uses to which the property is adapted and for which it is capable of being used.[3] Real and personal property is assessed for taxation at its full appraised value, with two exceptions. Certain agricultural, horticultural, and forestry property is assessed for taxation based upon its value in its present use, rather than its market value. Public service company system property is assessed by the Department of Revenue based in part on the effective rates of taxation in a given county.[4]

4.1 Appraising Real Property

4.1.1 Reappraisal Cycle for Real Property

Traditionally, all North Carolina counties were required to conduct countywide reappraisals of all real property at least every eight years, though counties were able to adopt a more frequent reappraisal schedule.[5] Beginning in 2009, counties with populations of 75,000 or more will be required to conduct reappraisals more frequently than every eight years if the ratio of arms-length sales prices to assessed value as calculated annually by the Department of Revenue drops below 0.85 or increases to more than 1.15.[6] A reappraisal mandated by such a drop or increase in assessed value must be effective the third year following the notice of the sales assessment ratio or the eighth year following the year of the county's last reappraisal, whichever is sooner. Suppose, for example, that Tarheel County, a county with a population of 75,000 or more, conducts a countywide reappraisal effective January 1, 2009. Suppose further that Tarheel County has adopted an eight-year reappraisal cycle. Thus the county intends for the next reappraisal to be effective January 1, 2017. If, however, the Department of Revenue sends notice to Tarheel County by April 15, 2011, of a sales assessment ratio of 0.84, Tarheel County will be required to carry out a countywide reappraisal effective no later than January 1, 2014—three years after the date of the notice—which is sooner than January 1, 2017, the date by which the county planned to reappraise property on an eight-year schedule. Had Tarheel County's sales assessment ratio remained in the acceptable range until 2015, when the county received notice of a sales assessment ratio of 0.84, the county could have adhered to the eight year reappraisal schedule, since January 1, 2017, is sooner than January 1, 2018—three years from the date of the sales assessment ratio notice.

Reappraisal is a labor- and time-intensive process. The typical county has about forty thousand parcels, all of which must be separately appraised and many of which contain buildings, structures, and fixtures that must be appraised along with land.[7] Counties must accomplish this task at a fraction of the cost for a single property or fee appraisal. About half of the state's counties have adopted resolutions shortening the number of years between reappraisals to periods ranging from four to seven years. Example 1 is a resolution advancing the reappraisal schedule for the next cycle by four years. Example 2 is a resolution that shortens the reappraisal schedule to four years for the next reappraisal and those to follow. If a county that has adopted a reappraisal schedule of shorter than eight years is required, due to its population and sales assessment ratio, to conduct more frequent reappraisals, the reappraisal cycle designated in the resolution continues in effect after the mandatory reappraisal unless the county adopts another resolution designating a different date for the county's next reappraisal.

In addition to being reappraised in a year of reappraisal, real property may be reappraised in a nonreappraisal year if the value of the property has changed for some reason other than an economic condition affecting the county in general, such as a rezoning of the property.[8] Personal property, as noted above, is appraised for taxation every year based on its value on January 1.[9]

Example 1.

RESOLUTION OF THE TARHEEL COUNTY BOARD OF COMMISSIONERS TO ADVANCE TARHEEL COUNTY'S REAPPRAISAL SCHEDULE FROM JANUARY 1, 2017, TO JANUARY 1, 2013

WHEREAS, Tarheel County completed and implemented its most recent octennial reappraisal of real property on January 1, 2009, utilizing its own staff and personnel; and

WHEREAS, Tarheel County desires to conduct a reappraisal of real property earlier than required by G.S. 105-286, to be effective January 1, 2013, and to implement subsequent reappraisals on a schedule to be determined by the Board of Commissioners in compliance with G.S. 105-286; and

WHEREAS, the reappraisal work will be conducted by the staff of the Tarheel County Tax Assessor's Office as part of its program of work each year;

NOW, THEREFORE BE IT RESOLVED by the Board of Commissioners of Tarheel County (the Board) that in the annual budget ordinance for fiscal year 2009–10, the Board shall include in the special reserve fund established for the reappraisal an appropriation for Tax Administration in the amount required for reappraisal work during that fiscal year consistent with a plan established for the reappraisal of real property, as required by G.S. 153A-150; and

BE IT FURTHER RESOLVED that when the County budget for each succeeding fiscal year is in preparation, the Board, with the County Manager and Tax Assessor, shall review the progress of the reappraisal work, and the Board shall appropriate to the special reappraisal reserve fund such funds for reappraisal work during that year as may be necessary to continue the reappraisal work and to assure the completion of the reappraisal work on schedule.

BE IT FURTHER RESOLVED that a copy of this resolution be forwarded promptly by the Clerk to the Board to the Department of Revenue as required by G.S. 105-286.

Adopted this ____ day of ________ 2009.

Example 2.

RESOLUTION OF THE TARHEEL COUNTY BOARD OF COMMISSIONERS TO ADVANCE TARHEEL COUNTY'S REAPPRAISAL SCHEDULE FROM JANUARY 1, 2017, TO JANUARY 1, 2013 AND TO IMPLEMENT SUBSEQUENT REAPPRAISALS EVERY FOUR YEARS

WHEREAS, Tarheel County completed and implemented its most recent octennial reappraisal of real property on January 1, 2009, utilizing its own staff and personnel; and

WHEREAS, Tarheel County desires to conduct a reappraisal of real property earlier than required by G.S. 105-286, to be effective January 1, 2013, and to implement subsequent reappraisals every four years; and

WHEREAS, the reappraisal work will be conducted by the staff of the Tarheel County Tax Assessor's Office as part of its program of work each year;

NOW, THEREFORE BE IT RESOLVED by the Board of Commissioners of Tarheel County (the Board) that in the annual budget ordinance for fiscal year 2009–10, the Board shall include in the special reserve fund established for the reappraisal an appropriation for Tax Administration in the amount required for reappraisal work during that fiscal year consistent with a plan established for the reappraisal of real property, as required by G.S. 153A-150; and

BE IT FURTHER RESOLVED that when the County budget for each succeeding fiscal year is in preparation, the Board, with the County Manager and Tax Assessor, shall review the progress of the reappraisal work, and the Board shall appropriate to the special reappraisal reserve fund such funds for reappraisal work during that year as may be necessary to continue the reappraisal work and to assure the completion of the reappraisal work on schedule.

BE IT FURTHER RESOLVED that a copy of this resolution be forwarded promptly by the Clerk to the Board to the Department of Revenue as required by G.S. 105-286.

Adopted this ____ day of _______ 2009.

4.1.2 Valuation Standard for Real Property

In appraising land, the assessor must consider "its advantages and disadvantages as to location; zoning; quality of soil; waterpower; water privileges; dedication as a nature preserve; conservation and preservation agreements; mineral, quarry, or other valuable deposits; fertility; adaptability for agricultural, timber-producing, commercial, industrial, or other uses; past income; probable future income; and any other factors that may affect its value, except growing crops of a seasonal or annual nature."[10] In appraising a building or other improvement, the assessor must consider "its location; type of construction; age; replacement cost; cost; adaptability for residence, commercial, industrial, or other uses; past income; probable future income; and any other factors that may affect its value."[11] Partially completed buildings are appraised based upon the degree to which they are completed on January 1.[12]

While governmental restrictions such as zoning provisions are routinely considered in appraising property, contractual agreements that encumber the value of property are not.[13] The assessor must value the total property interest, regardless of whether that interest is divided among multiple parties with differing ownership interests.[14]

To accomplish the task of valuing tens of thousands of parcels as of the January 1 reappraisal date, a county must utilize the methodology of mass appraisal rather than the methodology employed in single-property appraisals, which are commonly performed at the behest of financial institutions.[15] Mass appraisal is the systematic appraisal of groups of properties, commonly referred to as neighborhoods, as of the controlling date (January 1 of the year of reappraisal), using standardized procedures and statistical testing.[16] The schedule for a large city may stratify property among thousands of neighborhoods.[17] In a mass appraisal system, the assessor must make valuation judgments about groups of properties rather than single properties and "must be able to develop, support, and explain standardized adjustments in a valuation model among use classes, construction types, neighborhoods, and other property groups."[18]

There are three generally recognized methodologies for valuing property, commonly referred to as *approaches to value*. They are the cost approach, the sales comparison approach, and the income approach.[19] The cost approach estimates value as the sum of the depreciated improvement cost and the value of the site, or land, as if the site were vacant and available for development at its highest and best use.[20] The sales comparison approach, as the title indicates, compares the property being appraised with similar properties that have recently sold.[21] This approach is most applicable when sufficient sales data are available for similar properties.[22] It is commonly used to appraise single-family residences and land but also is an effective approach for valuing multifamily and commercial properties where sufficient sales data for these types of property are available.[23] The third approach, the income approach, is generally accepted as the most reliable method for determining the market value of investment property.[24] This approach "is based on the principle that something is worth what it will earn."[25] Under the income approach, the assessor "arrives at valuation by applying a capitalization rate to the property's potential to generate income, plus or minus certain adjustments."[26] The analysis must be based upon market rents rather than contractually restricted rents.[27] To value property under the income approach, the assessor must analyze the quantity, quality, and duration of the income stream and apply an appropriate capitalization rate to convert the stream to market value.[28] Stated in terms of an equation, value equals income divided by rate.[29] Thus "the capitalized value of a given income stream varies directly with the amount of income and inversely with the capitalization rate." Even "[s]light variations in the capitalization rate can result in large variations in value."[30]

4.1.3 Schedule of Values

To conduct a countywide reappraisal, an assessor must prepare uniform schedules of values, standards, and rules to be used in appraising real property at its true value and at its present-use value.[31] The schedules of values, standards, and rules serve as the county's mass appraisal model and are implemented by means of a computer assisted mass appraisal system (CAMA).[32] The schedules incorporate building cost figures derived from national data that have been adjusted to reflect local costs,[33] sales data based upon qualifying arm's-length sales of property grouped by appraisal neighborhood,[34] and income and expense formulas applicable to commercial property and derived from local and national sources.[35] The schedule of values, standards, and rules sets forth values per appropriate unit of measurement for use in calculating the value of land and buildings. For example, the value of a dwelling typically is based on an established amount per square foot, while the value of land may be based upon a set amount per front foot, square foot, lot, or acre depending upon the highest and best use of the land.[36] The land value per appropriate unit of measurement also will vary depending upon the neighborhood in which the land is situated.[37] A schedule of values, standards, and rules also typically sets forth factors warranting adjustments in valuations for various types of property. For example, a schedule may provide for adjustments to the base value of dwellings to account for square footage included in an upper story or a basement, which typically has a lower value per square foot. Schedules of values also typically provide for adjustments to value based upon the grade—or quality—of construction. Standard values per square foot typically are based upon an average, or grade C, quality of construction. As the quality, or grade, increases, so does the price per square foot. Likewise, as the grade decreases, so does the price per square foot. Schedules also provide for a reduction in value for depreciation based upon the age of the structure. Schedules also assign values to other amenities that make property more valuable, such as fireplaces and air conditioning.[38] A schedule of values also typically authorizes adjustments to land value based upon factors such as homesite size, excess acreage, road frontage, topography, zoning, and the presence of easements.[39] A schedule also typically prescribes ranges of characteristics and corresponding percentage adjustments for recognized factors.[40]

The schedules of values, standards, and rules must be reviewed and approved by the board of county commissioners before January 1 of the year they are applied, though the assessor may collect data needed to apply the schedules, standards, and rules before they are adopted by the board.[41] The assessor is required to submit the proposed schedules, standards, and rules to the board at least twenty-one days before the meeting at which the board will consider the schedule.[42] On the same day the schedules are submitted to the board, the assessor must file a copy of the proposed schedules in the assessor's office to be available for public inspection. Upon receipt of the schedules, the board of commissioners must publish a statement in a newspaper with general circulation in the county stating that the schedules have been submitted and are available for inspection.[43] The newspaper notice also must specify the time and place of the public hearing regarding the proposed schedules.[44] The board must hold this public hearing at least seven days before adopting the final schedules.[45] The true value and present-use value schedules may be approved separately or simultaneously, in the board's discretion.[46]

When the board approves the final schedules of values, standards and rules, it must issue an order adopting the schedules.[47] Notice of the order must be published once a week for four consecutive weeks in a newspaper with general circulation in the county, with the last publication taking place at least seven days before the last day for challenging the validity of the schedule by appeal to the Property Tax Commission, which is the statewide board of equalization and review.[48] The published notice must state that the schedules have been adopted and are open to examination in the office of the assessor and that a property owner who asserts that the schedules are invalid may appeal to the Property Tax Commission within thirty days of the first publication of the notice.

4.2 Appraising Personal Property

Personal property is appraised annually as of January 1.[49] The appraisal of personal property is governed by G.S. 105-317.1, which requires the appraiser to consider the following factors: (1) the replacement cost of the property; (2) the sale price of similar property; (3) the age of the property; (4) the physical condition of the property; (5) the productivity of the property; (6) the remaining life of the property; (7) the effect of obsolescence[50] on the property; (8) the economic utility of the property—that is, its usability and adaptability for industrial, commercial, or other purposes; and (9) any other factor that may affect the value of the property.[51]

In appraising taxable tangible personal property held and used in connection with the mercantile, manufacturing, producing, processing, or other business enterprise of any taxpayer, the appraiser must consider information in the books and records of the taxpayer as well as information reported by the taxpayer for federal and state income tax purposes.[52] In considering such information, the appraiser must take into account the accuracy of the taxpayer's records, the taxpayer's method of accounting, and the level of trade at which the taxpayer does business.[53] The appraiser must consider the level of trade because property usually increases in value as it moves from the production level in the hands of the manufacturer to the wholesale level to the retail level.[54] Consideration of the level of trade takes into account markups to prices as property moves from manufacturer to retailer, which may include costs such as freight, handling, overhead, and installation as well as profit markups.[55] As a practical matter, business personal property in North Carolina is taxed at the retail level of trade since inventories of contractors, manufacturers, and retail and wholesale merchants are excluded from taxation.[56]

The three approaches to value—the cost approach, the sales comparison approach, and the income approach—applicable to appraisal of real property also apply to the appraisal of personal property.[57] The cost approach arrives at an estimate of market value by determining the replacement cost new of the property, which is the cost to replace the property with comparable property of like utility,[58] and subtracting depreciation from that amount.[59] The replacement cost new of the property is based upon the application of trending factors to the original, or historical, cost of the property, which "includes all costs involved with bringing the property into operation," including costs such as installation, freight, and taxes.[60] The Property Tax Division of the North Carolina Department of Revenue annually publishes trending schedules for use in appraising business personal property and certain other taxable personal property in North Carolina.[61] The cost approach is considered particularly well-suited to the appraisal of machinery and equipment.[62]

The sales comparison approach has limited application because sales of many types of taxable personal property are limited.[63] Nevertheless, the sales comparison approach can be used when reliable sales data are available, as is the case for aircraft, manufactured homes, motor vehicles, and watercraft.[64] Most North Carolina counties use industry pricing guides to appraise these types of property.[65] These guides are based upon sales of such property throughout the United States, with regional adjustments.[66]

The income approach can be applied to the appraisal of personal property in two ways.[67] The first is the gross income multiplier method.[68] Under this method, the sales price of comparable items of property is divided by gross rental incomes for those items.[69] The product of this division is the gross income multiplier, which is then multiplied by the rental income of the subject item to arrive at an estimate of value.[70] The other method for applying the income approach to personal property is more akin to the income approach methodology for real property.[71] Under this method, the appraiser applies a capitalization rate to the expected income stream resulting from the use of the property, which typically is an item of machinery or equipment, for its remaining economic life.[72]

4.3 Assessment of Public Service Company Property

Real and personal property owned or leased by a public service company is appraised and assessed at the state rather than county level.[73] *Public service companies* are defined as "[a] railroad company, a pipeline company, a gas company, an electric power company, an electric membership corporation, a telephone company, a telegraph company, a busline company, an airline company, or a motor freight carrier company."[74] Public service companies that have property taxable in North Carolina must provide to the state Department of Revenue each year a report showing, as of January 1, information regarding the property they own and the system property they lease.[75] *System property* is real and personal property used by public service companies in their public service activities and includes property under construction.[76] Companies must file their reports by the last day of March, and a principal officer of the company must sign an affirmation declaring that the company's listing is accurate and complete.[77] The Department of Revenue may grant "reasonable extensions of time for filing the required reports for good cause and may require the company to submit additional information or reports it needs to properly assess the property.[78]

Each year, the Department of Revenue must appraise the true value as of January 1 of each public service company other than bus lines, motor freight carriers, or airlines,[79] as a *system*.[80] The department must appraise system property at true value, taking into consideration system property both inside and outside North Carolina and, if necessary, leased property. In determining the value of a public service company as a system, the department must consider the market value of the company's capital stock and debt; the book value of the company's system property and what it would cost to replace or reproduce the system property, less depreciation; and the gross receipts and operating income of the company.[81] The department may, of course, consider other factors that affect the true value of system property.[82]

If a public service company operates inside and outside of North Carolina, the Department of Revenue must apportion for taxation in North Carolina a "fair and reasonable share of the value of the company as a system or its rolling stock or flight equipment."[83] The department reaches the apportioned figure by applying property, business, and mileage factors[84] to the appraised value in accordance with the ratio that the company's property, business, or mileage in North Carolina bears to its total property, business, or mileage.[85]

The Machinery Act also specifies how the Department of Revenue must allocate the appraised value of system property among local taxing units in the state.[86] The appraised valuation of the distributable system of railroad property is allocated to local taxing units in accordance with the ratio of the miles of all the company's tracks in the local taxing unit to the total miles of all the company's tracks in the state, adjusted to reflect density of traffic in the local taxing unit. The system property of telephone companies must be divided into two classes. Class 1 consists of central office equipment; large private branch exchange equipment; motor vehicles; tools and work equipment; office furniture and equipment; materials and supplies; and land, towers, and structures. All other property is Class 2 property. After dividing the property, the department must determine the original cost of the property and the percentage represented by the property in each class. The department then applies these percentages to the appraised value of the system property and apportions that valuation among the classes. Class 1 property is allocated among the local taxing units in which the Class 1 property is situated on January 1 in the proportion that the original cost of such property in the taxing unit bears to the original cost of all such property in the state. Class 2 property is allocated among the local taxing units in which the company operates based upon the proportion that company wire miles located in the unit bears to the total of company wire miles in the state. The system property of public service companies other than railroad, telephone, bus line, motor freight carrier, and airline companies is allocated for taxation to the local taxing units in which the company operates in the proportion that the original cost of the taxable system property in the local taxing unit on January 1 bears to the original cost of all the taxable system property in North Carolina.[87] The appraised valuation of a bus line company's rolling stock is allocated for taxation to each local taxing unit according to the ratio of the company's scheduled miles during the calendar year preceding January 1 in each such unit to the company's total schedule miles in this state for the same period.[88] The appraised valuation of the rolling stock owned or leased by a motor freight carrier company is allocated to each local taxing unit in which the company has a terminal according to the ratio of the tons of freight handled in the calendar year preceding January 1 at the company's terminals within the taxing unit to the total tons of freight handled by the company in the state in the same period. If a North Carolina interstate motor freight carrier company has no terminal outside the state but has been required to pay property tax to other taxing units, the North Carolina valuation is reduced by a the ratio of the rolling stock taxed by other states to all of the carrier's rolling stock.

The appraised valuation of an airline company's flight equipment is allocated for taxation to each local taxing unit in which an airport used by the company is situated according to the ratio obtained by averaging two ratios: (1) the ratio of the company's ground hours in the taxing unit in the year preceding January 1 to the company's ground hours in the state in the same period, and (2) the ratio of the company's gross revenue in the taxing unit in the year preceding January 1 to the company's gross revenue in the state in the same period.[89]

4.3.1 Sales Assessment Ratios and the Assessment of Public Service Company Property

For many years public service companies complained that because their system property was assessed annually at its true value by the Department of Revenue, they bore a disproportionate share of the local tax burden, given that property was frequently locally assessed at a fraction of its value.[90] The General Assembly responded to those concerns in 1985 by enacting Chapter 601 of the 1985 Session Laws, "An Act to Equalize the Tax Burden."[91] The net effect of the legislation was to ensure "that the spread between the level of appraisal of public service company system property and locally assessed property will never be more than 10 per cent, no matter what the quality of local appraisal practices may be."[92] This was accomplished by tying the assessment of public service company property to the percentage of true value represented by the appraised value of property in a taxing unit, as calculated by the Department of Revenue based upon sales assessment ratio studies. If the median ratio for real property assessments in a county falls below 90 percent in the year of reappraisal or in the fifth or eighth year thereafter, then the valuation of public service company system property allocated to the county is reduced by a corresponding percentage until the next sales ratio study year.[93]

The process works like this: The Department of Revenue selects a representative sample of sales of real property in the county based upon transfers recorded with the county register of deeds during the previous calendar year and provides that list to the county assessor.[94] The county assessor reviews the list and eliminates sales that do not represent arm's-length transactions. The assessor also makes any adjustments to the reported sales price, as indicated by the revenue stamps on the deed, to ensure that it reflects only the amount paid for real property.[95] The assessor then compares the assessed value of the property to its sales price and calculates the ratio of assessed value to the sales price for that particular parcel.[96] For example, if a parcel of real property assessed at $90,000 sells for $100,000, the resulting ratio is 90/100, or, stated as a percentage, 90 percent. For each transaction, the assessor lists the ratios in ascending order.[97] The median number in the array is the county's real property assessment ratio.[98] The median is the number in the mid-point of all the ratios.[99] If there are an odd number of ratios, the median number is the ratio for which there are even numbers of higher and lower ratios.[100] If there are an even number of ratios, the median number is the average of the two ratios in the middle of the array.[101] The department must complete its annual sales ratio study for every county by April 15 of the following calendar year.[102]

If a county's sales assessment ratio falls below 90 percent in the year of a reappraisal or in the fifth or eighth year thereafter, the assessed value of a public service company allocated by the county is reduced. The reduction is based on one of two percentages, either (1) the median ratio, or (2) a weighted average percentage based on the median ratio and a 100 percent ratio for personal property.[103] The weighted average percentage (the higher of the two) will be applied if the county assessor provides information that satisfies the Department of Revenue that the county follows accepted guidelines and practices in assessing business personal property. Application of the weighted average percentage prevents the value of public service company system property, which consists of real *and* personal property, from being reduced solely based on the ratio of the county's real property assessments to true value when the county can demonstrate its use of procedures generally accepted for assessing business personal property at its true value. The Department of Revenue calculates the weighted average based upon the assessed value figures for real and personal property reported by the county to the Local Government Commission (LGC) for the previous year.

The following example illustrates the calculation and application of the weighted average percentage. Suppose that the Department of Revenue calculates a median sales assessment ratio of 85/100, or 85 percent, for Tarheel County in 2008, the fourth year after its 2004 revaluation. Tarheel County reported to the LGC in 2007 $80,000,000 in assessed value of real property and $20,000,000 in assessed value of personal property. Tarheel County has satisfied the Department of Revenue that it follows accepted guidelines and practices in the assessment of business personal property. The public service company system property value allocated to Tarheel County is $1,000,000. The weighted average percentage that will be applied to this value is calculated as set forth in table 4.1. The public service company system property valuation must be multiplied by the weighted average percentage (88 percent), resulting in a taxable value of $880,000. This percentage is applied until the next study is conducted by the Department of Revenue pursuant to G.S. 105-284. Thus, if a percentage reduction is applied to public service company property in the fourth year after reappraisal, that percentage will apply each year until the department conducts its next study, which will occur the year of the county's next reappraisal or the seventh year after the last reappraisal, whichever is first.[104]

The Department of Revenue must notify the chairperson of the county board of commissioners of the median ratio and the percentage to be applied for each county by April 15 of the year for which it is effective.[105] The department also must give notice to the public service companies whose values are subject to adjustment.[106] The county or an affected public service company may challenge the real property ratio or the percentage established by the department by giving notice of exception within thirty days after the mailing of the department's notice.[107] After receiving such notice, the department must arrange a conference with the challenging party or parties to review the matter.[108] The department then must notify the challenging party or parties of its final determination.[109] Either party may appeal to the Property Tax Commission within of days after the mailing of the department's decision.[110]

4.3.2 Assessment of Railroad Property

The Railroad Revitalization and Regulatory Reform Act of 1976 (4-R Act) prohibits states and their political subdivisions from assessing rail transportation property[111] at a value that has a higher ratio to the true market value of the rail transportation property than the ratio that the assessed value of other commercial and industrial property in the same jurisdiction has to the

Table 4.1 Sample Calculation of a Weighted Average Percentage to be Applied to Public Service Company System Property Value

$$(80{,}000{,}000^{a}/100{,}000{,}000^{b}) * (.85^{c}) = .68$$
$$+(20{,}000{,}000^{d}/100{,}000{,}000^{e}) * (100) = .20$$
$$= .88$$

a. Assessed value of real property.
b. Total assessed value.
c. Median sales assessment ratio.
d. Assessed value of personal property.
e. Total assessed value.

true market value of the other commercial and industrial property.[112] In other words, counties in North Carolina cannot assess railroad property at its true value if commercial and industrial property within the county is assessed at less than true value. Furthermore, because the accepted method of proving discrimination under the 4-R Act is by conducting a sales assessment ratio, only the ratio of the assessed value of commercial and industrial *real* property to true value may be compared to the assessment of railroad property, since accepted methods of completing sales assessment ratio studies include only real property for which records of arm's-length transactions can be readily sampled and analyzed.[113] This means that a county cannot increase the ratio applied to railroad property values by using a weighted average based upon a deemed assessment ratio of 100 percent for personal property. Moreover, railroads are entitled to relief under federal law if the ratio of assessed value to market value of rail transportation property exceeds by at least 5 percent the ratio of assessed value to market value of other commercial and industrial real property.[114] As well, railroads are entitled to this relief if the sales assessment ratio for such property drops below 95 percent in *any* year.

Notes

1. Between 1996 and 2005 housing prices nationwide increased by 45 percent. Dean Baker, *The Housing Bubble Fact Sheet,* ISSUE BRIEF for CENTER FOR ECON. AND POL'Y RES. (July 2005), *available at* www.cepr.net/content/view/104/8/.

2. While revaluations may be politically unpopular, infrequent reassessments of real property have been linked to systematic bias against certain groups of property owners in the property tax structure, see Jerome F. Heavey, *Patterns of Property Tax Exploitation Produced by Infrequent Assessments*, 42 AM. J. OF ECON. AND SOC. 441–49 (1983) (reporting findings from study of tax assessments in thirty-five counties in Pennsylvania school districts indicating that assessment ratios were systematically biased against cities), as well as general lack of assessment uniformity, *see* Ta Ho Eom, *A Comprehensive Model of Determinants of Property Tax Assessment Quality: Evidence in New York State*, 28:1 Public Budgeting and Finance 58 (Spring 2008).

3. G.S. 105-283.

4. G.S. 105-284.

5. N.C. GEN. STAT. 105-286(a) (hereinafter G.S.).

6. S.L. 2008-146 (S 1878).

7. According to data maintained by the Department of Revenue, Property Tax Division, as of September 2007, the mean number of parcels per county was 50,844.71 and the median was 37,250.

8. G.S. 105-287.

9. G.S. 105-285. The value of a registered motor vehicle is determined annually as of January 1 of the year the taxes become due. G.S. 105-330.2. Taxes on registered motor vehicles are due the first day of the fourth month following the date the registration expires. G.S. 105-330.4(a).

10. G.S. 105-317(a)(1).

11. G.S. 105-317(a)(2).

12. G.S. 105-317(a)(3).

13. *In re* Greens of Pine Glen, 356 N.C. 642, 651, 576 S.E.2d 316, 321 (2003).

14. *In re* Greensboro Office P'ship, 72 N.C. App. 635, 325 S.E.2d 24 (1985).

15. INT'L ASS'N OF ASSESSING OFFICERS, PROPERTY ASSESSMENT VALUATION 285 (2d ed. 1996) (hereinafter PROPERTY ASSESSMENT VALUATION).

16. *Id.*

17. *See, e.g.*, WAKE COUNTY, WHAT'S YOUR PROPERTY WORTH? THE ABCS OF WAKE COUNTY'S 2008 PROPERTY REVALUATION PROJECT (2007) (stating that Wake County had 4,200 appraisal neighborhoods in 2008 revaluation).

18. PROPERTY ASSESSMENT VALUATION at 285.

19. *Id.* at 42.

20. *Id.* at 42–44.

21. *Id.* at 45; *see also In re* Lane Co.,153 N.C. App. 119, 127, 571 S.E.2d 224, 229 (2002) (holding that comparative sales occurring after January 1 of the revaluation year, adjusted for changing values over time, are a proper basis for a sales comparison valuation of property).

22. *In re* Lane Co., 153 N.C. App. at 127, 571 S.E.2d at 229.
23. Property Assessment Valuation at 46.
24. *In re* Belk-Broome, 119 N.C. App. 470, 474, 458 S.E.2d 921, 924 (1995).
25. *In re* S. R.R., 313 N.C. 177, 185, 328 S.E.2d 235, 241 (1985).
26. *In re* Belk Broome, 119 N.C. App. at 474, 458 S.E.2d at 474.
27. *In re Greens of Pine Glen*, 356 N.C. at 649, 576 S.E.2d at 320.
28. Property Assessment Valuation at 46.
29. *In re* S. R.R., 313 N.C. at 185, 328 S.E.2d at 241.
30. *Id.*
31. G.S. 105-317(b)(1).
32. See Property Assessment Valuation at 288.
33. *Id.* at 132–37.
34. *Id.* at 72, 84.
35. *See, e.g.*, Forsyth County 2005 Schedule of Values, Standards and Rules as adopted September 27, 2004 (2004) (hereinafter Forsyth County 2005 Schedule of Values).
36. Forsyth County 2005 Schedule of Values at 305–29; Property Assessment Valuation at 70, 73, 104.
37. Property Assessment Valuation at 54–67.
38. *See, e.g.*, Forsyth County 2005 Schedule of Values at 65–69, 109, 111.
39. Forsyth County 2005 Schedule of Values at 42–48.
40. *See generally* Forsyth County 2005 Schedule of Values.
41. G.S. 105-317(c).
42. G.S. 105-317(c)(1).
43. G.S. 105-317(c)(2).
44. *Id.*
45. *Id.*
46. G.S. 105-317(c).
47. G.S. 105-317(c)(3).
48. *Id.*
49. G.S. 105-285(b).
50. Obsolescence is "[a] decrease in the value of a property occasioned solely by shifts in demand from properties of this type to other types of property and/or to personal services." Int'l Ass'n of Assessing Officers, Glossary for Property Appraisal and Assessment 95 (1997) (emphasis in original omitted). Obsolescence may be economic or functional. Economic, or external, obsolescence is "[a] cause of depreciation that is a loss in value as a result of impairment in utility and desirability caused by factors outside the property's boundaries, or loss in value of a property (relative to the cost of replacing it with a property of equal utility) that stems from factors external to the property." *Id.* at 48 (emphasis in original omitted). An example is a buggy-whip factory that "to the extent that it could not be used for anything else suffered substantial economic obsolescence when automobiles replaced horse-drawn buggies." *Id.* Functional

obsolescence, on the other hand, is "[l]oss in value of a property resulting from changes in tastes, preferences, technical innovations, or market standards." *Id.* at 59.

51. G.S. 105-317.1(a).

52. G.S. 105-317.1(b).

53. *Id.*

54. Property Assessment Valuation at 342–43.

55. *Id.*

56. North Carolina Department of Revenue, Property Tax Division, Personal Property Appraisal and Assessment § 8, at 15 (June 2007), *available at* www.dornc.com/publications/appraisalassessment2007.pdf (hereinafter Personal Property Appraisal and Assessment) (noting that taxable business personal property owned and used by the manufacturer who produced the product, such as computers used in the offices of the manufacturer who produced the computers, should be appraised based upon the retail cost of the property rather than the manufacturer's cost).

57. Property Assessment Valuation at 360.

58. Personal Property Appraisal and Assessment § 8, at 15.

59. Property Assessment Valuation at 360; *see also* North Carolina Department of Revenue, Property Tax Division, 2009 Cost Index & Depreciation Schedules i (January 1, 2009), *available at* www.dornc.com/publications/2009cost_index.pdf (hereinafter 2009 Cost Index & Depreciation Schedules) (explaining use of trending schedules in cost approach to value).

60. 2009 Cost Index & Depreciation Schedules at i.

61. *See, e.g.,* 2009 Cost Index & Depreciation Schedules; *see also* Memorandum from Kirk F. Boone, PPS, Property Valuation Specialist II, Property Tax Division, North Carolina Department of Revenue, to Users of Cost Index and Depreciation Schedules (December 19, 2008), *available at* www.dornc.com/publications/2009cost_memo.pdf (last visited March 17, 2009) (recommending use of schedules in valuation of business personal property and certain taxable personal property).

62. Property Assessment Valuation at 360.

63. *Id.* at 361.

64. *Id.* at 362; *see also* Personal Property Appraisal and Assessment § 7, at 9, 12, 14, 21 (recognizing that sales comparison approach is best method for appraising these types of property when sufficient sales are available).

65. Personal Property Appraisal and Assessment § 7, at 9, 12, 14, 21.

66. *Id.*

67. Personal Property Appraisal and Assessment § 8, at 5.

68. *Id.*

69. *Id.*

70. *Id.*

71. *Id.*

72. Property Assessment Valuation at 362–63; *see also* Personal Property Appraisal and Assessment § 8, at 5–6 (setting forth detailed explanation and sample application of this approach).

73. G.S. 105-335(a).

74. G.S. 105-333(14). The term also includes companies that perform a public service regulated by the U.S. Department of Energy, the U.S. Department of Transportation, the Federal Communications Commission, the Federal Aviation Agency, or the North Carolina Utilities Commission but does not include water companies, radio common carriers, cable television companies, or radio or television broadcasting companies.

75. G.S. 105-334(a).

76. G.S. 105-333(17).

77. G.S. 105-334(a).

78. G.S. 105-334 (c), (d).

79. The state also appraises the rolling stock of bus and motor freight carrier companies along with airlines' flight equipment, but all other property of these three types of companies is listed, appraised, and assessed in the normal manner by county assessors. G.S. 105-335(a), (c). The department must consider the book value and replacement cost in appraising rolling stock and flight equipment. G.S. 105-336(b).

80. G.S. 105-335(a), (b).

81. G.S. 105-336(a).

82. G.S. 105-336(a)(4).

83. G.S. 105-337.

84. G.S. 105-337 provides that:

1. The term *business* factor means data that reflect the use of the company's property, such as gross revenue, net income, tons of freight carried, revenue ton miles, passenger miles, car miles, ground hours, and comparable data.
2. The term *mileage factor* means factual information as to the linear miles of the company's track, wire, lines, pipes, routes, and similar operational routes and factual information as to the miles traveled by the company's rolling stock.
3. The term *property factor* means investment in property; it may be either gross or net investment or any other reasonable figure reflecting the company's investment in property.

85. G.S. 105-337.

86. G.S. 105-338.

87. G.S. 105-338(b)(3).

88. Valuations of less than $500 to a taxing unit are not allocated. G.S. 105-338(c)(1).

89. G.S. 105-338(c).

90. *See* Joseph S. Ferrell and William A. Campbell, *Local Taxes and Tax Collection, in* North Carolina Legislation 1985 25, 126 (Robert P. Joyce ed., 1986) (hereinafter NC Legislation 1985).

91. *Id.*

92. *Id.*

93. G.S. 105-284(b)(2).

94. NC Legislation 1985 at 126.

95. *Id.*; *see also* Clinchfield R.R. Co. v. Lynch, 527 F. Supp. 784, 786 (E.D.N.C. 1981) (describing proper methodology for calculating sales assessment ratio).

96. NC Legislation 1985 at 126.
97. *Id.*
98. *Id.*
99. *Id.* at n.3.
100. *Id.*
101. *Id.*
102. G.S. 105-289(h).
103. G.S. 105-284(b).
104. G.S. 105-284(b)(1).
105. G.S. 105-284(c).
106. *Id.*
107. *Id.*
108. *Id.*
109. *Id.*
110. *Id.*
111. *Rail transportation property* is defined as "property, as defined by the [Surface Transportation] Board, owned or used by a rail carrier providing transportation subject to the jurisdiction of the [Surface Transportation] Board under this part." 49 U.S.C. § 11501(a)(3) (incorporating definition of *Board* as "Surface Transportation Board" in 49 U.S.C. § 10102(a)).
112. 49 U.S.C. § 11501.
113. Clinchfield R.R. Co. v. Lynch, 527 F. Supp. 784, 788 (E.D.N.C. 1981).
114. 49 U.S.C. 11501(c).

5 Review and Appeal

5.1 Notification regarding Applications for Exemption or Exclusion 113

5.2 Notification of the Assessed Value of Property 114

5.3 Review of Assessments 114

5.3.1 Proceedings before the Board of Equalization and Review 116

5.3.2 Appeals from the Board of Equalization and Review to the Property Tax Commission 120

5.3.3 Settlement of Property Tax Appeals 132

5.3.4 Enforced Collection 133

5.3.5 Appeal to the Court of Appeals from the Decision of the Property Tax Commission 133

5.4 Changes to the Value of Real Property in a Nonreappraisal Year 136

5 Review and Appeal

Once property has been listed, appraised, and assessed, taxpayers must be notified of the resulting assessed value and provided an opportunity for review of that determination. Taxpayers who have applied for the exemption or exclusion of property from taxation likewise must be notified regarding whether the request has been granted and must be provided an opportunity to appeal. This chapter describes the process for providing such notification to taxpayers, for review of assessments, and for appealing determinations of the county assessor.

5.1 Notification regarding Applications for Exemption or Exclusion

The Machinery Act does not specify when a property owner must be notified that an application for exemption or exclusion from property taxation has been denied. Nonetheless, the county's need to determine its tax base before setting its tax rate, and the constitutional requirement that a taxpayer be provided due process—that is, notice and an opportunity to be heard before being deprived of property[1]—require that such notice be provided before the board of equalization and review adjourns. As noted in Chapter 2, the board of equalization and review is the quasi-judicial body charged at the local level with considering and ruling upon taxpayer appeals of valuation and exemption/exclusion denials. As a practical matter, most counties notify taxpayers of their decisions within a few weeks after receiving the application.

5.2 Notification of the Assessed Value of Property

An assessor must provide written notice of a change in the assessment of property to the taxpayer[2]—that is, the owner of the property—at his or her last known address before the first meeting of the board of equalization and review.[3] Notice of the value of personal property must be provided no later than the date of the property tax bill.[4] An owner of personal property has the right to appeal the value, situs, or taxability of property within thirty days after the date of the initial notice of value, which, again, often is the date of the tax bill.[5]

Though not required by the Machinery Act, most assessors provide an informal appeal process to afford taxpayers an opportunity to inform the assessor of their objections to an appraisal or assessment or the denial of a request for exemption. If the assessor finds the taxpayer's objection well-founded, the assessor may correct the error in the assessment of property before the board of equalization and review convenes.

5.3 Review of Assessments

Each county has a board of equalization and review responsible for reviewing tax lists and hearing taxpayer appeals. The board of commissioners serves as the county board of equalization and review unless it appoints by resolution a special board to carry out these duties.[6] Many boards of commissioners find that appointing a separate board of equalization and review permits review of county assessments by a more representative cross-section of the community. For instance, the board of equalization and review might be made up of private appraisers, real estate professionals, and others with particular expertise in the valuation of property. The appointment of a separate board also shields the review process from political pressures. In a handful of counties, boards of equalization and review were created and continue to operate pursuant to the provisions of a local act enacted by the General Assembly.[7] The board of equalization and review must convene no earlier than the first Monday in April and no later than the first Monday in May. While the Machinery Act provides that the board, in a nonreappraisal year, "shall complete its duties on or before the third Monday following its first meeting unless . . . a longer period of time is necessary," the act is not explicit about the shortest amount of time the board may meet.[8] In some counties, the board convenes and adjourns the same day. The Machinery Act's reference to meetings held "[f]rom the time of [the board of equalization and review's] first meeting until its adjournment"[9] appears to contemplate that there will be more than one meeting. It bears noting that the very purpose of the board is to provide taxpayers an opportunity for a meaningful hearing and review of the assessment of their property. Convening and adjourning on the same day is not a practice designed to meet that objective. The author's interpretation of the statute, in light of its vague language and its underlying purpose, is that the board must have at least two meetings, though a contrary interpretation certainly is plausible.

In reappraisal years, the board must adjourn by December 1; in other years it must adjourn by July 1. This adjournment signals the end of the appeal period for real property, but not the end of the board's work. The board may remain in session after adjournment to consider the following: appeals filed before adjournment; appeals from personal property valuations; timely appeals from valuation changes made by the board itself, notice of which was mailed fifteen days before the board's adjournment; appeals relating to discovered property; appeals related to the appraisal, situs, and taxability of classified motor vehicles; and appeals relating to audits of exempted or excluded property. The board may continue to meet to hear and decide such appeals, since the taxpayer will frequently not have been notified of the assessment until after the board adjourns from its regular duties of reviewing tax lists and accepting taxpayer appeals.[10] If the board of equalization and review does not continue for the purposes of hearing such appeals, the board of commissioners must hear the appeals. County commissioners should specify by resolution which body will hear these types of appeals. A taxpayer may appeal to the board of equalization and review by submitting a written request for a hearing or by personally appearing before the board at one of its sessions.[11]

The consideration of taxpayer appeals comprises the lion's share of the work of all boards of equalization and review. The boards are required by statute "to hear appeals from any taxpayer who owns or controls property taxable in the county with respect to the listing or appraisal of the taxpayer's property or the property of others."[12] While the statute is broadly written, the courts have determined that the legal doctrine of standing permits a taxpayer to contest the valuation of property of others *only* when the appellant taxpayer is in some way aggrieved by that valuation.[13] Given that " '[t]he purpose of the statutory requirement that all property be appraised at its true value in money is to assure, as far as practicable, a distribution of the burden of taxation in proportion to the true values of the respective taxpayers' property holdings,'" a taxpayer is only aggrieved by the valuation of another's property where that property has been *undervalued* or *underassessed* by the county assessor, thereby resulting in the taxpayer bearing a disproportionately greater share of the overall tax burden.[14] The *overvaluation* of another's property, which would, in fact, *lessen* the tax burden borne by other property owners, including the taxpayer, is not a matter that aggrieves the taxpayer and, as such, is not a matter that the taxpayer may appeal.[15]

5.3.1 Proceedings before the Board of Equalization and Review

The procedures generally followed by the board of equalization and review are relatively informal, at least when compared to proceedings before the Property Tax Commission or courts of general justice. Unlike the Property Tax Commission, whose deliberations as a quasi-judicial state agency are excepted from the open meetings law,[16] county boards of equalization and review, as quasi-judicial local agencies, must deliberate as well as hear taxpayer appeals in open session.[17]

Boards of equalization and review have discretionary authority to examine any witnesses and documents and to place witnesses under oath.[18] In addition, the board may subpoena witnesses or documents on its own motion. The board must subpoena witnesses or documents if an appellant taxpayer so requests and there is a reasonable basis for believing that the witnesses have, or the documents contain, information relevant to the decision of the appeal.

The board may appoint committees composed of its own members or other persons to assist it in making investigations necessary to its work.[19] The board also may employ expert appraisers in its discretion and may make such an appointment either on its own motion or upon the demand of the appealing taxpayer.[20] If experts are employed upon a taxpayer's demand, the board may require the taxpayer to reimburse the county for the expense if the expert's appraisal does not result in a material reduction of the value of the property by the local board or by the Property Tax Commission upon appeal.[21]

The county assessor serves as clerk to the board of equalization and review.[22] The assessor must be present at all board of equalization and review meetings and must maintain accurate minutes of the board's actions.[23] In addition, the assessor must provide the board with all information related to the listing and valuation of taxable property in the county. At the hearing, the board of equalization and review may receive and consider evidence offered by the taxpayer, the assessor, and other county officials.[24]

As previously noted, the board may examine witnesses and documents, may place witnesses under oath, and may subpoena documents on its own motion.[25] The board must subpoena witnesses and documents upon request of the taxpayer if there is a reasonable basis for believing that the witnesses have, or the documents contain, information relevant to the appeal.[26] The willful failure to appear, produce documents, or testify when appearing in response to a subpoena is a Class 1 misdemeanor.[27] The board must enter into its minutes any order reducing, increasing, or confirming an appraisal and any order that lists or removes property from a tax list. The board must notify the taxpayer by mail as to the action taken on the appeal no later than thirty days after the board's adjournment.[28]

All changes in listings, names, descriptions, appraisals, and assessments made by the board of equalization and review must be noted in the tax records, which then must be totaled. A majority of the board of equalization and review then must sign the following statement to be included at the end of the tax records:

> State of North Carolina
> County of ______________________
>
> We, the undersigned members of the Board of Equalization and Review of ________ County, hereby certify that these tax records constitute the fixed and permanent tax list and assessment roll and record of taxes due for the year ______, subject to only such changes as may be allowed by law.
>
> ____________________________________
> ____________________________________
> ________________________________
> Members of the Board of Equalization and Review of _______ County

5.3.1.1 Post-Adjournment Changes. After the board of equalization and review certifies the fixed and permanent tax list and assessment roll and record, the board of county commissioners (and the assessor, upon delegation of the power from the board) has sole authority to authorize changes to the abstracts and tax records.[29] A board of county commissioners may authorize changes for the following purposes: (1) to give effect to decisions of the Property Tax Commission; (2) to add to the tax records any valuation certified or corrected by the Department of Revenue; (3) to correct the names and descriptions appearing on abstracts or tax records; (4) to correct appraisals, assessments, and tax amounts resulting from clerical or mathematical errors; (5) to add discovered property to tax records and abstracts; and (6) to appraise or reappraise property when the assessor reports that since adjournment of the board of equalization and review, facts have come to his or her attention that warrant changing the appraisal of property in the current calendar year.[30] The board of commissioners may delegate to the assessor the authority to make the changes authorized in categories (1) through (5). While Section 105-325(a)(6) of the North Carolina General Statutes (hereinafter G.S.) specifically limits its reach to the current calendar year, subdivisions (1) through (5) do not contain that restriction. This makes sense for the provisions requiring that the assessor implement decisions of the property tax commission. After all, those decisions typically relate to taxes for a previous year. Certified values from the Department of Revenue relate only to the current year, and taxpayer name changes do not result in refunds or releases. Subdivision (5) relating to adding discovered property may involve taxes for a prior year, but it involves a current year discovery bill. The import of G.S. 105-325(4) is, however, more open to interpretation. G.S. 105-325(4) permits the governing body—or the assessor, upon delegation of such authority—to correct clerical or mathematical errors. Obviously, such errors may have existed in previous years as well as the current year. Thus a question arises as to whether the board or the assessor may correct clerical and mathematical errors so as to effect a release or refund of taxes for prior years. That interpretation and result would be at odds with the other provisions of G.S. 105-325 and the Machinery Act relating to the time for review and appeal. After all, the provisions of G.S. 105-325 become effective only after the board of equalization and review has adjourned, and the board of equalization and review can make changes effective only for the current tax year. It seems unlikely, given other provisions of the Machinery Act clearly designed to promote stability in the tax base,[31] that such changes may be made retroactively.

Changes of the sort authorized in G.S. 105-325(a)(6) may be made only by the governing board and only if such changes could have been made by the board of equalization and review had the same facts been brought to its attention. The board of county commissioners may not appraise or reappraise property to account for changes that have occurred since the listing date. If a reappraisal demonstrates that property was listed at a substantial understatement in value, quantity, or other measurement, the provisions of G.S. 105-312 providing for a discovery of property listed at a substantial understatement in value apply. The taxpayer must be provided written notice of any appraisal or reappraisal that will adversely affect his or her interests and must be afforded an opportunity to be heard before any such appraisal becomes final. Orders of the board of county commissioners and actions of the assessor, upon delegation of the board's authority pursuant to G.S. 105-325, may be appealed to the Property Tax Commission.

If a change made by the board or assessor pursuant to G.S. 105-325 results in a reduction in a tax that has been paid, the board or assessor should direct the finance officer to refund the amount of the overpayment.[32]

5.3.1.2 Standing. Given that someone other than the owner of property may appeal the undervaluation or exemption of the property, the owner of the property must be notified of the challenge to the value or assessment and provided an opportunity to be heard in a new (or de novo) hearing in which none of the board's previous judgments are binding. This may require the board of equalization and review to conduct two proceedings: an initial hearing to hear the party bringing the appeal, and a subsequent hearing in which the property owner may be heard.

In *In re Whiteside Estates*,[33] a Jackson County taxpayer filed an appeal with the county board of equalization and review challenging the classification of a 227-acre parcel owned by Whiteside Estates, a family corporation, for taxation based upon its present-use value as forestland. The board determined that the property did not meet present-use value requirements and notified Whiteside of its right to a hearing. At Whiteside's request, the board conducted another hearing and again determined that the property had been improperly classified as forestland qualifying for present-use value taxation. The board ordered the property assessed at its market value of $719,000 rather than its present-use value of $102,800. Whiteside appealed to the Property Tax Commission, contending that the initial appeal to the county board should have been dismissed as the taxpayer who challenged the classification had no standing to do so. The Property Tax Commission denied Whiteside's motion to dismiss and heard the merits of the case regarding the property's present-use classification. The commission affirmed the county board's decision taxing the property at market value. Whiteside appealed to the court of appeals on the basis that the appealing taxpayer, as a general taxpayer in

Jackson County who did not own property in the present-use program or that adjoined the Whiteside property, had no standing to appeal the classification of the Whiteside property. The court of appeals rejected Whiteside's contention. The court reasoned that as the owner of property in Jackson County, the appellant taxpayer was aggrieved by the reduction in assessed value of the Whiteside property (from market to present-use) that resulted from the allegedly improper classification of the property as forestland. Thus the court concluded that the taxpayer had standing to appeal to the county board for a reappraisal of the Whiteside property. Upon consideration of the merits of the classification issue, the court affirmed the Property Tax Commission's determination that the property was not eligible for appraisal at present-use value.

When property in a county appreciates rapidly from one reappraisal year to the next, towns within the county sometimes join taxpayers' refrain by objecting to increases in appraised value of real property. On such occasions, towns or their representatives may attempt to appeal the valuation of all property within the town limits on behalf of taxpayers in the town. Given that no property owned by the town is taxable, by virtue of the exemption granted in the North Carolina Constitution for property owned by municipalities, codified in G.S. 105-278.1, towns have no standing to appeal the valuation of their own property or the property of others. Likewise, an individual property owner in the town lacks standing to challenge the valuation of *all* property within the town on behalf of all of the owners of such property since, as previously noted, a taxpayer may contest the valuation of others' property only when the taxpayer is in some way aggrieved by that valuation.[34] A property owner is aggrieved by the *undervaluation* of another taxpayer's property, which results in the appellant taxpayer paying more than his fair share of taxes. The *overvaluation* of another's property, in contrast, is not a matter that a taxpayer may appeal.[35] Thus an individual does not have standing to appeal an alleged overvaluation of the property of others within a particular town.

5.3.2 Appeals from the Board of Equalization and Review to the Property Tax Commission

A county board of commissioners may, by resolution, permit a taxpayer to appeal a decision of a separate board of equalization and review to the board of commissioners.[36] If the board of commissioners also serves as the board of equalization and review, or if the board of commissioners elects not to provide this appeal route, a taxpayer may appeal a decision of the board of equalization and review to the Property Tax Commission, which functions as the state board of equalization and review.[37] Only a *taxpayer* may appeal a decision of the board of equalization and review. If the board of equalization and review reduces the valuation of property or grants an exemption or exclusion upon the taxpayer's appeal, the *county* may not seek review of that determination by the Property Tax Commission. A taxpayer must file a notice of appeal, specifying the grounds for appeal, from an order of a board of county commissioners (other than an order adopting a uniform schedule of values) or from a board of equalization and review with the Property Tax Commission within thirty days after the date the board mailed notice of its decision to the property owner.[38] The property owner also must send a copy of the notice to the county assessor. A notice of appeal is considered filed on the date it is postmarked by the United States Postal Service or, if there is no such postmark, on the date it is received in the office of the Property Tax Commission.[39] A property owner bears the burden of proving that the appeal is timely.[40]

The Property Tax Commission consists of five members, three appointed by the governor and two appointed by the General Assembly.[41] Of the two appointments made by the General Assembly, one is made upon the recommendation of the speaker of the House of Representatives and the other is made upon the recommendation of the president pro tempore of the Senate.[42] For all appointments to the commission made after July 1, 2007, each member has a four-year term. Formerly the term of the commission member appointed upon recommendation of the speaker of the House of Representatives was two years, while other members served four-year terms, two of which expired on June 30 of each odd-numbered year. The Property Tax Commission is required to meet at least once in each quarter and may hold special meetings at any time and place within the state at the call of the chairperson or upon the written request of at least three members.

Joint owners of property may file separate appeals or may jointly appeal the listing, appraisal, or assessment of property. In addition, a taxpayer may file a single appeal to contest the listing or valuation of more than one item of personal property or more than one tract or parcel of real property.[43] Upon receiving an appeal filed by a taxpayer, the Property Tax Commission must provide a hearing before one or more representatives of the commission[44] (followed by a review of representatives' findings of fact and conclusions of law by the full commission) or, in the alternative, before the full commission.[45]

The commission sets the time and place for the hearing of an appeal and must provide written notice of either type of hearing to the taxpayer and to the clerk of the board of commissioners of the county from which the appeal arises at least ten days before the hearing. At the hearing, the commission or its representative(s) must hear evidence and affidavits offered by the appellant taxpayer and the county. The commission must determine the weight and sufficiency of the evidence and the credibility of the witnesses, draw inferences from facts, and appraise conflicting and circumstantial evidence.[46]

The Property Tax Commission is not bound by findings and conclusions of the county board of equalization and review; instead, the hearing before the commission is de novo, meaning that it is based solely on the record before the commission. Nevertheless, the court of appeals held in *MAO/Pines Associates Ltd. v. New Hanover County Board of Equalization*[47] that the Property Tax Commission is not required to consider evidence of a factor affecting the value of a taxpayer's property unless the taxpayer alerts the county assessor of the factor within the tax year in question, alerts the board of equalization and review of the factor upon appeal, or states the factor in its application for hearing to the Property Tax Commission. In other words, a taxpayer may not withhold material information from the county assessor and the local board of equalization and review with plans to present the information to the commission in an appeal from the local decision. In *MAO/Pines*, the taxpayer learned of asbestos contamination before the board of equalization and review heard its valuation appeal. The taxpayer did not alert the board or the county assessor of the presence of asbestos on the property and appealed the board's decision affirming the county's appraisal to the Property Tax Commission on the basis that "'excessive expenses and low rents'"[48] warranted a reduction in value. The taxpayer later moved to amend its petition to the commission to introduce an appraisal that took into account the presence of asbestos on the property, though the motion itself did not specifically refer to asbestos. The commission affirmed the county's valuation, declining to consider the asbestos contamination. The court of appeals affirmed the commission, holding that company representatives' statements to the county assessor regarding asbestos contamination nearly sixteenth months after the effective date of the appraisal and almost four months after the end of the calendar year of the appraisal, as well as the proffer to the commission regarding asbestos contamination, "came too late to qualify as proper and timely notification."[49] The court explained that the Machinery Act provides for appeal to a local board to "provide opportunity at the local level to deal with taxpayer-presented information and to modify appraisals as such information requires before any appeal need be heard by the Commission."[50]

The taxpayer must appear in person at the hearing or be represented by an attorney.[51] While individuals may represent themselves before the commission, corporate taxpayers and the county must be represented by an attorney.[52] The commission and its individual members, as well as Department of Revenue employees so authorized by the commission, may subpoena witnesses and documents upon a subpoena signed by the chairperson of the commission. Proceedings before the commission are governed by the rules of evidence that apply in the courts of general justice.[53] The Property Tax Commission must make findings of fact and conclusions of law and, based upon these findings and conclusions, enter an order reducing, increasing, or confirming the valuation appealed or listing or removing the property from the tax lists. A certified copy of the order must be delivered to the appellant and to the clerk of the board of commissioners of the county from which the appeal was taken, and the abstracts and tax records of the county must be corrected to reflect the commission's order.[54] When the Property Tax Commission reduces the valuation of property or removes the property from the tax lists and, based on the commission's order, the taxpayer is owed a refund, the taxpayer is entitled to receive the overpayment with interest.[55] Overpayments bear interest at the rate set pursuant to G.S. 105-241.21 from the date interest begins to accrue until a refund is paid.[56] Interest accrues from the later of the date the tax was paid or the date the tax would have been considered delinquent.[57] Thus an overpayment of a 2008 tax made on December 20, 2008, begins to accrue interest on January 6, 2009, the date the tax would have been delinquent.[58] An overpayment for a 2008 tax bill made on February 1, 2009, would, in contrast, bear interest from the date of payment, since payment was made after the taxes became delinquent. A refund is considered paid on a date determined by the governing body of the taxing unit that is no sooner than five days after a refund check is mailed.[59]

5.3.2.1 Standard Governing Review of Assessment. There is a well-established presumption under North Carolina law that the county tax assessor has acted in good faith and that the assessor's assessments are correct.[60] Because of this presumption, a taxpayer seeking to challenge an assessment bears the burden of proving that the assessment is erroneous.[61] Without this presumption of correctness, every taxpayer would have an unlimited ability to attack the assessment of his or her property. The administrative and fiscal burden imposed upon local governments in a system permitting unbridled taxpayer challenges would be insurmountable.[62] To say, however, that the county's assessment is presumed correct does not imply that a taxpayer may never demonstrate otherwise. A taxpayer may rebut the factual presumption that the county's assessment is valid by producing competent, material, and substantial evidence that tends to show that (1) the tax assessor used an arbitrary or illegal method of valuation *and* (2) that the assessment substantially exceeded the true value in money of the property. In other words, the resulting value is more important than the methodology used to establish the value. To prevail on appeal, the taxpayer must produce evidence demonstrating that flawed methodology resulted in an assessment that substantially exceeded the property's true value in money. Once the taxpayer produces such evidence, the presumption of correctness is rebutted. The taxing unit then must produce evidence and persuade the finder of fact that its methods will produce true values.[63]

The leading case on the standard of review of assessments is *In re Amp*.[64] Amp owned and operated a plant in Greensboro where it manufactured electronic parts and components.[65] Amp filed business property abstracts with the Guilford County tax supervisor (the title held by a county assessor before 1987) for 1964–68, which included values for its inventories.[66] In August 1969 the tax supervisor notified Amp of a discovery resulting from Amp's undervaluation of inventory from 1964 to 1968.[67] Amp appealed the discovery to the county board of commissioners, which approved and confirmed the assessment.[68] Both the tax assessor and the county board valued the inventories based upon the values reported on Amp's state income tax returns.[69] Amp appealed to the State Board of Assessment (the predecessor to today's Property Tax Commission).[70]

Amp's tax manager testified before the State Board of Assessment that the book values recorded by Amp exceeded the true cash values of its inventories because Amp could sell in-process inventory only for scrap prices.[71] Since Amp had no finished goods on hand as of January 1 of any of the listing years at issue, Amp's tax manager testified that all of his computations for those years included in-process and raw material inventories, all of which were valued as scrap.[72] The tax manager testified that if Amp had finished goods as of January 1, 1968, the book value of such goods would have equaled their true value.[73] Indeed, the values testified to by Amp's tax manager before the State Board of Assessment were lower even than the values listed by Amp for the years in question.[74] Amp explained that its outside accountant had improperly overvalued its inventory for the years in question.[75]

The Guilford County tax supervisor testified that he believed the values of inventory listed with the county should match the taxpayer's books as well as the values reported on a taxpayer's state income and franchise tax returns.[76] The tax supervisor testified as to his assumption that there was no difference between the amount to be reported as ad valorem tax value and the amount reported on state corporate income and franchise tax returns, though he conceded that he had made no inquiry to determine the correctness of this view.[77] The State Board of Assessment determined that the value of Amp's inventories for property tax purposes was represented by the values reported in its books for the years in question.[78] The difference between book value and the value reported by Amp thus constituted unlisted property subject to discovery and assessment of additional taxes and penalties. Amp appealed the State Board of Assessment's decision to the Superior Court Division of Guilford County,[79] which reversed the state board's determination.[80] Guilford County appealed the superior court's decision to the court of appeals, which reversed the superior court. Amp then appealed to the North Carolina Supreme Court.

The supreme court began its analysis by reciting the appropriate standard of review for decisions by the State Board of Assessment and noting that "no court of the General Courts of Justice could weigh the evidence presented to the State Board and substitute its evaluation of the evidence for that of the Board."[81] The court then recognized the factual presumption that property tax assessments are presumed to be correct and held that in order to rebut the presumption, the taxpayer had to produce competent, material, and substantial evidence tending to show that the county tax assessor used an arbitrary or illegal method of valuation and that the assessment substantially exceeded the true value in money of the property.[82]

The court noted that the record demonstrated that the tax supervisor had used an illegal method of valuation given his erroneous assumption that the true value of property equaled its book value.[83] The court then addressed the question of whether Amp produced competent, material, and substantial evidence demonstrating that Guilford County's assessment increasing the value of its inventories from 1964 to 1968 was substantially greater than the true value in money of the property.

The court noted that Amp's tax manager testified that Amp hired an outside accounting firm to prepare its abstracts for the years in question because it did not know how to compute the true cash value of its inventories.[84] Moreover, Amp's tax manager testified that when Amp figured out how to compute the value of its inventory, it concluded that the calculations of the outside accounting firm were incorrect.[85] Thus, the court concluded, there was no evidence to substantiate the values reported by Amp from 1964 through 1968.[86] The court further determined that Amp's subsequently calculated values were unreasonable, since Amp valued all of its material as scrap.[87] The court rejected Amp's interpretation that its property was to be valued as though it was required to sell all of its inventory on January 1 of each year, whether such material was raw or in-process, so that the only potential buyers are scrap mills.[88] The court noted that property was to be valued at its true value in money rather than its value in a forced sale.[89]

The court then considered whether the Machinery Act permitted a county assessor, as a per se rule, to equate the book value of property as listed on a state income tax return with the true value in money of such property for purposes of property taxation.[90] The court concluded that such a per se rule was not statutorily sanctioned.[91] Nevertheless, the court noted that book value was the appropriate measure of value for certain property such as business inventories and that the result reached was more important than the method used to determine valuation.[92] The book values used by Guilford County were based upon figures Amp itself furnished to the state for income and franchise tax purposes. Amp defined *book value* as the lower of cost or market value; thus, by its own definition, the reported values adopted by the county did not exceed market value.[93] Moreover, the expert accountant testifying for Amp before the state board explained that Amp based book value on replacement cost plus labor and overhead.[94] Thus the court agreed with the state board's conclusion that, in this case, book value was evidence of the property's true value in money and concluded that the difference between the values originally listed by Amp and book value was subject to discovery.[95]

5.3.2.2 Two-Part Test for Challenging Assessment. A North Carolina Court of Appeals decision involving the assessment of property in a country club community in Davie County further demonstrates why improper appraisal methodology alone will not satisfy a taxpayer's burden on appeal.[96] Persons who purchased property in several subdivisions in Davie County were required by the terms of restrictive covenants encumbering their properties to join the Bermuda Run Country Club. The covenants provided that country club membership was not a personal right "'but shall run with the ownership of a Dwelling Unit.'"[97] The initiation fee for the country club was due at the time title to an encumbered parcel of property was transferred. The purchaser received a credit toward the total initiation fee in the amount of the fee in effect at the time the previous owner acquired the property. The new purchaser was then obligated to pay the difference, if any, between the previous and current initiation fee. The Davie County Tax Assessor included $10,000 in the appraised value of each parcel of residential real estate to represent the initiation fee as of the date of the county's last reappraisal. Several property owners objected to the inclusion of this amount and appealed the valuations to the county board of equalization and review and then to the Property Tax Commission, both of which affirmed the county's assessments. The property owners then appealed to the court of appeals, arguing that the county improperly included the values of the country club memberships in the assessment of their property, given that the memberships were intangible personal property not subject to taxation. The court never reached this issue, instead concluding as a preliminary matter that the appellants failed to produce any evidence that the county's assessments exceeded the true value in money of the properties. The property owners conceded in their written brief to the court of appeals that, while they objected to the inclusion of the initiation fees in the valuation of their properties, they were "'not otherwise contesting the appraised value of their real property.'"[98] The taxpayers' attorney affirmed at the hearing before the Property Tax Commission that he planned to present no evidence as to the value of the specific properties. The attorney explained that since he was representing more than eighty taxpayers, the presentation of such valuation evidence was "'just not practical.'"[99] Based on the lack of evidence that the specific properties had been substantially overvalued by the tax assessor, the court held that the taxpayers failed to carry their burden to demonstrate that the assessments were invalid. Thus the court affirmed the order of the Property Tax Commission upholding the county's assessments.

5.3.2.3 Immaterial Irregularities. Akin to the principle that taxpayers may not invalidate a county's assessment merely by attacking the methodology of assessment—without showing a corresponding unwarranted increase in value—is the notion that an assessment will not be invalidated because of a procedural irregularity in the assessment process. The Machinery Act provides that such *immaterial irregularities*, which range from clerical errors by the assessor to failure to advertise, list, appraise, or assess any property for taxation, do not invalidate the tax imposed on any property.[100]

Property "not properly listed" during the regular listing period, property listed at a substantial understatement in value, and property granted an exemption or exclusion for which it did not qualify are subject to discovery under G.S. 105-312; yet, on occasion, property may escape assessment and taxation without meeting any of these criteria. For instance, a taxpayer may properly list property, but the assessor may inadvertently neglect to assess such property. A question then arises as to whether the omitted assessment and resulting taxes may be imposed at a later date under the theory that the failure to timely assess the property was an immaterial irregularity.

The North Carolina Court of Appeals addressed such a situation in *In re Notice of Attachment and Garnishment Issued by Catawba County Tax Collector Against Nuzum-Cross Chevrolet, Inc.*[101] Nuzum-Cross Chevrolet timely listed its business personal property with the Catawba County tax supervisor (now, the tax assessor) in 1976, 1977, and 1978. The tax department transposed numbers when calculating the total assessment. As a result, Nuzum-Cross Chevrolet was taxed on a lower figure than it should have been in 1976, 1977, and 1978. The county tax supervisor recognized the error in September 1978 and billed Nuzum Cross for the unpaid taxes. When Nuzum-Cross did not pay, the tax collector attached one of the company's bank accounts for $5,087.67, the amount of the additional taxes plus interest.

At a hearing, a district court judge ordered the bank to remit the total taxes due, minus penalties and interest. The taxpayer appealed to the court of appeals. The appellate court held that the tax supervisor's error was an immaterial irregularity under G.S. 105-394 that did not invalidate the tax imposed. Recognizing that its holding permitted the county to "go back two years (from 1978 to 1976) to correct its error," the court noted that under the Machinery Act "all property is subject to taxation unless subject to an exemption." The appellate court acknowledged the taxpayer's argument that a taxpayer who intentionally fails to list property might be better off than one whose property is not assessed due to an immaterial irregularity since discoveries cannot go back more than five years, while the immaterial irregularities clause contains no such time limitation. The court noted, however, that it was the role of the legislature, not the court, to impose such time limits. Thus the court of appeals affirmed the district court's order, which, as previously mentioned, did not award interest or penalties.

Another case defining the circumstances in which the immaterial irregularities clause permits the retroactive assessment of property is *In re Dickey*, which involved an appeal from a Forsyth County assessment.[102] The Dickeys purchased a new home in Forsyth County in October 1988 for $272,500 and submitted a listing form in January 1989. The Dickeys listed their house on a portion of the form separated by perforation. When tax office personnel received the form, someone threw away the perforated portion, which was the proper procedure if nothing was listed on that portion of the form. That, of course, was not the case on the Dickeys' form. The Dickeys received a 1989 tax bill imposing taxes only on the value of their unimproved lot, $37,500. In June 1990, the assessor's office realized its mistake and discovered $185,500 in value. The assessor then billed the Dickeys for an additional $2,094.30 in taxes. The Dickeys alleged that the assessment was untimely and appealed to the county board of equalization and review, which dismissed their appeal. The Dickeys then appealed to the Property Tax Commission, which concluded that the value of the Dickeys' house was not discoverable pursuant to G.S. 105-312 as the Dickeys had properly listed the house with the tax office. The commission further concluded that the assessor had "appraised" the house at a value of $0 for 1989. While the assessor could *reappraise* the house for 1990–91 and subsequent tax years,[103] the commission concluded that this value was not retroactive. The commission ordered the assessor to revise its tax records to reflect a value of $0 for the Dickeys' house in 1989. The county appealed the commission's decision to the court of appeals. While the court of appeals agreed with the commission that discovery of property listed by the taxpayer was improper, the court disagreed with the commission's conclusion that the assessor had appraised the house at a value of $0 in 1989. The court cited the lack of evidence that the assessor had attempted to determine the value of the Dickeys' home before 1990 and noted that no one contended that the home purchased by the Dickeys for more than $250,000 was actually worth nothing. Instead, the court noted that the record demonstrated that the assessor was unaware that the house existed because a portion of the Dickeys' listing form was inadvertently removed and destroyed. Because the assessor could not have appraised a house that he did not know existed, the court determined that the provisions of G.S. 105-287 prohibiting retroactive increases in appraised property values did not preclude the assessor from levying the challenged tax. Furthermore, the court held that the administrative error that resulted in the failure to assess the Dickeys' house for 1989 taxes was an immaterial irregularity within the meaning of G.S. 105-394.

The court concluded that such an irregularity did not invalidate the taxes owed by the Dickeys for 1989 and levied by the assessor in 1990 and reversed the decision of the Property Tax Commission. The court further stated that G.S. 105-394 imposed no time restriction on the correction of immaterial irregularities from previous years, noting that the imposition of time limits was the exclusive province of the legislature.

The North Carolina Supreme Court in *In re Morgan*[104] clarified that the immaterial irregularities clause allows a tax assessor to assess property for prior years even when gross negligence by the assessor resulted in the previous failure to assess. In a per curiam opinion, the supreme court reversed the majority opinion of the court of appeals, for the reasons set forth in the dissenting opinion.[105] Tyleta Morgan and her husband owned property in Henderson County and, beginning in 1986 and continuing until 1993, built a home on the property.[106] Mr. Morgan, who died before the house was assessed, obtained all required building permits from the county. The county inspected the home in 1986. In 1993, when the house was 80 percent complete, Mr. Morgan listed the house with the Henderson County Tax Assessor. The county performed a countywide reappraisal effective January 1, 1999, and another effective January 1, 2003. An appraiser for the county visited the Morgan's property during both reappraisals; yet the Morgans' house was not assessed. In 2004 the county assessed taxes on the residence and informed Mrs. Morgan that she owed taxes and interest totaling $8,533.61 for tax years 1995 through 2003. The Property Tax Commission determined that the county should have assessed the property before 2004 and that its failure to do so was not an immaterial irregularity.[107] Thus the commission barred the county from attempting to collect the back taxes.[108]

The court of appeals, in an opinion joined by two of three panel judges, reviewed the Property Tax Commission's decision under the whole record test, considering only whether the commission's decision had a rational basis in the evidence.[109] Because legal issues are subject to de novo review in the court of appeals, the court of appeals majority's application of this deferential standard signaled its approval of the commission's view that only clerical and administrative errors may be corrected pursuant to G.S. 105-394. The appellate court majority proceeded to find that the commission's conclusion was supported by substantial evidence that the county botched multiple opportunities to assess the residence over more than a decade after it was properly listed by Mr. Morgan.[110]

Judge Geer dissented on the basis that "the Commission and majority opinion have improperly imposed their view of appropriate public policy—fairness to individual taxpayers—to override other public policies promoted by the statute's plain language such as equality of taxation and reduction of tax rates."[111] Noting that G.S. 105-394 defines *immaterial irregularity* as a " 'failure to assess any property for taxation . . . within the time prescribed by law' " and does not explicitly require that this failure result from a clerical or administrative error, the dissent concluded that the county's failure to assess Mrs. Morgan's residence fell squarely within the statutory definition of immaterial irregularity.[112] Moreover, the dissent concluded that because interest automatically applies to taxes paid after the date they became due, interest also applies to taxes assessed after their due date due to an immaterial irregularity.[113] While noting that it was the responsibility of the General Assembly, not the court, to determine the public policy of the state, the dissent nevertheless cited several "public policy advantages of construing the statute as written."[114] The dissent quoted liberally from a brief filed in support of the county's position by the North Carolina Association of County Commissioners recognizing that correcting past assessment errors " '*avoids the inequity of one property owner not being taxed on some or all of his or her property while all other property owners in that county are taxed*' " and " '*avoids any incentive on the part of the property owner to allow an assessment oversight to persist.*' "[115] Finally, the dissent cited the association's argument that the full assessment of all property permits the tax rate to be set as low as possible, recognizing that "[i]t is the province of the General Assembly—and not this Court or the Property Tax Commission—to determine whether these policies outweigh the fairness to individual taxpayers."[116] The state supreme court's adoption of the reasoning in the dissent forecloses a restrictive reading of the immaterial irregularities clause and subjects taxpayers to assessment of property in subsequent years, with interest calculated from the date the taxes originally would have become due.

Because the assessor could not have made a discovery of the property in *In re Morgan*—since it *was* listed, though not assessed—it is unclear whether an assessor may use the more generous immaterial irregularity provisions of G.S. 105-394 in lieu of the discovery provisions of G.S. 105-312 if the discovery statute is applicable. An assessor might prefer to assess property under G.S. 105-394, given that there is no stated statute of limitations (though the dissent in *In re Morgan* referenced the assessor's ability to "*go back 10 years* to assess property that the authority has neglected to assess in a timely fashion through no fault of the taxpayer")[117] and that interest applies from the original due date,[118] whereas a discovery may only be made for the current and five previous years and no penalty applies to a discovery of real property subject to permanent listing.[119] Likewise, one might question whether the broad language in G.S. 105-394 allowing correction of errors resulting from the "failure to . . . appraise . . . any property . . . or levy any tax" trumps other Machinery Act provisions permitting prospective, but not retroactive, changes to the appraised value of real property.[120] The court of appeals' opinion in *In re Dickey* indicates, however, that G.S. 105-394 will not be construed so broadly as to overwrite the G.S. 105-287 provision prohibiting retroactive changes in appraised value.[121]

5.3.3 Settlement of Property Tax Appeals

Occasionally, a taxpayer proposes to settle a matter appealed to the Property Tax Commission by paying some portion of the tax owed before the case is heard by the Property Tax Commission. A taxpayer might, for instance, offer to withdraw the appeal and pay the principal amount of taxes owed on the condition that the board of commissioners waive accrued interest. In such a circumstance, a governing board might wish to enter into the agreement and save the costs of litigation.

While normally a county board of commissioners has no authority to compromise interest or any other portion of a tax absent a showing that the tax was imposed through clerical error, the tax was illegal, or the tax was levied for an illegal purpose,[122] a board is implicitly empowered to settle pending litigation.[123] Notwithstanding this power, a board of commissioners does not have unfettered authority to enter into such settlements with respect to taxes that are the subject of an appeal to the Property Tax Commission. If the board had unlimited discretion to settle appeals, the mere filing of an appeal with the Property Tax Commission would provide the taxpayer and the board with an end-run around the Machinery Act's prohibition against compromising taxes. If a board has the power to compromise taxes simply by virtue of the appeal, then a taxpayer could readily avoid the prohibition against compromise of taxes by appealing the assessment of taxes to the Property Tax Commission and thereby creating litigation that a board has authority to settle.

Given that a provision of state law prohibits a local governing body from compromising taxes (including accrued interest), a board may not circumvent that state law prohibition through its power to settle pending litigation.[124]

Governing boards are, however, authorized to appraise or reappraise property in the current calendar year upon the assessor's report that, since adjournment of the board of equalization and review, facts have come to his or her attention that warrant raising or lowering the value of property.[125] If a governing board finds that reduction in the value of the property is authorized to comport with the market value standard or other provisions of the Machinery Act, it is authorized to enter into a settlement agreement that alters the property's assessed value as provided by law.

A staff member of the Property Tax Division of the Department of Revenue reviews all appeals filed with the Property Tax Commission.[126] This entails reviewing the issues on appeal with the taxpayer, counsel for the taxpayer, the county assessor, and the county attorney. These discussions sometimes result in an agreement about the appropriate valuation or exempt status of the property, which may be formalized in a settlement agreement prepared as a consent order signed by the director of the Property Tax Division of the Department of Revenue or as a formal order signed by the chairperson of the Property Tax Commission. Such settlement agreements are afforded the same status as a post-hearing decision by the commission; thus, the refund and release provisions of G.S. 105-380 and 105-381 do not apply.

5.3.4 Enforced Collection

Tax receipts for assessments appealed to the Property Tax Commission are delivered to the tax collector along with all other tax receipts, but the tax collector may not use enforced collection remedies to collect such taxes nor advertise the taxes as delinquent until the appeal is resolved.[127]

5.3.5 Appeal to the Court of Appeals from the Decision of the Property Tax Commission

Either the taxpayer or the county, or both, may appeal to the North Carolina Court of Appeals from an adverse decision rendered by the Property Tax Commission.[128] A party seeking to appeal an order of the Property Tax Commission must file with the Property Tax Commission within thirty days after entry of the final order a notice of appeal and exceptions setting forth the basis on which the order is unlawful, unjust, unreasonable, or unwarranted and including errors alleged to have been committed by the Property Tax Commission.[129] The Property Tax Commission may then, upon its own motion or the motion of any party, set a hearing on the exceptions to the final order upon which the appeal is based. If the Property Tax Commission does not set such a hearing, the appeal proceeds directly to the North Carolina Court of Appeals for hearing and determination. The appellant may not rely upon any grounds for relief on appeal that are not set forth in the notice of appeal filed with the Property Tax Commission.

5.3.5.1 Appellate Standard of Review. The appellate court considers questions of law under the standard of de novo review, pursuant to which the court "consider[s] the matter anew and freely substitute[s] its own judgment for that of the Commission."[130] Other issues, such as sufficiency of the evidence to support the commission's decision, are reviewed under the whole record test, which requires the appellate court to determine whether the Property Tax Commission's decision has a rational basis in the evidence.[131] The whole record test does not permit the reviewing court to substitute its view and assessment of the matter for that of the Property Tax Commission where both views are reasonable, regardless of whether the court justifiably could have reached a different result had the matter been before it under the de novo standard. Instead, the whole record rule requires the court, in determining the substantiality of the commission's decision, to consider items in the record that detract from the weight of the evidence supporting the decision. Under the whole record rule, the court must consider the evidence that justifies the commission's decision along with contradictory evidence.[132] By applying this analysis, a reviewing court can determine whether the commission's decision has a rational basis in the evidence.[133]

The court of appeals bases its determination upon the record and proceedings of the Property Tax Commission and may not receive additional evidence. If a party can demonstrate to the court that it discovered evidence after the Property Tax Commission hearing that it could not through reasonable efforts have obtained for use at the Property Tax Commission hearing and the evidence will materially affect the merits of the case, the court of appeals may remand the record and proceedings to the Property Tax Commission for consideration of the new evidence.[134]

The court of appeals must review the record and exception and assignments of error in accordance with the Rules of Appellate Procedure. The appellate court must decide all questions of law presented by the appeal, interpret constitutional and statutory provisions, and determine the meaning and applicability of the terms of any commission action.[135] The court may affirm, reverse, or declare null and void the decision of the Property Tax Commission, or it may remand the case for further proceedings.

The appellate court may reverse or modify the Property Tax Commission's decision regarding a disputed assessment if it determines that the substantial rights of the appellants have been prejudiced because the Property Tax Commission's findings, inferences, conclusions, or decisions are (1) in violation of constitutional provisions; (2) in excess of the commission's jurisdiction or statutory authority; (3) made upon unlawful proceedings; (4) affected by other errors of law; (5) not supported by competent, material, and substantial evidence in view of the entire record; or (6) arbitrary or capricious.[136]

The taxpayer or county, or both, may appeal an adverse decision by the court of appeals to the North Carolina Supreme Court if the case directly involves a substantial question arising under the state or federal constitution (this might be the case, for example, if the issue involved an attempt to tax property within the exclusive jurisdiction of the federal government) or in a case in which a dissent is filed by a court of appeals judge.[137] In cases in which there is no appeal of right from the court of appeals decision, a party may petition the supreme court for discretionary review after the court of appeals renders its decision.[138] The supreme court may only agree to review the case if it determines that the subject matter of the appeal has significant public interest, the case involves legal principles of major significance to the jurisprudence of the state, or the court of appeals decision conflicts with a supreme court decision.[139] A petition for appeal of right to or for discretionary review by the state supreme court must be filed within fifteen days after the mandate of the court of appeals has been issued to the Property Tax Commission.[140] The mandate of the court consists of certified copies of its judgment and opinion, which are issued by the clerk of the court to the clerk of the Property Tax Commission.[141] The clerk of court enters judgment and issues the mandate twenty days after the written opinion of the court is filed with the clerk.[142]

Recall that a tax collector may not seek to collect taxes or enforce a tax lien resulting from an assessment appealed to the Property Tax Commission until the appeal is "finally adjudicated."[143] Though various arguments could be raised regarding the time at which the appeal is finally adjudicated,[144] the most conservative and prudent course of action for tax collectors is to refrain from enforcing payment of taxes subject to an appeal either (1) until the entry of an opinion by the state supreme court or (2) until the time to file an appeal as of right or a petition for discretionary review to either the state court of appeals or the state supreme court has expired.

5.4 Changes to the Value of Real Property in a Nonreappraisal Year

As noted at the outset of this chapter, the Machinery Act provides for annual appraisal of personal property and at least octennial appraisal of real property. Yet for the sake of equity and uniformity, some parcels of real property must be reappraised in a year in which general reappraisal of real property is not undertaken. Property may be rezoned from residential to commercial, bringing about a change to its highest and best use and the resulting valuation. Buildings may be constructed, improved, or expanded, and portions of existing parcels may be transferred, which can result in a change in the portion of property valued as residual acreage.[145] While most of the aforementioned changes increase the value of property in a nonreappraisal year, property also must be reappraised for qualifying changes that *reduce* its value, such as damage or destruction of property by tornados, floods, or fires. G.S. 105-287 directs the assessor to reappraise specific parcels in a nonreappraisal year in order to (1) correct clerical or mathematical errors in the former appraisal; (2) correct appraisal errors resulting from misapplication of the county's appraisal manual; or (3)recognize an increase or a decrease in value resulting from some factor other than normal depreciation, economic changes affecting property in general, or certain listed improvements such as repainting and landscaping. If the circumstance that causes the increase or decrease in valuation is not specifically *excluded* from reappraisal, the assessor is required to reappraise the property to recognize the impact of that circumstance.[146]

An appraisal change may only be made based upon a factor that has affected the property by January 1 of the year in which the property is reappraised. Thus, if a county conducts a countywide reappraisal effective January 1, 2007, and a house is destroyed by fire on January 2, 2008, the property may not be reappraised until 2009.

Reappraisals made under the authority of G.S. 105-287 must conform to the appraisal manual adopted in the last reappraisal year so that they will represent the property's market or present-use value as of January 1 of the reappraisal year, rather than its current value. A fee appraiser's independent determination of value may be relied upon only to the extent that it correlates to the applicable schedule of values.[147] Thus, in the example above in which a house is destroyed by fire on January 2, 2008, the reappraisal of the affected parcel in 2009 will be based upon the 2007 schedule of values. Nonreappraisal year appraisals take effect as of January 1 of the year in which they are made and do not affect previous tax years.

Property may not be reappraised in a nonreappraisal year based upon an increase or decrease in value evidenced by a sale of the property that occurs after the January 1 reappraisal date.[148] While the transfer of some portion of a larger parcel requires reappraisal to assign value to the resulting parcels, the sale of an entire parcel does not. Such a sale is not a factor from which the increase or decrease in value results.[149]

The county assessor must complete all reappraisals warranted under G.S. 105-287 before the board of equalization and review convenes. Once the board of equalization and review is in session, reappraisal may occur only at its direction. Any reappraisal by the board of equalization and review must conform to the standards and procedures set forth in G.S. 105-287. The Property Tax Commission's authority to change property valuations is limited to the same extent as the assessor's; thus any reappraisal ordered by the commission must likewise conform to G.S. 105-287.[150]

As noted earlier, after adjournment, the board of equalization and review's authority is limited to considering appeals filed before adjournment along with appeals from personal property valuations; timely appeals from valuation changes made by the board itself; appeals relating to discovered property; appeals related to the appraisal, situs, and taxability of classified motor vehicles; and appeals relating to audits of exempted or excluded property. At this stage in the assessment cycle, only the board of county commissioners may make or authorize changes to the tax records, including reappraisal.[151] The board of county commissioners may authorize the reappraisal of property when the assessor reports that, since the adjournment of the board of equalization and review, facts have come to his or her attention rendering it advisable to raise or lower the appraisal of property in the current calendar year. The assessor has discretion over whether make such a report to the board.

Notes

1. U.S. Const. amend. XIV, § 1.

2. The term t*axpayer* is defined as "any person whose property is subject to ad valorem property taxation by any county or municipality and any person who, under the terms of this Subchapter, has a duty to list property for taxation." N.C. Gen. Stat. § 105-273(17) (hereinafter G.S.).

3. G.S. 105-296(i).

4. G.S. 105-317.1(c).

5. *Id.*

6. G.S 105-322.

7. 1989 N.C. Sess. Laws ch. 605 (Cumberland County); 1981 N.C. Sess. Laws ch. 509 (Mecklenburg County); 1975 N.C. Sess. Laws ch. 155 (Henderson County).

8. 7. G.S. 105-322(e).

9. *Id.*

10. G.S. 105-322(g)(5).

11. Notice of the date, hours, place, and purpose of the board's first meeting must be published at least three times in a newspaper with general circulation in the county, with the first publication at least ten days before the first meeting. The notice also must state the dates and hours of the board's subsequent meetings and the date on which it expects to adjourn. G.S. 105-322(f).

12. G.S. 105-322(g)(2).

13. *In re* Whiteside Estates, 136 N.C. App. 360, 365–66, 525 S.E.2d 196, 199 (2000).

14. *Id.* at 365, 525 S.E.2d at 199 (quoting *In re* King, 281 N.C. 533, 539, 189 S.E.2d 158, 161 (1972)).

15. Brock v. Prop. Tax Comm'n, 290 N.C. 731, 228 S.E.2d 254 (1976). Brock and several unidentified property owners appeared before the Jones County Board of Equalization and Review to request a 25 percent reduction of all farm property in Jones County. When their request was denied, Brock and eleven other taxpayers appealed to the Property Tax Commission. Brock later sought to have ninety-nine additional landowners added to the complaint. The Property Tax Commission dismissed all of the appeals on the basis that the taxpayers sought to attack the schedule of values rather than the appraised value of their own property and thus lacked standing to pursue the appeal. The taxpayers appealed to Wake Superior Court (which was, at that time, the body to which Property Tax Commission appeals were filed), which affirmed the Property Tax Commission. The taxpayers then appealed to the court of appeals, which also affirmed the Property Tax Commission's decision, though one judge dissented from the opinion. The taxpayers then appealed to the North Carolina Supreme Court, which reversed the lower court's decision, determining that the initial taxpayers had challenged the appraisal of their property rather than the schedule of values and, therefore, were entitled to a full hearing on the merits before the Property Tax Commission. The supreme court held, however, that the Property Tax Commission had properly dismissed the appeal as to the ninety-nine property owners who sought to join the appeal in process. Noting that the Machinery Act permitted *any* property owner to appeal an order of the county board of equalization and review to the

Property Tax Commission, the court held that this statutory provision presupposed a ruling by the county board adverse to the appellant taxpayer with respect to the listing or appraisal of his property or the property of others, after a hearing requested by the taxpayer. Since the additional taxpayers had not requested a hearing before the county board or filed a timely notice of appeal, the dismissal of the case was proper. The original eleven appellants argued that even if the ninety-nine additional plaintiffs lacked standing, they could appeal the appraisal of this additional property under the authority to appeal the appraisal of others' property. The court rejected this argument on the basis that there had been no showing that the original eleven appellants had been aggrieved by those appraisals.

16. G.S. 143-318.18(7).

17. *See* David M. Lawrence, Open Meetings and Local Governments in North Carolina: Some Questions and Answers, Question 140 at 32 (6th ed. 2002).

18. G.S. 105-322(g)(3)(b).

19. G.S. 105-322(g)(3)(a).

20. *Id.*

21. *Id.*

22. G.S. 105-322(d).

23. *Id.*

24. G.S. 105-322(g)(2)(c). Ethical concerns may arise when persons, other than attorneys, seek to represent parties in connection with an appeal to the board of equalization and review. This issue arises in the context of appeals filed by corporations as well as individuals, particularly elderly individuals who may wish to have a younger relative explain or articulate the basis for the appeal. The North Carolina State Bar issued an advisory opinion concluding that only lawyers may represent another party before a planning board, board of adjustment, or other government body conducting quasi-judicial hearings since the representation of another person at a quasi-judicial hearing constitutes the practice of law. N.C. State Bar Comm. On Ethics and Prof'l Responsibility, Formal Ethics Op. 3 (2007).

25. A subpoena issued by the board must be signed by the chair of the board, directed to the witness or to the person having custody of the document, and served by an officer authorized to serve subpoenas. G.S. 105-322(g)(3)(b).

26. G.S. 105-322(g)(2)(c).

27. G.S. 105-322(g)(3)(b).

28. G.S. 105-322(g)(2)(d).

29. G.S. 105-325(a).

30. *Id.*

31. *See* G.S. 105-282.1(a1) (permitting approval of late application for exemption, but only for current calendar year); G.S. 105-381 (setting strict procedures and limits on refunds and release of taxes).

32. *See* William A. Campbell, Property Tax Collection in North Carolina 107–08 (4th ed. 1998).

33. 136 N.C. App. 360, 525 S.E.2d 196 (2000).
34. *In re* Whiteside Estates, 136 N.C. App. at 365–66, 525 S.E.2d at 199.
35. Brock v. Prop. Tax Comm'n, 290 N.C. 731, 228 S.E.2d 254 (1976).
36. G.S. 105-322(a).
37. G.S. 105-290.
38. G.S. 105-290(e).
39. G.S. 105-290(g).
40. *Id.*
41. G.S. 105-288(a).
42. *Id.*
43. G.S. 105-290.
44. G.S. 105-290(b)(2)(a) (permitting the Property Tax Commission to authorize one or more members of the commission or employees of the Department of Revenue to hear an appeal, make examinations and investigations, have made a record of the evidence offered at the hearing, and make recommended findings of fact and conclusions of law).
45. G.S. 105-290(b)(2).
46. *In re* McElwee, 304 N.C. 68, 87, 283 S.E.2d 115, 126–27 (1981).
47. 116 N.C. App. 551, 449 S.E.2d 196 (1994).
48. *Id.* at 552, 449 S.E.2d at 197.
49. *Id.* at 560, 449 S.E.2d at 202.
50. *Id.* at 558, 449 S.E.2d at 201.
51. N.C. Admin. Code tit. 17, ch. 11, § .0217 (2008).
52. N.C. Admin. Code tit. 17, ch. 11, § .0216 (2008).
53. *Id.*
54. G.S. 105-290(b)(3).
55. G.S. 105-290(b)(4).
56. *Id.*
57. *Id.*
58. Taxes are payable at par—that is, without interest—until January 5 of the fiscal year for which they are levied.
59. G.S. 105-290(b)(4).
60. *In re* Amp, 287 N.C. 547, 215 S.E.2d 752 (1975).
61. *Id.*
62. *Id.*
63. *In re* S. Ry. Co., 313 N.C. 177, 182, 328 S.E.2d 235, 239 (1985); *In re* IBM Credit Corp., ___ N.C. App.___, 650 S.E.2d 828 (2007), *aff'd*, No. 520A07, 2008 WL 616118 (N.C. S. Ct. March 7, 2008) (per curiam).
64. 287 N.C. 547, 215 S.E.2d 752 (1975).
65. *Id.* at 549, 215 S.E.2d at 754.
66. 287 N.C. at 549, 215 S.E. 2d at 754. Inventories are now excluded from taxation by G.S. 105-275(33).
67. 287 N.C. at 550, 215 S.E.2d at 754.
68. *Id.* at 551, 215 S.E.2d at 755.
69. *Id.*

70. *Id.*
71. *Id.* at 554–56, 215 S.E.2d at 757–58.
72. *Id.* at 555, 215 S.E.2d at 757.
73. 287 N.C. at 555, 215 S.E.2d at 757.
74. *Id.* at 555–56, 215 S.E.2d at 757–58.
75. *Id.* at 555–56, 215 S.E.2d at 758.
76. *Id.* at 558, 215 S.E.2d at 759.
77. *Id.*
78. *Id.* at 559, 215 S.E.2d at 760.
79. Appeals from decisions of the Property Tax Commission now lie directly to the North Carolina Court of Appeals rather than to superior court.
80. 287 N.C. at 559–60, 215 S.E. 2d at 760.
81. *Id.* at 562, 215 S.E.2d at 761.
82. *Id.* at 562, 215 S.E.2d at 761–62.
83. *Id.* at 563, 215 S.E.2d at 762.
84. *Id.* at 565–66, 215 S.E.2d at 763.
85. *Id.* at 566, 215 S.E.2d at 764.
86. 287 N.C. at 566, 215 S.E.2d at 764.
87. *Id.* at 567–75, 215 S.E. 2d at 765–70.
88. *Id.*
89. *Id.*
90. *Id.* at 575, 215 S.E.2d at 769.
91. *Id.*
92. 287 N.C. at 575, 215 S.E.2d at 769.
93. *Id.* at 575, 215 S.E.2d at 769–70.
94. *Id.* at 576, 215 S.E.2d at 770.
95. *Id.*
96. *In re* Bermuda Run Prop. Owners, 145 N.C. App. 672, 551 S.E.2d 541 (2001).
97. *Id.* at 673, 551 S.E.2d at 542.
98. *Id.* at 677, 551 S.E.2d at 545.
99. *Id.*
100. G.S. 105-394.
101. 59 N.C. App. 332, 296 S.E.2d 499 (1982).
102. *In re* Dickey, 110 N.C. App. 823, 431 S.E.2d 203 (1993).
103. G.S. 105-287.
104. 362 N.C. 339, 661 S.E.2d 733 (2008).
105. *Id.* at 340, 661 S.E.2d at 734.
106. *In re* Morgan, 186 N.C. App. 567, 568, 652 S.E.2d 655, 656 (2007), *rev'd*, 362 N.C. 339, 661 N.C. 733 (2008).
107. *Id.*
108. *Id.*
109. *Id.* at 568–69, 652 S.E.2d at 656.
110. *Id.* at 570, 652 S.E.2d at 657.
111. 186 N.C. App. at 572, 652 S.E.2d at 658 (Geer, J., dissenting).

112. *Id.* at 574, 652 S.E.2d at 659 (Geer, J., dissenting).

113. *Id.* at 575, 652 S.E.2d at 660 (Geer, J., dissenting).

114. *Id.* (Geer, J., dissenting)

115. *Id.* (Geer, J., dissenting)

116. *Id.* (Geer, J., dissenting).

117. 186 N.C. App. at 576, 652 S.E.2d at 660 (Geer, J., dissenting) (emphasis added).

118. *See In re* Morgan, 362 N.C. 339, 340, 661 S.E.2d 733, 734 (adopting reasoning of dissenting opinion in *In re Morgan*, 186 N.C. App. at 572–76, 652 S.E.2d at 658–60 (Geer, J., dissenting)).

119. *See* G.S. 105-303(b)(3)(providing that penalties imposed by G.S. 105-308 and 105-312 do not apply to a failure to list real property for taxation, with the exception of failure to report newly constructed or acquired improvements or separate rights).

120. *See* G.S. 105-287(c).

121. *See In re* Dickey, 110 N.C. App. at 828–29, 431 S.E.2d at 206–07 (relying on immaterial irregularities clause to justify change in assessment for previous years given that the assessor did not appraise the residence in prior years and therefore concluding that G.S. 105-287 was inapplicable).

122. G.S. 105-380; G.S. 105-381.

123. G.S. 153A-11 sets out the corporate powers of counties, which include the power to sue and be sued and to contract and be contracted with. G.S. 153A-12 gives the board of commissioners authority to exercise the corporate powers of the county. The authority to settle a claim is implicit in suing or being sued.

124. *See, e.g.*, Cleveland County Ass'n for Gov't by the People v. Cleveland County Bd. of Comm'rs, 142 F.3d 468 (D.C. Cir. 1998) (holding that a North Carolina county could not enter into a consent decree that circumvented state elections law).

125. G.S. 105-325(a)(6).

126. North Carolina Department of Revenue, Property Tax Division, Property Tax Appeals Manual 21 (2006), *available at* www.dor.state.nc.us/publications/appeals_manual_2006.pdf.

127. An appeal is resolved when all rights to appeal are exhausted or the time for filing an appeal has expired.

128. G.S. 105-345.

129. *Id.*

130. *In re* Greens of Pine Glen, 356 N.C. 642, 647, 576 S.E.2d 316, 319 (2003) (internal quotations omitted).

131. *Id.*

132. *In re* McElwee, 304 N.C. 68, 87–88, 283 S.E.2d 115, 127 (1981).

133. *In re* Owens, 132 N.C. App. 281, 511 S.E.2d 319 (1999).

134. G.S. 105-345.1.

135. G.S. 105-345.2.

136. *Id.*

137. G.S. 7A-30.

138. G.S. 105-345.4.

139. G.S. 7A-31.

140. N.C. R. App. P. 14; N.C. R. App. P. 15.

141. N.C. R. App. P. 32.

142. *Id.*

143. G.S. 105-378(d).

144. N.C. R. Civ. P. 54.

145. *See In re* Corbett, 355 N.C. 181, 558 S.E.2d 82 (2002) (approving the reappraisal of residual acreage from a larger parcel as a residential homesite after transfer of that acreage to a new owner in a non-revaluation year).

146. *Id.* at 185, 558 S.E.2d at 84.

147. *In re* Allred, 351 N.C. 1,10, 519 S.E.2d 52, 57 (1999).

148. *In re Allred*, 351 N.C. 1, 519 S.E.2d 52 (1999).

149. *Compare In re* Corbett, 355 N.C. 181, 558 S.E.2d 82 (revaluation year reappraisal affirmed when parcel split into two smaller buildable lots) *with In re* Allred, 351 N.C. 1, 519 S.E.2d 52 (holding that a sale after January 1 of the revaluation year is not a factor from which an increase or decrease in value results within the meaning of G.S. 105-287(a)(3)).

150. *In re Allred*, 351 N.C. at 3, 519 S.E.2d at 53.

151. G.S. 105-325.

6 Classified Motor Vehicles

6.1 **Classified Motor Vehicles** 148

6.2 **Listing and Assessment of Registered Classified Motor Vehicles** 149

6.2.1 Appraisal, Ownership, and Situs 150

6.2.2 Municipal Vehicle Taxes 151

6.2.3 Exempt Vehicles 154

6.2.4 Collection 154

6.2.5 Enforcement 155

6.2.6 The Tax Year 156

6.2.7 Deadlines 158

6.2.8 Antique Vehicles 158

6.2.9 Registration Consolidation 159

6.3 **Amended Article 22A, Effective 2011** 159

6 Classified Motor Vehicles

Nearly every general rule of property taxation has an exception for registered motor vehicles. The General Assembly designated all motor vehicles as a special class of property in 1991 and enacted special procedures, contained in Article 22A of the Machinery Act, for levying and collecting taxes on classified motor vehicles. Most of the procedures governing listing and assessment of taxes on unregistered motor vehicles mirror those for the taxation of other types of personal property, but the procedures for listing and assessing taxes on registered motor vehicles differ significantly since the Machinery Act links the schedule for and taxation of such motor vehicles directly to their registration.

Before the enactment of Article 22A, owners of motor vehicles, were responsible for listing those vehicles, like other taxable property, for taxation. Not surprisingly, many motor vehicles were never taxed or were taxed only after being discovered by the assessor.[1] Even when those vehicles ultimately were listed and taxed, many car owners did not pay the taxes. Tax collectors could, of course, use enforced collection remedies, but only at an administrative cost that sometimes exceeded the value of the taxes collected. Article 22A solved the listing problem by requiring the Division of Motor Vehicles (DMV) to send to each county a monthly list of motor vehicles registered in that county. Counties then generate a bill for such vehicles—including city taxes, if applicable—that is due four months after the date of registration. Article 22A created a remedy designed to address the difficulty of collecting motor vehicle taxes as well. If taxes are not paid four months after they became due, the tax collector notifies the Division of Motor Vehicles, which then places a block on the registration, preventing the registration from being renewed until the taxes are paid.

6.1 Classified Motor Vehicles

Article 22A of the Machinery Act consists of the statutes codified from Sections 105-330 through 150-330.9 of the North Carolina General Statutes (hereinafter G.S.) and applies to classified motor vehicles, which includes most private passenger vehicles, both registered and unregistered. The article adopts the definition of *motor vehicles* from Article 20 of the North Carolina General Statutes, which contains the laws governing the registration of vehicles and the operation of those vehicles on the public highways.[2] This definition includes "[e]very vehicle which is self-propelled and every vehicle designed to run upon the highways which is pulled by a self-propelled vehicle" but specifically excludes mopeds. All automobiles, motorcycles, trucks, and trailers are thus classified for taxation under Article 22A, with the exception of (1) manufactured homes, mobile classrooms, and mobile offices; (2) semitrailers or trailers registered on a multiyear basis; (3) vehicles owned or leased by a public service company; and (4) vehicles exempt from registration, which include farm tractors and other farm vehicles, mopeds, motorized wheelchairs, certain self-balancing nontandem two-wheeled devices, tow dollies, and vehicles owned by manufacturers, dealers, the United States government, and nonresidents.[3] These categories of excepted vehicles continue to be listed and taxed the same as other kinds of personal property.

While both registered and unregistered vehicles are *classified* by Article 22A, unregistered vehicles continue to be listed and taxed under the article in much the same manner as other kinds of personal property. That is, they must be listed by the owner during the regular listing period, they are subject to discovery if not listed, they are valued as of January 1, and taxes on them are due September 1 of each year and delinquent the following January 6. One key procedural difference in the ad valorem taxation of unregistered classified motor vehicles and that of other personal property is that the tax assessor must provide separate notice of taxes due on unregistered motor vehicles, whereas owners of other types of personal property are presumed to have notice of taxes owed.[4] The tax notice prepared by the assessor must include all county and special district taxes owed on the unregistered classified motor vehicle. Municipalities are required to provide their own tax notices for such vehicles.[5] While the notice requirement creates a slight difference in the procedure for taxing unregistered classified motor vehicles from that used to tax other personal property, *registered* classified motor vehicles are subject to significantly different procedures for taxation.

6.2 Listing and Assessment of Registered Classified Motor Vehicles

As mentioned above, owners of unregistered classified motor vehicles must list those vehicles during the annual listing period along with any other taxable personal property. The registration of an unregistered motor vehicle during the calendar year for which it is listed for taxation has no property tax consequences.[6] Instead, the vehicle remains subject to taxation in the ensuing fiscal year as an unregistered motor vehicle.[7]

Owners of registered classified motor vehicles, in contrast, have no duty to list their vehicles. Instead, the county assessor is responsible for listing these vehicles pursuant to the procedures set forth in Article 22A of the Machinery Act.

Most motor vehicles are registered under a staggered system, under which registrations for vehicles expire in varying months over each of the twelve months of the calendar year. Because registered motor vehicles are listed by taxing units based upon records of new and renewed registrations compiled by the Division of Motor Vehicles, taxes likewise are levied upon registered motor vehicles on a staggered monthly basis.

Here is how the process works: By the tenth day of each month, the Division of Motor Vehicles sends to each county assessor a list of vehicles for which registration was renewed or for which a new registration was obtained under the staggered system in the county during the second preceding month.[8] For example, by September 10, 2008, DMV will mail the lists of vehicles registered in July 2008. For the few remaining vehicles registered under the annual system (certain vehicles whose registration always expires at the end of December), DMV forwards the registration lists of those that are renewed to the assessor by March 10. The assessor then audits the list and appraises listed vehicles based upon their value as of January 1 of the year in which the taxes become due. The discovery provisions in G.S. 105-312 do not apply to the failure to list a registered motor vehicle for taxation.[9]

The assessor then prepares a separate tax notice for each vehicle.[10] The notice requirement applies to both registered and unregistered motor vehicles. The notice for registered motor vehicles must contain all county, city, and special district taxes,[11] while the notice for unregistered motor vehicles must contain all county and special district (but not city) taxes.[12] This is because cities remain responsible for listing, assessing, and taxing unregistered classified motor vehicles and must send notices of city taxes.[13] In preparing the tax

Table 6.1 Calendar for Listing and Assessing Motor Vehicles Registered in July

June 10	Division of Motor Vehicles (DMV) mails renewal notices and cards to vehicle owners whose registrations expire in July.
September 10	DMV sends to county assessors a list of renewals of registrations that expired in July.
October 15 (approximately)	Tax collectors mail bills for renewals of registrations that expired in July.
November 1	Due date for renewals of registrations that expired the previous July.
December 1	Interest begins to accrue on unpaid bills for renewals of registrations that expired the previous July.
March 10	Tax collector mails to DMV list of delinquent taxpayers for renewals of registrations that expired the previous July.

notices for registered motor vehicles, the assessor uses the tax rates in effect as of the first day of the month in which the new registration was applied for or the existing registration expired (regardless of what day during the month the registration was actually obtained or renewed).[14]

Table 6.1 sets forth a calendar of important listing, assessment, and billing dates applicable to motor vehicles that are registered in July.

6.2.1 Appraisal, Ownership, and Situs

The ownership, situs, and taxability (that is, whether the vehicle qualifies for an exemption or exclusion from taxation) of a registered motor vehicle are determined as of the day on which the vehicle registration is renewed or the date a new registration is applied for.[15] The applicable tax rate is determined as of the first day of the month in which the current vehicle registration expired or the new registration was applied for.[16] An owner may appeal the situs assigned to a particular motor vehicle or its taxation by filing a request for refund or release pursuant to G.S. 105-381.[17]

The value of a classified motor vehicle registered under the staggered system, in contrast, is determined as of January 1 of the year in which the taxes become due.[18] Since taxes on registered motor vehicles are due on the first day of the fourth month after the date the current registration expires, vehicles for which the registration expires in September, October, November, and

December are valued as of January 1 of the following year, while vehicles registered from January through August are valued as of January 1 of the current year.[19] If the value of a new motor vehicle cannot be determined as of January 1 of the year in which the taxes become due, the value must be determined as of the date that model vehicle was first offered for sale at retail in North Carolina.[20] County assessors must appraise and assess motor vehicles at market value, pursuant to the appraisal standards governing the appraisal of all other property, but must exclude highway use taxes paid by the purchaser from any valuation of a motor vehicle based upon its purchase price when the cost approach is utilized.[21] Table 6.2 sets forth the controlling dates for assessment and collection of taxes on registered motor vehicles.

A vehicle owner may appeal the appraised value of a vehicle but must pay the tax when it comes due, regardless of any pending appeal.[22] The vehicle owner must file the appeal within thirty days of the date on the tax bill for the vehicle.[23] The assessor must then arrange a conference with the vehicle owner to permit the owner to present evidence and argument regarding the appeal.[24] Within fifteen days after the conference, the assessor must provide written notice to the taxpayer of his final decision unless the taxpayer signs an agreement accepting the listing and appraisal.[25] If written agreement is not reached, the taxpayer has fifteen days from the date of the notice to request review of the assessor's decision by the board of equalization and review, the board of commissioners, or a special committee appointed by the board of commissioners to hear motor vehicle appeals.[26] If the appeal is decided in favor of the vehicle owner, the owner is entitled to a refund of the excess taxes paid.[27]

A vehicle owner may appeal situs (that is, whether the taxing unit has jurisdiction to tax the vehicle) and taxability (that is, whether the vehicle is exempt from taxation) by following the procedures for requesting a refund or release of taxes.[28] This requires that the taxpayer appeal the listing or assessment of the vehicle to the board of county commissioners or special motor vehicle appeal committee on one of three bases: (1) the tax was imposed through clerical error, (2) the tax was illegal, or (3) the tax was levied for an illegal purpose.[29]

6.2.2 Municipal Vehicle Taxes

Cities and towns may levy a municipal license tax of up to $5.00 per year on any vehicle resident in the city or town.[30] Many cities and towns are authorized by local act to levy taxes exceeding this amount.[31] Cities and towns

Table 6.2 Controlling Dates for the Assessment and Collection of Taxes on Registered Classified Motor Vehicles

New Registrations	Value G.S. 105-330.2(a)	Tax Rate G.S. 105-330.5(a)	Tax Year G.S. 105-330.6(a)	Levy Year G.S. 105-330.5(d)	Ownership, Situs, Taxability G.S. 105-330.2(a)	Due Date G.S. 105-330.4(a)	Block Date G.S. 105-330.7
Staggered Registrations	January 1 of the year taxes are due	Rate in effect 1st day of month in which registration applied for	Begins 1st day of 1st month that follows the date the new registration is applied for—ends on the last day of the month in which new registration expires	Included in levy for fiscal year in which taxes become due unless tax notice is prepared after due date—then include taxes in levy for current fiscal year	Date registration applied for	1st day of 4th month following last day of month in which new registration applied for	1st day of 4th month after month taxes become due
Annual Registrations			Begins 1st day of 1st month following the date new registration applied for and ends Dec. 31				

Table 6.2 *(continued)*

Renewed Registrations	**Value G.S. 105-330.2(a)**	**Tax Rate G.S. 105-330.5(a)**	**Tax Year G.S. 105-330.6(a)**	**Levy Year G.S. 105-330.5(d)**	**Ownership, Situs, Taxability G.S. 105-330.2(a)**	**Due Date G.S. 105-330.4(a)**	**Block Date G.S. 105-330.7**
Staggered Registrations	January 1 of the year taxes are due	Rate in effect 1st day of month in which former registration expired	Begins 1st day of 1st month following date registration expires—ends on the last day of the month in which the current registration expires	Included in levy for fiscal year in which taxes become due unless tax notice is prepared after due date—then include taxes in levy for current fiscal year	Date of renewal (even if renewed after registration expires)	1st day of 4th month following date former registration expires	1st day of 4th month after month taxes become due
Annual Registrations			Begins 1st day of 1st month following the date the registration expires—ends December 31			May 1 following date former registration expires	

that operate a public transportation system may levy an additional $5.00 per vehicle tax to be allocated to the public transportation system.[32] The additional tax, when combined with the rate of tax levied under G.S. 20-97(b) and any local legislation, may not exceed $30 per year.[33] These taxes are not ad valorem property taxes; instead, they are privilege taxes, imposed for the privilege of owning a motor vehicle that is situated for tax purposes within a city or town.[34]

6.2.3 Exempt Vehicles

The owner of a vehicle who claims an exemption or exclusion from taxes for a vehicle (for instance, a church or a private school) must file an application with the assessor, which may cover one or several vehicles.[35] Machinery Act provisions governing applications for exemption of other property do not apply to classified motor vehicles.[36] Thus an application requesting exemption for other personal property is insufficient to request exemption for a motor vehicle. Once the assessor approves the application, the property described in the application is omitted from the tax records and will not be taxed.[37] The Machinery Act does not specify when an application for exemption of a classified motor vehicle must be filed. The interpretation that most closely aligns with the statutory scheme for imposing taxes on motor vehicles is that applications for exemption must be filed within thirty days after the date of the tax notice for registered motor vehicles and within the statutory listing period for unregistered motor vehicles. The owner of an exempted vehicle must report to the assessor when the vehicle no longer qualifies for exemption.[38] For registered vehicles, the owner must report disqualification within thirty days after the registration is renewed or initially applied for. For unregistered vehicles, the owner must report the changed status on or before January 31. If the owner fails to report that the vehicle is no longer exempt, the vehicle is subject to discovery, but instead of the normal 10 percent late-listing penalty, the penalty is $100 for each registration period that elapsed before the disqualification was discovered.[39]

6.2.4 Collection

As soon as the bills are prepared each month, the county tax collector mails them to the vehicle owners. For vehicles registered under the staggered system, taxes are due on the first day of the fourth month following the date the registration expired or following the last day of the month in which the new registration was applied for.[40] For example, if a vehicle's registration expired in June or a vehicle was newly registered in June, the taxes on that vehicle will be due the following October 1. Taxes for vehicles registered under the annual system are due May 1.[41] The taxes are included in the tax levy for the fiscal year in which they become due and are charged to the tax collector for that year, unless the tax notice is prepared after the date the taxes are due.[42] In the example given above, if a vehicle is registered in June 2008, the taxes on the vehicle are due October 1, 2008, and will be included in the 2008 tax levy. The county may retain up to 1.5 percent of municipal and special district taxes collected as an administrative charge.[43] Taxes collected for municipalities and special districts must be remitted to them at least once each month.[44]

6.2.5 Enforcement

If taxes remain unpaid one month after the due date, interest accrues at the rate of 5 percent for the first month of delinquency and 0.75 percent a month thereafter unless the tax bill was prepared after the due date.[45] For example, if the tax bill is prepared in September and the due date is October 1, interest begins to accrue at the rate of 5 percent a month on November 1 and continues to accrue at 0.75 percent per month thereafter until the taxes are paid. If the tax bill is prepared after the due date, interest accrues beginning the second month following the date of the bill. Thus, if the tax bill in the previous example is prepared October 15, taxes are delinquent and 5 percent interest accrues on December 1. The tax collector may use any of the normal means of enforcing collection of taxes from personal property, but, unlike taxes on other personal property, the taxes on a motor vehicle do not become a lien on the owner's real property.[46]

In addition to the normal collection remedies, a special enforcement provision applies for taxes on classified registered motor vehicles. On or before the tenth day of each month, the tax collector must send to the Division of Motor Vehicles a list with the owner's name and address and the vehicle identification number of each vehicle on which taxes remain unpaid on that date and which were due on the first day of the fourth month preceding that date.[47] For example, on December 10 the collector will forward to the division a list of unpaid taxes that became due on August 1 (these are vehicles for which the registration expired in April). The division will then refuse to renew the registration of any vehicle on the list until the taxes are paid.[48] A person to whom a listed vehicle was transferred in good faith may obtain renewal without paying the taxes.[49]

6.2.6 The Tax Year

The tax year for a classified motor vehicle registered under the staggered system begins on the first day of the month following the date the registration expires or a new registration is applied for and runs for the registration renewal period, which is generally twelve months.[50] The tax year for a classified motor vehicle registered under the annual system begins the first day of the first month following the date the new registration is applied for or following the date the former registration expires and ends December 31.[51] The tax year for an unregistered motor vehicle is the fiscal year that opens in the calendar year in which the vehicle is required to be listed.[52] If a vehicle owner transfers the registration plate from one vehicle to another during the first vehicle's tax year, the vehicle to which the plates are transferred is not taxed until the current registration expires or is renewed.[53] At that time, the owner will be unable to renew the registration of the second vehicle until the taxes on the first vehicle are paid.

An owner of a vehicle who transfers it to another person and surrenders the registration plate to the Division of Motor Vehicles or who moves out of state and registers the vehicle in the new state during the vehicle's tax year is entitled to a prorated refund of taxes paid on the vehicle for the current tax year if at least one full month remains in the tax year at the time of the transfer. The refund is in proportion to the number of full months remaining in the tax year after the surrender.[54] The refund is calculated by multiplying the total tax liability by a fraction with a denominator of the number of months in the vehicle's tax year and a numerator equaling the number of full months remaining in the vehicle's tax year.[55] The application for the refund or release must be made to the tax collector within one year after the plate is surrendered.[56]

For example, suppose Jane Jones, the owner of a classified registered motor vehicle, renews the registration on her vehicle on July 3, 2007, three days after it expired on June 30, 2007. In September 2007, Jane received a bill for property taxes on the vehicle. Taxes were due October 1, 2007. Jane paid the taxes October 28, 2007. She sold the vehicle December 12, 2007, and surrendered the plates. Jane presents the receipt from the surrender of plates to her county tax office September 10, 2008, and requests a prorated refund of taxes. What is the amount of the proration?

The tax year for Jane's vehicle began July 1, the first month after the registration expired, and extended twelve months, through June 30. After the December sale, six full months remained in the vehicle tax year (January through June). Since Jane presented the receipt within one year of surrendering the plates, she is entitled to a refund for 6/12, or ½, of the vehicle taxes paid.

What is the result if Jane sells the vehicle listed with the tax office and transfers the plates to another vehicle? As previously discussed, Jane will pay taxes on the listed vehicle for the remainder of the calendar year, regardless of whether the new vehicle has a higher or lower market value than the listed vehicle. But suppose Jane sells the second vehicle in December, surrenders the plates, and presents a receipt evidencing the surrender of plates to the tax office, along with a request for a refund of prorated taxes. Is Jane entitled to a refund?

The applicable statute requires that the taxpayer transfer the listed vehicle to a new owner (or move out of state and register the vehicle there) and surrender the plates from that vehicle.[57] In the above example, Jane transferred the vehicle listed with the tax office and subsequently surrendered the plates that once were on the listed vehicle. The question is whether the intervening transfer of the plates to the second vehicle disqualifies Jane from proration on the basis that the plates transferred were no longer "from the listed vehicle." The statute lends itself to conflicting interpretations, and policy arguments can be made for either interpretation. Prorating the bill seems reasonable since Jane should not have to pay an entire year of taxes on a vehicle she no longer owns. On the other hand, Jane already received a benefit from the transfer if the second vehicle was more valuable than the first by continuing to pay taxes based on the value of the first vehicle. An argument can be made that that benefit should not be increased by prorating the taxes for the months remaining after Jane surrenders the plates. Given that the taxing unit never considered the second vehicle, the best interpretation of this statutory provision is probably the former; that is, Jane may receive a proration of the bill.

Vehicle owners may also be entitled to a release of taxes when the tax year for a vehicle changes for a reason other than the transfer of plates to another vehicle. Suppose, for example, that on January 29, 2007, Joe Jones renewed the registration on his Land Rover, which expired on January 31, 2007. In May, Joe pays the tax bill for his Land Rover for the tax year February 1, 2007, through January 30, 2008. Joe plans to leave the county in July for a backpacking trip in the Swiss Alps. He surrenders the plates on the Land Rover on June 5, 2007. Joe is not entitled to a proration of the taxes levied on his Land Rover upon surrender of the plates because he did not transfer the vehicle to a new owner. When Joe returns from the Swiss Alps in September 2007, he applies for a new registration for the Land Rover. Joe receives a bill, due in January, for the tax year September 1, 2007, through August 31, 2008. Joe is eligible for a credit against the taxes on the vehicle for the new tax year equal to a proportion of the taxes already paid on the vehicle for the February 1, 2007, through January 31, 2008, tax year. The proportion is the number of full months remaining in the original tax year when the new tax year began, divided by twelve. Because four months remained in the old tax year when the new tax year began, Joe is entitled to a credit of $^4/_{12}$, or ⅓, of the original tax bill to be applied to the most current tax bill on the Land Rover. To receive the credit, Joe must apply within thirty days after the taxes for the new year are due and must provide the county tax collector information establishing the original tax year of the vehicle, the amount of taxes paid on the vehicle for that year, and the reason for the change in registration.[58]

6.2.7 Deadlines

Generally under North Carolina law, when the deadline for completing an act falls on a weekend or holiday, the act is considered timely if completed the next business day.[59] This rule does not apply to obligations under Article 22A of the Machinery Act other than the deadline for paying taxes at par. Thus, when the time for performing an act related to the taxation of registered motor vehicles occurs on a weekend or holiday, the act must be performed on the last business day preceding the statutory deadline. Thus applications for releases or refunds of motor vehicle taxes, as well as taxpayer appeals, must be filed before the expiration of the statutory period if the last day of the period falls on a weekend or holiday.

6.2.8 Antique Vehicles

Antique vehicles are designated a special class of property.[60] As such, they are not subject to provisions governing the taxation of other vehicles, including the law that a vehicle be assessed at market value.[61] Antique vehicles are assessed at the lower of market value or $500.[62] To qualify for this reduced assessment, a vehicle must be owned by an individual and satisfy three additional conditions.[63] First, the vehicle must be registered with the Division of Motor Vehicles and have a historic vehicle special license plate. Second, the vehicle must be maintained primarily for use in exhibitions, club activities, parades, and other public interest functions and be used only occasionally for other purposes. Third, the vehicle must not be used to produce income or in connection with a business.

6.2.9 Registration Consolidation

An owner of multiple vehicles who desires to be billed simultaneously for all of the vehicles may place all vehicles on the same tax year by renewing registration for all of the vehicles during the annual renewal period for one of the vehicles.[64] When a vehicle owner seeks to renew a registration that has not yet expired for the purpose of consolidating property taxes, the Division of Motor Vehicles must honor the request.

6.3 Amended Article 22A, Effective 2011

After Article 22A was implemented in 1993, the rate of timely payment of motor vehicles bills rose to about 80 percent. By 2005 the rate of timely payment had declined to about 66 percent.[65] The North Carolina Tax Collectors' Association estimated in 2005 that the failure to timely pay resulted in about $80 million in delinquent, uncollected motor vehicle taxes at the end of each fiscal year.[66] While some of these taxes certainly are collected after the close of the fiscal year, such collection may require the use of enforced collection remedies such as attachment and garnishment. Many owners of registered motor vehicles simply wait to pay taxes until they need to renew their registrations. At that time, the block for unpaid taxes prevents them from doing so, so the taxes must be paid. At this juncture, eight months have passed since the taxes became due.

The 2005 General Assembly took substantial steps toward solving the problems associated with the collection of taxes for registered motor vehicles by establishing funding and launching a process for the full integration of vehicle taxation and registration.[67] Beginning on July 1, 2011, taxes will be billed *simultaneously* with registration fees and must be paid *before* a vehicle's registration is renewed.

Amended Article 22A of G.S. Chapter 105 fully integrates the registration and taxation of motor vehicles as of July 1, 2011, or upon the earlier creation of a combined registration renewal and tax collection computer system within DMV. Funding for the new DMV property tax collection system was created by increasing the first month's interest on delinquent registered motor vehicle taxes from 2 to 5 percent effective January 1, 2006, and by allocating 60 percent of those funds (that is, the increase) to a Combined Motor Vehicle and Registration Account under the control of the Office of State Budget and Management to fund the development of the integrated computer system.[68]

Under the combined system, the Property Tax Division of the Department of Revenue must annually adopt a schedule of motor vehicle values for use by all county assessors. The schedule must account for local market conditions and allow adjustments for mileage and condition. Taxes on registered motor vehicles become due on the date a new registration is applied for or at the end of the grace period following the expiration of a vehicle's current registration. A person may, however, obtain a limited registration plate without paying property taxes upon submitting an application for title and registration fees to DMV.[69] Limited registrations expire on the last day of the second month following the date on which the registration was applied for. Limited registrations become valid for the remainder of the year upon payment of county and municipal taxes and fees.[70] A person may opt to pay property taxes at the time the application for title is submitted and registration fees are paid and thereby obtain a twelve-month rather than a limited registration.[71] The integrated statutory scheme eliminates the need to block registrations by making payment of taxes a prerequisite to issuance or renewal of the registration for the taxable period.

The new system requires the Property Tax Division of the Department of Revenue to prepare a combined registration renewal and tax notice for each registered motor vehicle. The notice must inform vehicle owners that limited registrations become valid for the remainder of the year upon payment of county and municipal taxes and fees.[72] The Department of Revenue may recoup its costs of sending the combined notice from the taxing unit or units in which the vehicle is registered. Interest collected on unpaid registration fees must be transferred monthly to the North Carolina Highway Fund to be used for technology improvements within DMV.

Taxes and registration fees may be collected by DMV or a DMV agent, defined as "collecting authorit[ies]" under G.S. 105-330(1a). The collecting authority may retain a fee equal to at least one-third of the compensation DMV agents currently receive for registration renewals pursuant to G.S. 20-63(h). Each collecting authority must provide a weekly financial report to taxing units and DMV.

Automobile dealers may register and obtain license plates for newly sold vehicles without collecting property taxes at the time of sale. G.S. 20-79.1A provides for the issuance of limited registration plates—license plates bearing a clear and visible marker denoting their temporary status—to dealers and others who submit applications for title and registration fees to DMV.

Limited registrations expire on the last day of the second month following the date on which the registration was applied for. New G.S. 105-330.5(a2) provides that limited registrations become valid for the remainder of the year upon payment of county and municipal taxes and fees and requires the Property Tax Division of the Department of Revenue to include this information in its notice to the vehicle's new owner. A dealer or any other person may opt to pay property taxes at the time the application for title is submitted and registration fees are paid and thereby obtain an annual rather than a limited registration.

Upon the full integration of the registration and taxation of motor vehicles, vehicles registered under the International Registration Plan (IRP) will no longer be *classified* motor vehicles.[73] This change divorces the taxation of IRP vehicles from the process of registering these vehicles. Thus taxpayers must list IRP vehicles with the county in which they are subject to taxation during the period for listing other taxable personal property (generally, the month of January) unless the vehicles are centrally assessed by the Department of Revenue as public service company property.

Notes

1. *See* William A. Campbell, *A New Day for Collecting Local Property Tax on Automobiles*, Popular Government, Fall 1992, at 28–31.

2. N.C. Gen. Stat. § 105-330 (hereinafter G.S.) (incorporating by reference G.S. 20-4.01(23)).

3. G.S. 105-330.1.

4. *Compare* G.S. 105-330.5(c) (separate notice of taxes required) *with* G.S. 105-348 (notice of taxes conclusively presumed).

5. G.S. 105-330.5(c).

6. G.S. 105-330.3(a)(2).

7. *Id.*

8. G.S. 20-50.3.

9. G.S. 105-330.3(a)(1).

10. G.S. 105-330.5(a).

11. *Id.*

12. G.S. 105-330.5(c).

13. *Id.*

14. G.S. 105-330.5(a).

15. G.S. 105-330.3(a)(1).

16. G.S. 105-330.5(a).

17. G.S. 105-330.2(b).

18. G.S. 105-330.2(a). The value of a classified motor vehicle registered under the annual system is determined January 1 of the period in which the vehicle is required to be listed. *Id.*

19. *See id.*

20. G.S. 105-330.2(a).

21. G.S. 105-330.2(b).

22. *Id.*

23. *Id.*

24. *Id.* (incorporating appeal procedures from G.S. 105-312(d) applicable to discovered property).

25. *Id.*

26. *Id.*; G.S. 105-325.1.

27. G.S. 105-330.2(b).

28. G.S. 105-330.2(b) (providing for situs and taxability appeals pursuant to procedures in G.S. 105-381).

29. G.S. 105-381(a)(1).

30. G.S. 20-97(b).

31. *See, e.g.*, City of Charlotte, 1985 N.C. Sess. Laws ch. 1009 (Reg. Sess., 1986), as amended 1991 N.C. Sess. Laws ch. 209, as amended 1993 N.C. Sess. Laws ch. 345; City of Durham, S.L. 2003-329, sec. 1, 3, 4, as amended S.L. 2004-103, sec. 1, 2.

32. G.S. 20-97(c).

33. *Id.*

34. G.S. 20-97(a).

35. G.S. 105-330.3(b). Pursuant to G.S. 105-282.1(a)(1)b., no application is required to claim exemption of short-term rental vehicles.

36. G.S. 105-330.3(d) (stating that G.S. 105-282.1 does not apply to classified motor vehicles).

37. G.S. 105-330.3(b).

38. G.S. 105-330.3(c).

39. *Id.*

40. G.S. 105-330.4(a)(1).

41. G.S. 105-330.4(a)(2).

42. G.S. 105-330.5(d).

43. G.S. 105-330.5(b); G.S. 105-330.5 provides that "[t]he county may retain the actual cost of collecting municipal and special district taxes collected *pursuant to this Article*, not to exceed one and one-half percent (1½%) of the amount of taxes collected." (emphasis added) A city's license tax on motor vehicles is imposed pursuant to G.S. 160A-213(a) and G.S. 20-97(b), rather than Article 22A of Chapter 105. Thus the question is whether it can be considered as "collected pursuant to this article." G.S. 105-330.5 requires that the tax notice prepared by the assessor for registered motor vehicle taxes "contain *all* county, municipal, and special district taxes due on the motor vehicle." (emphasis added). This reference to all taxes appears to require that the notice contain city license taxes as well as ad valorem taxes. Thus the county must collect all taxes—not just ad valorem taxes. G.S. 105-330.5 therefore may be fairly interpreted as permitting the county to retain the actual cost of collecting city license taxes as well as other municipal and special district taxes not to exceed 1.5 percent of the amount collected.

44. G.S. 105-330.5(b).

45. G.S. 105-330.4(b).

46. G.S. 105-330.4(c).

47. G.S. 105-330.7.

48. G.S. 20-50.4(a).

49. *Id.*

50. G.S. 105-330.6(a). Certain annual registrations were converted to staggered registrations in 2006. DMV implemented that changes by renewing annual registrations in 2006 for periods ranging from seven to eighteen months. The registrations expired in varying months, from July 2006 to June 2007. To permit taxing units to tax registered motor vehicles for the full registration renewal period, the definition of tax year was amended to correspond to the period of registration. S.L. 2005-313.

51. G.S. 105-330.6(a).

52. *Id.*

53. G.S. 105-330.6(b).

54. G.S. 105-330.6(c).

55. *Id.*

56. *Id.*

57. *Id.*

58. G.S. 105-330.6(a1).
59. G.S. 105-395.1.
60. G.S. 105-330.9(b).
61. *Id.*
62. *Id.*
63. G.S. 105-330.9(a).
64. G.S. 20-66(i).
65. Memorandum from the N.C. Ass'n of Tax Assessors and N.C. Ass'n of Tax Collectors, H 1779 Impact Statement (April 5, 2006) (on file with author).
66. *Id.*
67. S.L. 2005-294; as amended S.L. 2006-259, sec. 31.5; as amended S.L. 2007-471; as amended S.L. 2007-527, sec. 22; as amended S.L. 2008-134, sec. 65.
68. Any funds remaining in the account after creation of the integrated system must be distributed to local governments on a pro rata basis. G.S. 105-330.10. Each jurisdiction's pro rata share is based on the first month's interest collected by the jurisdiction and paid into the account. *Id.*
69. G.S. 20-79.1A.
70. G.S. 105-330.5(a2).
71. G.S. 20-79.1A(b).
72. G.S. 105-330.5(a2).
73. G.S. 105-330.1(b). The International Registration Plan is a registration reciprocity agreement among forty-eight states, the District of Columbia, and provinces of Canada providing for payment of apportioned registration fees for fleet vehicles on the basis of total distance operated in all jurisdictions. INT'L REGISTRATION PLAN© (IRP) with Official Commentary 6, 34, 84–85 (amended 2008), *available at* www.irponline.org; *see also* N.C. ADMIN. CODE tit. 19A, ch. 3E, § .0401 (2008) (providing that apportionable vehicles used or intended for use in two or more jurisdictions that allocate or proportionally register vehicles must be registered in accordance with the provisions of the IRP).

7 Exemptions and Exclusions

7.1 Exemptions 167

7.1.1 Property Owned by the State, Counties, and Municipalities 168

7.1.2 Property Owned by the Federal Government 170

7.1.3 Property Situated on Federal Lands 170

7.1.4 Exemptions for Burial, Religious, Educational, Charitable, and Other Qualifying Property 176

7.2 Exclusions 187

7.2.1 Homestead Exclusion 188

7.2.2 Circuit Breaker Benefit 191

7.2.3 Disabled Veteran Benefit 193

7.3 Applying for Special Tax Treatment 194

7.3.1 No Application Requirement 194

7.3.2 Single Application Requirement 195

7.3.3 Annual Application Requirement 197

7.3.4 Late Applications 197

7.4 Discovery of Property Entitled to Exemption or Exclusion 198

7.5 Special Rules for Classified Motor Vehicles 198

7.6 Review of Exempt Property 199

7.6.1 Roster of Exempt Property 199

7.7 Assessment at Present-Use Value 200

7.7.1 Application Requirement 202

7.7.2 Appeal Process 203

7.7.3 Classes of Property Eligible for Present-Use Taxation 203

7 Exemptions and Exclusions

As discussed in Chapter 1, the North Carolina Constitution, Article V, Section 2(3), exempts from taxation property belonging to the state, counties, and municipal corporations and authorizes the General Assembly to exempt from taxation cemeteries; property held for educational, scientific, literary, cultural, charitable, or religious purposes; personal property to a value not exceeding $300; and $1,000 in property held and used as the place of residence of the owner.

A separate subsection of Article V, Section 2(2), permits the General Assembly to classify property for special tax treatment, including exclusion from taxation. The General Assembly has exercised both forms of authority to exempt some property from taxation and to classify and exclude other forms of property. Both exemptions and classifications must be enacted by general law, rather than local legislation, that uniformly applies in every unit of local government. Thus, for example, an act exempting all cemeteries in a particular county would be unconstitutional. In contrast, the General Assembly *may* constitutionally enact a statute exempting *all* cemeteries from taxation or, in the alternative, designating burial grounds as a special class of property to be assessed based on its value as a burial ground. The General Assembly has, in fact, both exempted burial property not held for sale and designated such property held for sale as a special class of property.[1] This chapter is dedicated to a discussion of exemptions and exclusions set forth in the Machinery Act.

7.1 Exemptions

The exemptions clause dates from the 1868 North Carolina Constitution, while the General Assembly did not gain the power to classify property for special tax treatment until 1936. While the power to classify and exclude certain types of property from taxation is broader than the power to exempt property, the exemptions clause remains important because of its provisions mandating the exemption of property belonging to the state and its political subdivisions and because of the statutory exemptions enacted by the General Assembly under the exemptions clause authorization and codified in the Machinery Act at Sections 105-278.1 through 105-278.8 of the North Carolina General Statutes (hereinafter G.S.).[2]

7.1.1 Property Owned by the State, Counties, and Municipalities

Nearly two decades after the adoption of the 1868 state constitution, the General Assembly enacted a statute exempting property belonging to the state and its political subdivisions so long as the property was "used for public purposes." The statutory limitation that property be held for a public purpose remained in effect even after the constitution was rewritten in 1970 to contain the same mandatory exemption for state, county, and municipal property, without the public-purpose limitation present in the 1868 constitution. In 1974 the tax assessor for Orange County assessed for taxation a hotel and the personal property therein owned by and located on the campus of the University of North Carolina at Chapel Hill, a state institution, on the basis that the hotel and associated personal property were being used for commercial purposes unrelated to the university's educational mission. The university objected, alleging that the hotel and personal property were exempt from property taxes pursuant to the state constitution as property owned by the state. The state supreme court in *In re University of North Carolina*[3] agreed with the university and found unconstitutional the public-purpose gloss placed by the legislature upon the constitutionally mandated exemption for state property. The court, like the constitution, put it simply, stating, "[S]tate-owned property is exempt from ad valorem taxation solely by reason of State ownership, regardless of the property's use."[4]

Today G.S. 105-278.1 carries out the constitutional directive by exempting real and personal property belonging to the state, counties, and municipalities from taxation, regardless of the purpose for which such property is used. The statute also specifies that departments, institutions, and agencies of a state, county, or municipality are considered one and the same as the unit of government. Subsections (c)(2) and (3) contain nonexclusive listings of boards, commissions, authorities, and institutions that are considered to be units of state and local government. The court of appeals interpreted what it means for property to "belong to" the state or to one of its political subdivisions in *In re Appalachian Student Housing Corp.*[5] In that case, Watauga County assessed taxes on a student housing complex owned and managed by a private nonprofit corporation, Appalachian Student Housing Corporation (ASHC), pursuant to a trust agreement with Appalachian State University (ASU), which is a member school of the University of North Carolina system.[6] The trust agreement provided in part: "All funds and property received by ASHC shall be held in trust and used or expended for the benefit of ASU to the extent such expenditure is not inconsistent with lawful restrictions . . . ASHC may, from time to time, transfer any net revenue from its operations to ASU for support of student housing acquisition, development and operation. ASHC shall not transfer any funds or other assets to any person or entity other than ASU except in exchange for capital assets, goods or services at fair market value." Thus, while ASHC had legal title to the property, ASU had equitable title pursuant to the terms of the trust agreement. The question before the court was whether this beneficial ownership interest was sufficient to exempt the property from taxation as property "belonging to" the state. Noting that legal and equitable titles in an active trust[7] do not merge, the court determined that property held in an active trust is owned by both the trustee and the beneficiary. The court held that ASU's equitable interest in the property was sufficient to establish ownership by the state and, thus, exemption from taxation.

In an earlier case, the state supreme court upheld the taxation of forestland owned by the North Carolina Forestry Foundation, Inc., a nonprofit corporation created to develop new forestry methods and improve timber growing while giving financial assistance to the Division of Forestry at North Carolina State University, another member school of the University of North Carolina system.[8] The court determined that the University of North Carolina had no legal or equitable title to the land and, thus, that the land did not "belong to" the state. Likewise, the state attorney general opined in a 2000 advisory opinion that the Town of Ocean Isle's leasehold interest in property used for public beach access and parking did not render the property exempt.[9]

Given that the court's holding in *Appalachian Student Housing* hinged upon the unusual circumstances that the state was an equitable owner of property held in an active trust, one might have assumed that an equitable interest in property held by the state or one of its political subdivisions short of an out-right legal ownership interest would be insufficient to render property exempt from taxation as "belonging to" the government.

The court of appeals in *In re Fayette Place*, LLC,[10] however, expanded the definition of equitable ownership by the government to encompass an interest in property not formalized by a trust agreement. The *Fayette Place* court concluded that property owned by a for-profit limited liability company operated as a public housing project for the benefit of the Housing Authority of the City of Durham belonged to the Housing Authority and therefore was exempt from property taxation. Fayette Place, LLC, was formed as a joint venture between Development Ventures, Inc. (DVI), which owned 99 percent of the company, and Creative Housing Development Strategies, Inc. (CHD), which owned 1 percent of the company.[11] DVI, a nonprofit corporation, was wholly owned by the Housing Authority, and CHD was wholly owned by DVI.[12] The Housing Authority transferred public housing property to Fayette Place subject to a declaration of restrictive covenants, which provided, in part, that Fayette Place would operate the property as a public housing project for the benefit of the Housing Authority.[13] Durham County denied Fayette Place's subsequent application to exempt the property from taxation.[14] The Property Tax Commission held that the property was exempt pursuant to GS 105-278.1 since it belonged to the Housing Authority.[15] The North Carolina Court of Appeals agreed with the Property Tax Commission.[16] Relying on *Appalachian Student Housing* for the proposition that "where the state possesses a sufficient interest in property, such as equitable title to the property, the property is said to belong to the state even where legal title to the property is held by another party," the court determined that "[u]nder this labyrinthine ownership structure, complete ownership of Fayette Place can be imputed to the Housing Authority."[17] Thus the court concluded that the property was exempt from taxation pursuant to Art. V, Section 2, of the North Carolina Constitution and G.S. 105-278.1.[18]

7.1.2 Property Owned by the Federal Government

G.S. 105-278.1(a) codifies the exemption of real and personal property owned by the United States that, by virtue of the supremacy clause of the United States Constitution,[19] is not subject to state or local taxation unless federal law expressly permits its taxation.

7.1.3 Property Situated on Federal Lands

The federal government owns more than one million acres of property in North Carolina, used for purposes ranging from federal military reservations to national parks to post offices. As noted in the previous section, property owned by the federal government, including property situated on federal military reservations, is exempt from taxation. However, not all property located on federal lands is owned by the federal government. Instead, some property is privately owned. This section addresses whether and under what circumstances privately owned property situated on land owned by the federal government is subject to taxation by local governments in North Carolina.

The federal government may hold or acquire title to property situated within a state in one of five ways:

1. through reservation of title from the time before creation of the state,
2. by a grant from the state,
3. by exercising the power of eminent domain,
4. by purchasing the property without the states consent, or
5. by purchasing the property from the state with the state's consent for "the Erection of Forts, Magazines, Arsenals, dock-Yards, and other needful Buildings," pursuant to Article 1, Section 8, Clause 17, of the United States Constitution (the enclaves clause).[20]

Regardless of the manner in which the property is acquired, the state must cede jurisdiction to the federal government in order for the lands to become subject to federal jurisdiction.[21] Where the state cedes jurisdiction over property acquired by the federal government and the federal government accepts exclusive jurisdiction, the state no longer retains the power to tax property located on the federal property, regardless of who owns the assessed property.[22]

Because the federal government acquired property in North Carolina at different times, pursuant to different cessions of jurisdiction, and under different provisions for federal acceptance of jurisdiction, the determination of whether a particular area is under the exclusive jurisdiction of the federal government or, instead, whether the state retained some or all jurisdiction over property in the defined area—including the power to tax—must be made on a case-by-case basis.

To determine the nature of federal jurisdiction over federal lands, one must first determine the extent of jurisdiction ceded by the state.[23] Before 1887, the North Carolina General Assembly authorized the sale of specific tracts to the federal government by individual public laws. Thus, to determine the jurisdiction of property granted to the federal government before 1887, one must examine the particular act transferring title to the United States. On March 2, 1887, the North Carolina General Assembly enacted legislation "to authorize the United States to acquire title to lands on which are to be erected certain public buildings," consenting to the United States' acquisition of property in the state for "the purpose of erecting thereon any custom-house, courthouse, post-office or other building, including lighthouses, light keeper's dwellings, life saving stations, buoys and coal depots and buildings connected therewith."[24] The act did not explicitly cede jurisdiction. The North Carolina Supreme Court subsequently held, however, that the federal government had exclusive jurisdiction over lands it acquired under the federal enclaves clause and pursuant to the 1887 act consenting to such acquisition.[25]

Effective August 1, 1905, the legislature enacted the provision currently codified as G.S. 104-1, which authorizes the federal government to acquire title to land in North Carolina for certain enumerated purposes but provides that the state "shall so far retain a concurrent jurisdiction with the United States over such lands as that all civil and criminal process issued from the courts of the State of North Carolina may be executed thereon in like manner as if this authority had not been given, and that the State of North Carolina also retains authority to punish all violations of its criminal laws committed on any such tract of land." This reservation of concurrent jurisdiction for certain criminal law and service of process purposes does not encompass the power to tax property located on federal lands acquired pursuant to its authorization.[26] Indeed, a separate section of the Revisal of 1905, Section 5428, provided that the "lots, parcels or tracts of land acquired under this chapter, together with the tenements and appurtenances for the purpose mentioned in this chapter, shall be exempt from taxation."

In 1907 the North Carolina General Assembly enacted the provision currently codified as G.S. 104-7, which consents, in accordance with Article 1, Section 8, Clause 17, of the United States Constitution, to acquisition of property by the federal government for certain specified purposes and cedes exclusive jurisdiction for all purposes except (1) the service of all civil and criminal process of the state courts; (2) the concurrent power to enforce the criminal law; (3) the power to enforce state laws for the protection of public health and the environment and for the conservation of natural resources; and (4) the legislative jurisdiction of the state with respect to marriage, divorce, annulment, adoption, commitment of the mentally incompetent, and descent and distribution of property. Thus cessions of state jurisdiction pursuant to G.S. 104-7 clearly forfeit state and local government authority to tax property situated on federal lands.

In enacting G.S. 104-7, the General Assembly did not repeal G.S. 104-1, leaving it unclear as to which jurisdictional provision governed properties conveyed before the enactment of G.S. 104-7. The North Carolina Supreme Court, in *State v. De Berry*,[27] reconciled the conflict among the jurisdictional provisions of the 1887 act, G.S. 104-1, and G.S. 104-7 by holding that each statute applied prospectively to lands acquired after its enactment.[28]

The rule of prospective application set forth in *De Berry* means that for federal land acquired from 1905 until 1907, concurrent state and federal jurisdiction is presumed over criminal offenses, but the state does not retain its power of taxation over such territory. For property acquired after the enactment of G.S. 104-7 from January 24, 1907, until February 1, 1940 (the effective date of a federal statute requiring that the United States formally accept jurisdiction ceded by a state), the federal government has exclusive jurisdiction over the property and the state retains only the limited powers reserved by that statutory provision over such property. As a result, neither the state nor local government has the power to tax property situated on such lands absent a federal statute that expressly permits such taxation.[29]

Another layer of analysis is required to determine the scope of federal government jurisdiction for property acquired by the United States on or after February 1, 1940, the effective date of former 40 U.S.C. § 255, currently codified at 40 U.S.C. § 3112, which requires the United States to formally accept state-ceded jurisdiction of property acquired under the federal enclaves clause by filing a notice of acceptance with the governor of the state or taking other steps prescribed by state law.[30]

Before the enactment of 40 U.S.C. § 255, the federal government was presumed to have accepted whatever jurisdiction was ceded by the state. Post-enactment, until the federal acceptance is filed, it is presumed that jurisdiction has not been accepted,[31] and the state retains jurisdiction—so long as the exercise of state authority does not interfere with the carrying out of the federal project.[32]

Federal jurisdiction, once obtained, does not necessarily last forever.[33] The federal government may expressly surrender jurisdiction over state lands to the state from which jurisdiction was acquired. Exclusive federal jurisdiction also terminates upon the federal government's transfer of lands without restriction to private entities or when the federal government ceases to use the property for the public purposes for which it was acquired.[34]

In summary, the following principles apply to a determination of whether local governments have the power to tax property located on federal lands.

If the property was acquired before March 2, 1887, the particular grant pursuant to which the property was acquired must be consulted to determine whether privately owned property located on such lands may be subject to local taxation.

No property taxes may be imposed on property situated on federal lands acquired by the United States pursuant to the enclaves clause between March 2, 1887, and July 31, 1905. Property taxes likewise may not be imposed on property situated on federal lands acquired (regardless of the authority under which they were acquired) from August 1, 1905, until January 31, 1940. If the United States accepted the state's cession of jurisdiction over lands acquired on or after February 1, 1940, property situated on such lands is not subject to property taxation.

Of course, if congress specifically authorizes the imposition of state or local taxes upon such lands, that authority may be exercised by the state or local government regardless of the general rules stated above regarding jurisdiction and date of acquisition.[35]

Table 7.1 sets forth this information in summary form.

7.1.3.1 Power of Local Taxation over Specified Federal Lands. As stated earlier, one must know the year in which the federal government acquired property to apply these principles. Depending upon the year the property was acquired, one may be required to make further determinations regarding, for example, whether the federal government formally accepted jurisdiction or the authority pursuant to which the property was acquired. In 1962 the General Services Administration published its Inventory Report on Jurisdictional Status of Federal Areas within the States, which can serve as a useful starting point for determining the scope of federal jurisdiction.[36] The report lists all federal property by county and includes the number of acres, the year of acquisition, and a jurisdictional code indicating whether jurisdiction is exclusive, concurrent or partial, or unknown, or whether the federal government has only a proprietary interest in the property.

7.1.3.1.1 Eastern Cherokee Indian Reservation. The Eastern Cherokee Indian Reservation (also known as the Qualla Boundary) is home to the Eastern Band of Cherokee Indians, a federally recognized Indian tribe. The reservation is situated in Jackson and Swain counties. Because the Eastern Band of Cherokee Indians is a federally recognized Indian tribe and the reservation land is held in trust by the United States, North Carolina and its

Table 7.1 Determinative Dates and Statutory Provisions Controlling Local Government's Ability to Impose Property Tax on Privately Owned Property Situated on Federal Lands

Date Acquired	Nature of Jurisdiction	Power to Impose Property Taxes	Controlling Authority
Before March 2, 1887	Depends upon language in grant	Depends upon language in grant	See particular act granting property
March 2, 1887, and July 31, 1905	Exclusive federal jurisdiction, if acquired pursuant to federal enclaves clause	No	G.S. 104-1; U.S. Const. art. 1, § 8, cl. 17
August 1, 1905, through January 31, 1940	Exclusive federal jurisdiction	No	G.S. 104-1; G.S. 104-7
February 1, 1940, through present	Exclusive federal jurisdiction, if acceptance filed with governor	No	40 U.S.C. § 3112 (former 40 U.S.C. § 255); G.S. 104-7

political subdivisions may impose taxes on the property of Indians located on the reservation only if such taxation is expressly authorized by the federal government.[37] The federal government has provided no such authorization, and neither Jackson nor Swain county may tax real or personal property, including motor vehicles, owned by Indians and situated upon the reservation.[38] Personal property situated upon the reservation but owned by non-Indians presumably is subject to taxation,[39] so long as the imposition of such a tax does not frustrate tribal self-government or impair a right granted or reserved by federal law.[40]

Pursuant to a July 27, 1984, agreement between the Governor of North Carolina and the Secretary of the Department of the Interior, the United States and North Carolina have concurrent jurisdiction in the following places: Blue Ridge Parkway, Cape Hatteras National Seashore, Cape Lookout National Seashore, Carl Sandburg Home National Historic Site, Fort Raleigh National Historic Site, Great Smoky Mountains National Park, Moores Creek National Military Park, and Wright Brothers National Monument. According to a July 27, 1984, letter from the director of the National Park Service to the North Carolina Governor, "the term 'concurrent legislative jurisdiction' is understood as vesting in the State and the United States all the rights accorded a sovereign, with the broad qualification that such authority is held concurrently over matters including, but not limited to criminal laws, police powers and tax laws."[41] This embodies the "parallel right of both the State and the Federal Government to legislate with respect to such land and persons present or residing on it, subject only to United States and State of North Carolina constitutional constraints such as . . . the prohibition of taxation on the property of one sovereign by another." Thus local governments may tax privately owned property located within such jurisdictions.

In addition, state and federal courts and the attorney general have, in a handful of opinions, addressed the status of the federal government's jurisdiction in particular areas.[42]

7.1.4 Exemptions for Burial, Religious, Educational, Charitable, and Other Qualifying Property

As a policy matter, exemptions from property taxation are created to allow religious, charitable, educational, and other qualifying organizations to redirect funds that would otherwise be allocated to the payment of taxes to beneficial purposes that serve the public interest.[43] A countervailing policy consideration is the increased financial burden on taxable property that results from the exclusion of some property from the tax base.[44] In recognition of these competing interests, when statutes exempting property are capable of more than one construction, courts construe such statutes strictly against exclusion and in favor of taxation.[45] While statutes exempting property from taxation must be strictly construed, courts must not employ a narrow or stinting construction.[46] Put another way, the words used in the statute must be given their natural and ordinary meaning.[47] As a result, courts will uphold the exemption of property only if it clearly falls within the scope of a statutory exemption.[48]

7.1.4.1 Burial Property. As previously mentioned, the General Assembly has exercised both its exemption and classification authority to provide for special property tax treatment of burial property. G.S. 105-278.2(a) exempts from taxation real property "set apart" for burial purposes *unless* it is owned and held for purposes of sale or rental or sale of burial rights therein. G.S. 105-278.2(b) designates taxable real property set apart for human burial purposes as a special class of property, regardless of whether it is held for sale of burial rights. The assessor must consider the following factors in appraising the property:

1. The effect on its value of its division and development into burial plots
2. Whether it is irrevocably dedicated for human burial purposes by a recorded plat
3. Whether the owner is prohibited or restricted from selling, leasing, or encumbering the property

Property is considered set apart for burial purposes and entitled to exemption under G.S. 105-278.2(a) when it is presently used for such purposes or when it is held by the owner for the owner's personal use for burial purposes.[49] Property located on a tract of land dedicated for use as a cemetery by persons other than the owner is considered held for the purpose of sale to others as burial sites and thus is taxable, even if the land is undeveloped and no grave sites have yet been mapped.[50]

7.1.4.2 Real and Personal Property Used for Religious, Educational, Scientific, Literary, or Charitable Purposes. Statutory provisions providing for the exemption of certain real and personal property used for religious purposes (G.S. 105-278.3);[51] educational purposes (G.S. 105-278.4); religious and educational purposes (G.S. 105-278.5); and educational, scientific, literary, or charitable purposes (G.S. 105-278.7) contain provisions sufficiently similar to warrant discussion of their common provisions as a group.

7.1.4.3 Exclusive Use. Because the legislature has deemed that no public purpose is served by permitting land to lie unused and untaxed, the present use of land and other property—rather than the intended use of such property—governs the analysis of whether the property is being used for a purpose that qualifies it for exemption from taxation.[52] For example, property owned by a church and held as a future site for construction of a sanctuary but currently unused is not considered used for a religious purpose within the meaning of G.S. 105-278.3.[53]

Moreover, as the state supreme court explained in *Rockingham County v. Elon College*,[54] property held for a purpose that qualifies for exemption is supposed to be withdrawn from the competitive field of commercial activity; thus it does not violate the rule of equality or uniformity to permit such property to be exempted from taxation. When such property is "thrust into the business life of the community, it loses is sheltered place, regardless of the character of the owner, for it is then held for profit or gain."[55] It is not the character of the corporation or association owning the property that determines its exempt status but the purpose for which the property is held.[56] The fact that a commercial enterprise devotes its profits to a charitable or other laudable purpose does not change the character of the business or the purpose for which property is held. It is still a commercial enterprise and, as such, its property is subject to taxation.[57] Thus the court determined in *Elon College* that buildings owned by a private college and rented for business purposes were taxable, regardless of the college's use of all profits for educational purposes. Use of the property, not use of the income, controls.

The exemption statutes require more than simple use of the property; they require "exclusive" use. This requirement is common to the exemption for religious property (G.S. 105-278.3); educational property (G.S. 105-278.4); religious educational property (G.S. 105-278.5); charitable property (G.S. 105-278.6); educational, scientific, literary, or charitable property (G.S. 105-278.7); and charitable hospital property (G.S. 105-278.8). Thus it is worthwhile to explore the concept in greater detail to determine exactly what is meant by exclusive use.

The North Carolina Supreme Court explored the meaning of the term *exclusive* in *In re North Carolina Forestry Foundation*,[58] a case in which the North Carolina Forestry Foundation, Inc., a not-for-profit corporation organized to promote the development and practice of improved forestry methods and to promote forest education and research at North Carolina State University, appealed the taxation of forestland that it leased to a for-profit paper company for a term of ninety-nine years pursuant to an agreement that gave the paper company operational control of the property, known as the Hofmann Forest.[59] The court noted that *sole* and *single* were synonyms for exclusive and purported to reject the North Carolina Forestry Foundation's argument that the term exclusive was not to be construed literally. Yet it bears noting that the *Forestry Foundation* court denied the exemption based upon its determinations that the paper company had "virtually complete operational control of the Forest" and that the educational and scientific use of the property was "incidental to the activities of the paper company." Because the paper company's use was primary, rather than incidental, the court was not required by the facts of the case to apply the strict standard endorsed by its opinion.

In two cases decided after *In re Forestry Foundation*, the court of appeals interpreted the exclusive-use requirement more broadly than a literal reading of the term would suggest.[60] In *In re Worley*, the court of appeals held that a five-acre parcel of natural, wooded property owned by a church was exempt as it was used wholly and exclusively for a religious purpose by virtue of the recreational activities that occurred on the property and the use of the property as a spiritual retreat, even though the property also was used for hunting, which was not a religious purpose. The court explained: "Although we decline to hold that permitting hunting on Lot 37 was an exempt religious purpose, we conclude that the other recreational activities that occurred there and the use of the property as a spiritual retreat together constituted sufficient present use wholly and exclusively for religious purposes to warrant exemption."[61] The court also held that use of the property as a "buffer zone to protect the sanctity and serenity of the church from encroaching industrial development was a permissible 'religious purpose' and 'present use' entitling the property to exemption."[62] The court "emphasize[d] the narrowness of [its] holding," but refused to "quantify the amount of acreage a church may reasonably purchase for purpose of establishing a buffer zone," predicting that "appellate courts will view with a careful eye any acquisition of extensive acreage under less compelling facts."[63]

In *In re Appeal of Southeastern Baptist Theological Seminary, Inc.*,[64] the court of appeals affirmed the Property Tax Commission's conclusion that approximately two hundred acres of property held by the seminary as a buffer zone against urban development were exempt as educational property pursuant to G.S. 105-287.4. In that case, the taxpayer had actually contracted to sell fifty-six acres of the buffer zone property, contingent upon the rezoning of the property. When the application to rezone the property for a highway business district was denied, the sale fell through. Based on the attempted sale and other property, including woods and a golf course that shielded the seminary from commercial development, the county disputed the seminary's need for the buffer zone property. The court determined, however, that the property was essential to maintaining the rural campus, that recreational use of the parcels was consistent with the seminary's educational philosophy, and that the land was "situated in such a way as to contribute to the intended buffering effect."[65] The court rejected the county's argument that a portion of the property was not used for educational purposes but instead was being held for sale at future profit, stating that present use of property rather than future intended use controls. Nonetheless, an argument certainly can be made that holding the property for sale at a profit *was* the seminary's present use of the property.

The court of appeals applied a more restrictive determination of whole and exclusive use and of the amount of property necessary for a buffer zone in

In re Master's Mission,[66] ruling that 100 acres of land rather than the 1,347 acres owned by the taxpayer provided a sufficient buffer zone for the training grounds for missionaries. The court also held that improvements on the taxpayer's property were not entitled to an educational exemption since they were used for other purposes in addition to educating missionaries.

Master's Mission (the taxpayer), a nonprofit corporation, owned 1,347 acres in Graham County along the Tennessee border, which it used to train missionaries and prepare them for mission trips to remote areas of the world. Several residential structures located in the center of the property surrounded a lake. These structures housed staff members, guests, and the main business office for the operation. Cabins for missionary trainees were located on a separate part of the property. School, community, and church groups used a campsite on one corner of the property for recreational purposes without charge. Most of the remaining land was undeveloped.

The taxpayer applied to the Graham County Tax Assessor for tax exempt status for all of its buildings and land for the 1997 tax year. The assessor granted an exemption for all structures used to house or train missionaries, along with 100 of the 1,347 acres, but denied exemption for the remaining property. The denial of the exemption was affirmed by the county board of equalization and review and the Property Tax Commission. The commission concluded that the taxpayer was not entitled to exemption for the 1,247 acres in dispute under the religious, charitable, or educational exemptions. With respect to the educational exemption set out in G.S. 105-278.4, the commission concluded that while the taxpayer was an educational institution, it failed to show that all of its buildings and land were wholly and exclusively used for educational purposes. Specifically, the commission noted that half of the buildings were used for staff and guest housing and for an office for general business. The commission found that on a typical day, as many as fifty people were present on the grounds of the taxpayer and that the missionary trainees and their instructors comprised a small minority of these individuals. The commission upheld the exemption for the training center, cabins for the missionary trainees, women's classrooms, and bunkhouse but affirmed the board's denial of the exemption for the owner's home, guest house, office building, duplex, and storage building. The commission rejected the taxpayer's argument for exemption of all of the land on the basis that extended buffers were required to create the remote setting necessary for missionary training. The commission found that the taxpayer failed to show that more than the one hundred exempted acres was necessary for the use of cabins or classrooms and noted that only three or four missionary families trained on the site in 1997. Furthermore, the commission held that the use of the campground by outside groups was not wholly and exclusively educational in nature as there was no showing of a course of study or other education during the campouts.

The taxpayer appealed to the court of appeals on the basis that the entire property was exempt pursuant to the G.S. 105-278.4 exemption for educational property. The court of appeals affirmed the commission's decision, finding that the buildings for which the exemption was denied were used for multiple purposes—as housing for the owner and director of the taxpayer, as lodging for guests who came to the property for any purpose, as a business office for daily business operations, and as storage for equipment used for many purposes on the property. The court found that the taxpayer's articulated purpose of sending missionaries to different parts of the world was not wholly and exclusively educational. The court also agreed with the commission's conclusion regarding the taxable nature of the 1,247 acres outside the 100-acre buffer zone. The court found that the campsite grounds, while used for an "arguably educational" purpose, were not wholly and exclusively used for such a purpose.[67]

With respect to the need for a buffer zone surrounding the training facility, the taxpayer's business manager testified that he was concerned about a water-bottling company bordering the property and that some neighboring property might be logged. The court found this insufficient to demonstrate that more than one hundred acres was required to buffer the training grounds from encroaching urbanization, development, or other forces that might compromise its educational purpose. The court distinguished *In re Appeal of Southeastern Baptist Theological Seminary, Inc.*, and *In re Appeal of Worley* on the basis that in those cases, exemption was warranted for buffer zones because "major highways and urban development came within a distance of only a few acres of the property used for educational or religious purposes."[68]

Master's Mission is significant for the limitations it places on the exempt status of buffer zone property, particularly in light of the generous manner in which courts had previously afforded exemptions for such property. After all, the evidence that the seminary-taxpayer in *Southeastern Baptist Theological Seminary* sought to convert a portion of the exempted property to commercial use appears to be a far stronger indication of the lack of real need for the buffer zone to preserve the educational nature of the property than any of the evidence cited in *Master's Mission*. The *Master's Mission* court ignored the potential uses that might have been made of the surrounding area had the taxpayer not retained ownership of that land.

The *Master's Mission* court also interpreted whole and exclusive use in the strict manner that the courts previously had endorsed as a stated standard but which they had failed to apply to cases involving nonexclusive use. The court in *Master's Mission* denied exemption for certain structures on the property—including the business office—on the basis that the buildings were used for purposes other than training the missionaries. Were the whole- and exclusive-use requirement applied so strictly in all settings, it would likely pose exemption problems for all private universities with business offices where noneducational activities are conducted.

All of the exemption statutes other than those exempting government-owned and burial property permit exemption of a portion of property that meets statutory requirements for exemption, even if the entire building or tract of land does not qualify.[69] Statutes exempting property used for religious, educational, scientific, literary, or charitable purposes provide that incidental use of the property by the general public "so long as there is no material amount of business or patronage" does not defeat the property's entitlement to exemption.[70] Neither the statutes nor any court has defined what constitutes a *material amount of business or patronage*.[71]

7.1.4.4 Property That Is Gratuitously Made Available to Another. Real and personal property owned by a qualifying entity may also qualify for exemption from taxation pursuant to G.S. 105-278.3 if it is "gratuitously made available to one other than the owner and wholly and exclusively used by the possessor for religious, charitable, or nonprofit educational, literary, scientific, or cultural purposes." Other exemption statutes contain comparable language: G.S. 105-278.4 exempts from taxation real and personal property owned by a qualifying institution and occupied gratuitously by another nonprofit educational institution and wholly and exclusively used by the occupant for nonprofit educational purposes, and G.S. 105-278.7 exempts real and personal property owned by a qualifying agency and occupied gratuitously by a qualifying agency other than the owner and wholly and exclusively used by the occupant for nonprofit educational, scientific, literary, charitable, or cultural purposes. The state supreme court held in *Wake County v. Ingle*[72] that a church's payment of expenses associated with its use of a leased church building and appurtenances did not prevent the church from occupying the property gratuitously when the church paid no rent for the property and merely maintained and paid expenses connected with its use of the leased property. The court explained that "[t]o adopt a contrary construction would mean a narrow and stinting construction of the statute."[73] The court of appeals addressed the same issue with respect to the exemption of charitable property pursuant to G.S. 105-278.7, holding that a charitable nursing home's payment of "rent" to a church—a sum which consisted of the interest on a mortgage used by the church to expand the nursing home and an amount for depreciation to be used by the church for future capital improvements—did not prevent the nursing home from occupying the property gratuitously.[74]

7.1.4.5 Requirement That Land Be Adjacent to Building. G.S. 105-278.3, 105-278.4, and 105-278.7—the statutes providing for exemption of certain property used for religious, educational, scientific, literary, or charitable purposes—exempt from taxation "buildings, the land they actually occupy, and additional adjacent land reasonably necessary for convenient use of any such building" if wholly owned by a qualifying entity.[75] Land upon which no buildings are situated may qualify for exemption under these provisions only if it is "adjacent" and "reasonably necessary for convenient use" of a building owned by the landowner and exempted from taxation under this provision.[76] G.S. 105-278.5—the statute governing exemption of property of religious educational assemblies used for religious educational purposes—is similar, though it provides for the exemption of "buildings, the land they actually occupy, and additional adjacent land reasonably necessary for convenient use of any such building *or for the religious educational programs of the owner*," thereby loosening the requisite tie between land and buildings for this type of property.[77] A bricks-and-mortar requirement thus underlies the exemption for qualifying real property used for religious, educational, scientific, literary, or charitable purposes.

It is clear that without an associated building, real property cannot qualify for exemption under any of the statutes mentioned in the preceding paragraph.[78] There is no requirement, however, that the building owned by a qualifying taxpayer and used for religious purposes be a building of worship, so long as the structure is used for a purpose pertaining to "practicing, teaching, and setting forth a religion."[79] Moreover, the state supreme court has liberally construed the "adjacent" and "reasonably necessary" requirements. In *Harrison v. Guilford County*,[80] the court ruled that a six-acre unimproved parcel four or five blocks from the existing church building was both adjacent to the building and reasonably necessary for its use.[81]

7.1.4.6 Defining the Purpose for Which Property Is Used. Though the statutes exempting from taxation certain property used for qualifying purposes define the terms *religious purpose, educational purpose, scientific purpose, literary purpose*, and *charitable purpose*, questions regarding whether a particular taxpayer's activities satisfy those definitions predictably arise. This section will explore those definitions and the manner in which they have been applied by state courts.

A religious purpose is "one that pertains to practicing, teaching, and setting forth a religion."[82] The Machinery Act recognizes that "although worship is the most common religious purpose," other activities "demonstrate and further the beliefs and objectives of a given church or religious body."[83] Thus the term encompasses "the ownership and maintenance of a general or promotional office or headquarters" by a qualifying owner and "the ownership and maintenance of residences for clergy, rabbis, priests or nuns assigned to or serving a congregation, parish, mission or similar local unit, or a conference, association, presbytery, diocese, district, synod, province or similar unit of a church or religious body."[84] The ownership and maintenance of residences for other employees is not, however, deemed a religious purpose. Yet, if a portion of property that otherwise qualifies for exemption is used as a residence for a person who provides guardian, janitorial, and custodial services for the property, or who oversees and supervises qualifying activities upon and in connection with the property, the entire property, including the portion used as the employee's residence, must be considered as wholly and exclusively used for a religious purpose.

A charitable purpose has "humane and philanthropic objectives" and consists of "activity that benefits humanity or a significant rather than limited segment of the community without expectation of pecuniary profit or reward."[85] The humane treatment of animals also constitutes a charitable purpose.[86]

An educational purpose has as its objective the education or instruction of human beings through the transmission of information and the training or development of the knowledge or skills of individual persons.[87] Operating a student housing or dining facility, golf course, tennis court, sports arena, or similar sports property also is an educational purpose, regardless of the extent to which the property is available to and patronized by the general public.[88]

A literary purpose "pertains to letters or literature, especially writing, publishing, and the study of literature" and includes "literature of the stage and screen as well as the performance or exhibition of works based on literature."[89] The exemption of property for literary purposes was first authorized in the state constitution of 1868, though the current statute implementing that exemption was enacted in 1973. Nonetheless, the types of literary purposes contemplated by the drafters in 1868—and incorporated by the drafters of G.S. 105-278.8 in 1973—were likely literary society groups involved in studying literature or letters or in publishing works for purposes of entertainment, study, or advancing the literary field, as contrasted with groups whose primary purpose is to publish works for commercial sale.

A cultural purpose is one that is conducive to the enlightenment and refinement of taste acquired through intellectual and aesthetic training, education, and discipline.[90]

A scientific purpose is one that yields knowledge systematically through research, experimentation, or other work done in one or more of the natural sciences.[91]

7.1.4.7 Nature of Entity That Owns Property. Legal disputes also arise regarding the requirements that govern ownership of property used for a purpose that qualifies for exemption.

The following types of entities may obtain exemption for property they own and use for a religious purpose (or that they permit another to occupy gratuitously and which is used for a qualifying purpose): a congregation, parish, mission, or similar local unit of a church or religious body, or a conference, association, presbytery, diocese, district, synod, or similar unit comprising local units of a church or religious body.[92]

Property used for educational purposes must be owned by a not-for-profit educational institution—a term that includes a university, a college, a school, a seminary, an academy, an industrial school, a public library, a museum, or a similar institution—or by a nonprofit entity for the sole benefit of a constituent or affiliated institution of The University of North Carolina, an institution as defined in G.S. 116-22,[93] a North Carolina community college, or a combination of these types of institutions.[94] To qualify, no officer, shareholder, member, employee of the owner, or any other person may be entitled to receive pecuniary profit from the institution's operations other than reasonable compensation for services.[95]

The court of appeals determined in *In re Atlantic Coast Conference*,[96] contingent upon the Property Tax Commission's review of the conference's expenditure of administrative funds, that property owned and used by Atlantic Coast Conference (ACC) for the operation of its administrative offices was exempt from taxation pursuant to G.S. 105-278.4 as property wholly and exclusively used for an educational purpose. The court based its finding on the ACC's existence as an unincorporated association consisting of eight member educational institutions and the legal premise that property titled in the name of an unincorporated association belongs to its members. Thus an office building owned by the ACC actually was owned by eight member institutions. The court noted that while the Machinery Act required that no employee or shareholder of an educational institution receive a "pecuniary profit other than reasonable compensation for services," *pecuniary profit* was not defined in the statute. The court therefore remanded the case to the commission for a review of balance sheets and audits to determine if any person or entity received pecuniary profit or if anyone received unreasonable compensation. Moreover, the court determined that "in collegiate athletics, the negotiation of network contracts and management of broadcasts"—the work done at the offices of the ACC—"are as necessarily incidental to the operation of educational institutions as is the maintenance of a parking lot, and it matters not whether these activities take place at the Landmark Center in Greensboro, in Duke Chapel, in Watauga Hall, at the Old Well or in the Worrell Professional Center."[97] The court further determined that the ACC's use of property for television contract negotiation and organization and administration of conference tournaments qualifies as educational.[98]

7.1.4.8 Charitable Institutions. G.S. 105-278.6 exempts from taxation certain property owned by any of the following types of organizations:

1. a Young Men's Christian Association or similar organization;
2. a home for the aged, sick, or infirm;
3. an orphanage or similar home;
4. a society for the prevention of cruelty to animals;
5. a reformatory or correctional institution;
6. a monastery, convent, or nunnery;
7. a nonprofit lifesaving, first aid, or rescue squad organization;
8. a nonprofit organization providing housing for individuals or families with low or moderate incomes.

G.S. 105-278.7 more broadly defines the category of permissible owners of exempt real and personal property used for educational, scientific, literary, or charitable purposes, listing the following types of agencies as permissible owners:

1. a charitable association or institution,
2. an historical association or institution,
3. a veterans' organization or association,
4. a scientific association or institution,
5. a literary association or institution,
6. a benevolent association or institution, or
7. a nonprofit community or neighborhood organization.

The determination of whether an agency is a qualified owner pursuant to G.S. 105-278.7 may hinge upon its organizational documents and its classification under other statutory schemes. For instance, the court of appeals in *In re Totsland Preschool, Inc.*,[99] determined that the corporation was a qualified owner based upon its incorporation under North Carolina's Non-Profit Corporations Act by reviewing its articles of incorporation and by-laws and by noting that the federal government recognized Totsland as a nonprofit organization, classified under 26 U.S.C. § 501(c)(3). The court further noted that the North Carolina Department of Revenue considered Totsland a charitable institution entitled to a refund of sales tax pursuant to G.S. 105-164.14(b).

7.2 Exclusions

As mentioned in Chapter 1, the granting in 1936 of the power to classify property overshadowed the earlier-granted authority to exempt certain limited types of property from taxation. This is so because the classification power rendered the General Assembly capable of excluding from taxation any type of property that it chose to designate as a special class of property. In 1985 the General Assembly used this authority to exclude from taxation household personal property by designating all nonbusiness personal property (other than motor vehicles, mobile homes, aircraft, watercraft, and watercraft engines) as a special class of property and excluding it from the tax base. Thus, through its classification power, the legislature exempted from taxation far more than the $300 in personal property authorized by the earlier constitutional provision. Similarly, the General Assembly acted pursuant to the classification power to exclude from taxation the greater of $25,000[100] or 50 percent of the value of the residence of a qualifying disabled or elderly person, again exceeding the $1,000 residence exemption authorized in the permissible exemptions clause. A laundry list of property classified for exclusion is codified in G.S. 105-275; other exclusions are codified in G.S. 105-277 through 105-277.13 and in G.S. 105-278.6A. Some of these provisions exclude property from taxation entirely, while others exclude a portion of value or set forth special rules for assessing property at less than market value. Given the number of statutory exclusions, it is not feasible to review all of them in this chapter. An exhaustive list of all exemptions and exclusions from taxation is contained in the Appendix. The detailed review in this chapter is confined to two of the most commonly employed and complex exclusion provisions: the homestead exclusion and circuit breaker benefits set forth in G.S. 105-277.1 and 105-277.1B and the provision for present-use taxation of certain qualifying farmland pursuant to G.S. 105-277.2 through 105-277.7.

7.2.1 Homestead Exclusion

Since 1972, qualifying low-income elderly and disabled property owners have been eligible to have a portion of the value of their homes excluded from property taxation. Current G.S. 105-277.1 excludes from taxation the greater of $25,000 or 50 percent of the appraised value of a qualifying individual's permanent residence, which includes the dwelling and the dwelling site (up to one acre) and related improvements. A *dwelling* may be a single family residence, a unit in a multifamily residential complex, or a manufactured home.

To qualify, the owner of the residence must (1) be at least sixty-five years old or be totally and permanently disabled,[101] (2) have an income for the preceding calendar year of not more than the income eligibility limit, and (3) be a North Carolina resident.

The income eligibility limit was set at $18,000 in 2002 and has been adjusted each year based on the Social Security cost-of-living index. For the 2007–08 tax year, the income eligibility limit, measured by 2006 income, was $20,500. For the 2008–09 tax year, the General Assembly increased the income eligibility limit to a base limit of $25,000, which likewise will be adjusted each year based on the Social Security cost-of-living index.

Income is defined as "[a]ll monies received from every source other than gifts or inheritances received from a spouse, lineal ancestor, or lineal descendant."[102] For married applicants who reside with their spouses the income of both spouses is included in the calculation, regardless of whether the property is owned by one or both spouses. The definition of income was amended effective for the 2008–09 fiscal year to remove a reference to adjusted gross income as defined by the Internal Revenue Code.[103] This change was enacted to prevent taxpayers from basing the homestead exclusion income amount on an adjusted gross income figure derived after subtracting business and other losses from income as allowed on the front page of a federal income tax return. Income is not limited under this broad definition to taxable income but includes nontaxable revenue such as Social Security income and distributions from an individual retirement account.

An otherwise qualifying owner does not lose the benefit of the exclusion if he or she is temporarily absent from the permanent residence for health reasons or upon being confined to a rest home or nursing home, as long as the residence remains unoccupied or is occupied by the owner's spouse or other dependent.

Persons at least sixty-five years old who are claiming the benefit of the exclusion must apply for the exclusion by providing the requested information on an application form provided by the assessor.

Persons applying for the exclusion based upon total and permanent disability must likewise complete the application form provided by the assessor but must also furnish proof of their disability. There are two acceptable forms of proof: (1) a certificate from a physician licensed to practice medicine in North Carolina or (2) a certificate from a government agency authorized to determine qualification for disability benefits. A disabled applicant is not required to furnish an additional certificate after qualifying for exclusion unless he or she recovers from the disability to such an extent that he or she is no longer entitled to relief.

A permanent residence owned and occupied by a husband and wife as tenants by the entirety may receive the full homestead exclusion, which is the greater of $25,000 or 50 percent of the value of the residence, even if only one spouse meets the age or disability requirements. Suppose, for example, that a sixty-year-old husband and his sixty-five-year-old wife meet the residency and income requirements for the homestead exclusion. Their house, which they own as tenants by the entirety, is situated upon a ½-acre lot. Together, the house and lot were appraised for $200,000 in the county's last reappraisal. Upon the wife's application for the homestead exclusion, 50 percent of the appraised value of the house, or $100,000, must be excluded from taxation.

Property owned by multiple persons who are not husband and wife also may receive the benefit of the homestead exclusion. Three rules govern the determination of the amount to be excluded from taxation when property ownership is shared in this manner. First, each owner is entitled to the full amount of the exclusion not to exceed his or her proportionate share of the valuation of the property. Second, no part of an exclusion available to one co-owner may be claimed by any other co-owner. Third, the total exclusion amount may not exceed the greater of $25,000 or 50 percent of the appraised value of the residence. An example may help illustrate the application of these principles.

Suppose two sisters, Maude and Clementine, own as tenants in common (each with a 50 percent interest) a house and .25-acre lot, where they have lived for forty years. The house and lot appraised for $100,000 in the county's last reappraisal. Maude is sixty-four years old; Clementine is sixty-eight. Maude had $15,000 in income last year, while Clementine's income was $18,000. What amount, if any, may be excluded from taxation pursuant to G.S. 105-277.1?

Only Clementine meets the age threshold for eligibility for the homestead exclusion. Maude's income does not disqualify Clementine, as the only provision for including others' income applies to spouses residing together. Thus we must apply the multiple ownership rules of G.S. 105-277.1(d). Clementine is entitled to the full amount of the exclusion, not to exceed her proportionate share of the value of the property. The full amount of the exclusion is $50,000 (50 percent of the appraised value); this amount equals, but does not exceed, Clementine's 50 percent ownership interest in the property. No part of the exclusion claimed by Clementine may be claimed by the other co-owner, Maude. Finally, the total exclusion does not exceed the greater of $25,000 or 50 percent of the appraised value of the residence.

How does the analysis change the next year when Maude is sixty-five and thus eligible for the homestead exclusion? Assuming each sister's income remains below the statutory threshold, each is now eligible for the exclusion. The full amount of the exclusion is $50,000, assuming no change in the appraised value of the residence. Because no part of an exclusion available to one co-owner may be claimed by another, each sister is eligible for one-half of the exclusion, or $25,000.[104]

Let us change the value of the residence and see how that affects the analysis. Suppose that Maude and Clementine jointly own and reside in a manufactured home appraised for $24,000. In year one, only Clementine qualifies for the homestead exclusion. What is the amount of the exclusion? The full exclusion amount is the greater of $25,000 or 50 percent of the value of the residence. In this case, $25,000 is the greater amount. Clementine may claim the full exclusion amount so long as it does not exceed her interest in the property. She has a 50 percent interest in the property, which equates to $12,000. Thus the exclusion in year one may not exceed $12,000. Once Maude becomes eligible for the homestead exclusion in year two, the entire assessed value of the manufactured home will be excluded from taxation.

7.2.2 Circuit Breaker Benefit

Beginning in 2009–10, qualifying elderly and disabled homeowners are eligible to defer a portion of property taxes assessed against their primary residences under a new circuit breaker benefit program.[105] Qualifying owners are North Carolina residents who (1) are at least sixty-five years old or are totally and permanently disabled,[106] (2) have occupied their property as a permanent residence for at least five years, and (3) have an annual income of no more than 150 percent of the income eligibility limit set for the homestead exclusion.[107] A qualifying owner with gross income at or under the eligibility limit for the homestead exclusion may defer taxes on his or her permanent residence to the extent those taxes exceed 4 percent of his or her gross income.[108] A qualifying owner who has an annual income over, but no more than 150 percent of, the income eligibility limit may defer taxes on his or her permanent residence that exceed 5 percent of his or her gross income. Based on the $25,600 homestead exclusion income eligibility limit for the 2009 tax year, the income limit for the circuit breaker benefit is $38,400.[109] Thus a taxpayer with an income of $30,000 who qualifies for and elects the circuit breaker benefit for his or her primary residence will be required to pay no more than $1,500 in taxes on the residence (5 percent of $30,000). If the taxes on the residence total $2,500, then $1,000 in taxes will be carried forward in the books of the taxing unit as deferred taxes. A permanent residence owned and occupied by spouses as tenants by the entirety is entitled to the full benefit of the circuit breaker even if only one spouse satisfies the eligibility requirements.[110] When a permanent residence is owned by two or more people who are not married, all of the owners must qualify for the homestead circuit breaker and must elect to defer taxes under its provisions.

Some owners may qualify for both the homestead exclusion and the new property tax circuit breaker benefit. An individual owner may elect the benefit he or she desires; however, when property is owned by two or more persons other than husband and wife, each person must qualify for both types of relief and each must elect the property tax circuit breaker in order for that benefit to be allowed instead of the homestead exclusion.

If a property owner elects the homestead circuit breaker benefit, the difference between the taxes due under the circuit breaker and the taxes that otherwise would have been payable are a lien on the real property. The three most recent previous years of deferred taxes are carried forward in the records of the taxing unit. Interest accrues on the deferred amounts as if they had been payable when the taxes originally became due. By September 1 of each year, the tax collector must notify a property owner whose property is in the circuit breaker program of the accumulated sum of deferred taxes and interest.[111]

Deferred taxes are payable within nine months after a disqualifying event, which occurs when the owner transfers the residence (other than certain transfers to a co-owner or made as part of a divorce proceeding), dies, or ceases to use the property as his or her permanent residence. The tax for the fiscal year that opens in the calendar year in which deferred taxes become due is computed as if the property were not eligible for the benefit.

Transfer of the property is not a disqualifying event if the owner transfers property to a co-owner or to his or her spouse as part of a divorce proceeding and the transferee occupies the residence. Death is not a disqualifying event if the owner's share passes to a spouse or co-owner who occupies the residence.

The homestead circuit breaker allows for gaps in deferral that do not trigger an obligation to pay deferred taxes. If the owner does not qualify for the circuit breaker for reasons other than a disqualifying event— for example, by exceeding the income eligibility limit—then deferred taxes are carried forward until a disqualifying event occurs. If the owner later requalifies for tax deferral, the taxing unit must disregard the years during which there was no deferral for purposes of determining the three fiscal years for which deferred taxes should be assessed.

As with homestead applications, the deadline for filing for the homestead circuit breaker is June 1 preceding the fiscal tax year for which relief is claimed. Assessors must inform taxpayers of the homestead circuit breaker provisions along with the homestead exclusion in an information sheet distributed with an abstract or on the abstract itself.[112]

7.2.3 Disabled Veteran Benefit

Qualifying disabled veterans and their surviving spouses also are eligible for exclusion of a portion of the value of their permanent residences from taxation. Beginning with the 2009–10 tax year, the first $45,000 in appraised value of the permanent residence owned and occupied by an honorably discharged disabled veteran or his or her unmarried surviving spouse is excluded from taxation.[113] For earlier tax years, the first $38,000 in assessed value of a residence owned by a disabled veteran was excluded from taxation by G.S. 105-275(21), which was repealed upon the enactment of the more generous homestead exclusion codified in G.S. 105-277.1C.[114] A disabled veteran is a veteran who, as of January 1 preceding the taxable year for which the exclusion is claimed, receives benefits under 38 U.S.C. § 2101 or has a veteran's disability certification.[115] A husband and wife who occupy and own a permanent residence as tenants by the entirety are entitled to the full benefit of the exclusion even if only one spouse is a disabled veteran.[116] In addition, a disabled veteran who shares ownership of a residence with a person other than his or her spouse may obtain the full amount of the exclusion so long as it does not exceed his or her proportionate share of the valuation of the property.[117] If more than one co-owner is eligible for the exclusion, the amount of the exclusion allowed to all co-owners may not exceed the total allowable amount.[118]

A qualifying disabled veteran may own a residence with someone other than his or her spouse who separately qualifies for the homestead exclusion provided under G.S. 105-277.1. In that case, each co-owner is entitled to the full amount of the exclusion so long as it does not exceed the co-owner's proportionate share of the valuation of the property.[119] Moreover, the amount of the exclusion allowed to all the co-owners cannot exceed the greater of $45,000 or the homestead exclusion in G.S. 105-277.1.[120]

A taxpayer applies for property tax relief based on his or her status as a disabled veteran or surviving spouse in much the same way that a taxpayer applies for the homestead exclusion under G.S. 105-277.1.[121] To establish eligibility for property tax relief as a disabled veteran or surviving spouse, a taxpayer must apply by June 1 preceding the tax year for which the exclusion is claimed and must provide a copy of the veteran's disability certification or evidence of benefits received under 38 U.S.C. § 2101, which provides for assistance to qualifying disabled veterans in acquiring housing with special features and with adapting existing residences.[122]

7.3 Applying for Special Tax Treatment

The Machinery Act provides that every owner of property claiming an exemption or exclusion bears the burden of establishing that the property is entitled to exemption or exclusion.[123] For property appraised by the Department of Revenue (public service company system property), applications for exemption must be filed with the department. Otherwise, applications for exemption, exclusion, or other special tax treatment must be filed with the assessor of the county in which the property is situated. The application must contain a "complete and accurate statement of the facts that entitle the property to the exemption or exclusion and must indicate the municipality, if any, in which the property is located."[124] It must be submitted on a form approved by the Department of Revenue, and the department and county assessors must make forms available to taxpayers.

There are three categories of application requirements for property entitled to special tax treatment, including exemption or exclusion from taxation: (1) no application required; (2) a single application required; or (3) annual application required.

7.3.1 No Application Requirement

No application need be filed for property exempted or excluded from taxation pursuant to the following provisions of the Machinery Act:

- G.S. 105-278.1 (real and personal property owned by units of government)
- G.S. 105-278.2 (burial property)
- G.S. 105-275(15) (standing timber, pulpwood, seedlings, saplings, and other forest growth)
- G.S. 105-275(16) (non-business personal property)
- G.S. 105-275(26) (tangible personal property manufactured in North Carolina for a nonresident and held by the manufacturer for shipment)
- G.S. 105-275(31) (intangible personal property)
- G.S. 105-275(32a) (contractors' inventories)
- G.S. 105-275(33) (manufacturers' inventories)
- G.S. 105-275(34) (merchants' inventories)
- G.S. 105-275(37) (poultry and livestock and feed used to produce poultry and livestock)

- G.S. 105-275(40) (computer software)
- G.S. 105-275(42) (short-term lease or rental vehicles)

Likewise, no application is required for property classified for taxation at a reduced valuation pursuant to G.S. 105-277(g) (buildings equipped with a solar energy heating or cooling system) or G.S. 105-277.9 (real property that lies within a transportation corridor).

7.3.2 Single Application Requirement

The owner of property eligible for a property tax benefit under certain statutory provisions must file a one-time application to receive the benefit. Once the application has been approved, the owner is not required to apply in subsequent years unless "new or additional property is acquired or improvements are added or removed, necessitating a change in the valuation of the property, or there is a change in the use of the property or the qualifications or eligibility of the taxpayer necessitating a review of the exemption or exclusion."[125]

The following statutory exemptions require a one-time application:

- G.S. 105-278.3 (real and personal property used for religious purposes)
- G.S. 105-278.4 (real and personal property used for educational purposes)
- G.S. 105-278.5 (real and personal property used for religious and educational purposes)
- G.S. 105-278.6 (real and personal property used for charitable purposes)
- G.S. 105-278.7 (real and personal property used for educational, scientific, literary, or charitable purposes)
- G.S. 105-278.8 (real and personal property used for charitable hospital purposes)
- G.S. 105-275(3) (real and personal property owned by nonprofit water or sewer associations or corporations)
- G.S. 105-275(7) (real and personal property owned by a nonprofit or charitable organization and appropriated for public parks and drives)
- G.S. 105-275(8) (real and personal property used for pollution abatement or recycling or resource recovery)
- G.S. 105-275(12) (real property used as a protected natural area)

- G.S. 105-275(17) (real and personal property belonging to the American Legion, Veterans of Foreign Wars, Disabled American Veterans, or similar veterans organizations and used exclusively for meeting or lodge purposes)
- G.S. 105-275(18) (real and personal property belonging to the Grand Lodge of Ancient, Free and Accepted Masons of North Carolina; the Prince Hall Masonic Grand Lodge of North Carolina; or their subordinate lodges and appendant bodies and used exclusively for meeting or lodge purposes)
- G.S. 105-275(19) (real and personal property belonging to the Loyal Order of the Moose, the Benevolent and Protective Order of Elks, the Knights of Pythias, the Odd Fellows, the Woodmen of the World, or similar fraternal or civic organizations and used exclusively for meeting or lodge purposes)
- G.S. 105-275(20) (real and personal property belonging to Goodwill Industries and other charities organized for the training and rehabilitation of disabled persons)
- G.S. 105-275(35) (severable development rights)
- G.S. 105-275(39) (real and personal property owned by a nonprofit corporation organized to finance projects for public use, leased to a state or local government, and used for a public purpose)
- G.S. 105-275(41) (objects of art held by the North Carolina State Art Society, Inc.)
- G.S. 131A-21 (health care facilities financed by Medical Care Commission bonds)
- G.S. 131E-28 (hospital authority property used for public purposes)
- G.S. 105-277(h) (private water company investment in contributions in aid of construction and acquisition adjustments)
- G.S. 105-277.1 (homestead exclusion)
- G.S. 105-277.1B (circuit breaker benefit)
- G.S. 105-277.10 (precious metals used in manufacturing or processing by manufacturer)
- G.S. 105-277.13 (qualifying improvements on brownfields)
- G.S. 105-278 (historic properties)
- G.S. 105-277.8 (property owned by nonprofit homeowners association)

7.3.3 Annual Application Requirement

To obtain a tax benefit under any provision of the Machinery Act not listed above—other than the statutes providing for taxation of certain qualifying farmland and working waterfront property at present-use value—the owner of the property must file an application each year during the listing period.

7.3.4 Late Applications

As noted above, one-time and annual applications for property tax benefits must be filed during the listing period, which, unless extended by the county board of commissioners, is the month of January. The deadline for applying for the homestead exclusion or circuit breaker benefit is June 1. Because income information is a critical component of an application for either benefit, the Machinery Act sets the filing deadline after the April 15 deadline for filing an income tax return, by which time most taxpayers, or their tax preparers, will have computed their income from the previous year.

G.S. 105-282.1(a1) permits the Department of Revenue, the board of equalization and review, the board of county commissioners, or the governing board of a municipality, as appropriate, to approve a late-filed application for exemption or exclusion "[u]pon a showing of good cause by the applicant for failure to make timely application." A late-filed application so approved applies only to property taxes levied by the city or county in the calendar year in which the untimely application is filed.

As previously noted, the last date for timely filing for the homestead exclusion or circuit breaker benefit is June 1, as set forth in G.S. 105-277.1 and 105-277.1B. Because these filing deadlines are set forth in the specific statutes providing these benefits, a question may arise as to whether the provision of G.S. 105-282.1 will operate to permit late filing of either type of application. The answer appears to be yes. G.S. 105-277.1(c) and 105-277.1B(m) provide that such applications "may be filed and must be accepted at any time up to and through June 1 preceding the tax year for which [the exclusion or benefit] is claimed." Given that G.S. 105-282.1 does not require a board to accept a late-filed application, it appears that its provisions allowing for the acceptance of a late filing complement, rather than contradict, the more specific filing provisions of G.S. 105-277.1(c) and 105-277.1B(m). Thus it is the author's opinion that the board may approve an application for homestead exclusion or circuit breaker benefits filed after the June 1 deadline upon the taxpayer's showing of good cause for failure to make timely application.

7.4 Discovery of Property Entitled to Exemption or Exclusion

An assessor may, on occasion, discover unlisted property that would have been entitled to exemption or exclusion had the owner applied for that benefit. If the owner of the property appeals the discovery and demonstrates that the property meets the conditions for exemption or exclusion, the body hearing the appeal may approve the exemption or exclusion.[126] The Machinery Act does not limit that approval to exemption or exclusion of the property from taxation only for the current year. Thus a property owner who never listed property or filed the requisite exemption application can avoid the subsequent assessment of taxes on the property in a discovery if he or she can demonstrate in response to the discovery that the property is, or was, entitled to exemption or exclusion in all or some of the years involved in the discovery.[127] However, a taxpayer who lists and pays taxes on property and then learns that the property is entitled to exemption or exclusion upon proper application may obtain exemption or exclusion only for the year in which the application is made, not prior years.[128] While the differing treatment of taxpayers may seem inequitable or, to an individual taxpayer, "absurd," it can be justified in part by the fact that discovered amounts were not previously included in the tax base for budgeting purposes.[129] The subsequent exemption or exclusion of property formerly included in the tax base and expended in previous years could jeopardize the taxing unit's fiscal stability.[130]

7.5 Special Rules for Classified Motor Vehicles

The application provisions of G.S. 105-282.1 that govern all other claims for property tax benefits do not apply to applications for exclusion or exemption of classified motor vehicles. The process for claiming a tax benefit for a classified motor vehicle instead is governed by G.S. 105-330.3, a provision in Article 22A of the Machinery Act. The owner of a classified motor vehicle who claims the vehicle should be exempted or excluded from taxation must file an application for exempt status with the tax assessor.[131] Taxability of a registered motor vehicle is determined as of the first day of the month in which registration is applied for or for which registration is renewed. When an approved application is on file, the assessor must omit from the tax records the vehicles described in the application. The owner of a motor vehicle that has been omitted from the tax records must report to the assessor any classified motor vehicle registered to or owned by him or her that does not qualify for exemption or exclusion for the current year.[132] The vehicle owner must make this report within thirty days after applying for or renewing the vehicle's registration or, for an unregistered motor vehicle, by January 31, the end of the regular statutory listing period.

A classified motor vehicle that does not qualify for exemption or exclusion but has been omitted upon application of the taxpayer is subject to discovery. Upon discovery of a vehicle, a penalty of $100 shall be assessed for each registration period that has elapsed before the disqualification was discovered.

7.6 Review of Exempt Property

The assessor must annually review at least one-eighth of the parcels in the county that are exempted or excluded from taxation to verify that these parcels still qualify for the exemption or exclusion.[133] Thus, in an eight-year period, a review of all exempted and excluded parcels should be completed. During this review, the assessor may request from the owner of exempt or excluded property information necessary to verify that the property still qualifies for the property tax benefit.[134] The owner has sixty days from the date a written request for information is made to submit the information to the assessor.[135] If the assessor determines that the owner failed to make the information available within the time allowed, without good cause for the failure, then the property loses its exemption or exclusion. If the property loses its exemption or exclusion for failure to provide requested information, the assessor must reinstate the benefit if the owner makes the information available within sixty days from the disqualification, unless the information discloses that the property is no longer eligible for exemption or exclusion.

Pursuant to G.S. 105-296(m), the assessor must annually review the transportation corridor official maps and amendments filed with the register of deeds and must indicate on all of the county's tax maps the property within a transportation corridor and note any variance granted for the property for the period that the designation remains effective. The assessor must tax property within a transportation corridor as required under G.S. 105-277.9.

7.6.1 Roster of Exempt Property

The assessor must prepare and maintain a roster of all property in the county that is granted tax relief through classification or exemption.[136] By November 1 of each year, the assessor must send a report to the Department of Revenue summarizing the information contained in the roster in the format required by the department.[137] The roster must contain the following information with respect to real and personal property that has received a property tax benefit:

1. The name of the owner of the property
2. A brief description of the property
3. A statement of the use of the property
4. The value of the property
5. The total value of exempt property in the county and in each city within the county[138]

7.7 Assessment at Present-Use Value

In 1973 the General Assembly classified property used for agricultural, horticultural, and forestry purposes that met certain land, ownership, and use requirements as a special class of property entitled to assessment based upon its value in its present use rather than its market value based upon a differing highest and best use.[139] By rendering such property eligible for tax assessment based upon a below-market value, the General Assembly eliminated the risk that large tax liabilities resulting from the assessment of undeveloped property based upon its use for development would force owners to discontinue farming and other nondevelopmental operations merely in order to satisfy the tax liability. A deferred tax provision enacted as part of the new statutory scheme was designed to discourage developers and persons holding the property for sale to developers from availing themselves of the benefits of the program while awaiting sale or development. The additional taxes that would have been owed had the property not been eligible for present-use taxation are carried forward in the books of the taxing unit; upon the property's removal from the program, taxes for the current year are assessed based on market value, and deferred taxes from the three previous years become due with interest. Today, taxes deferred based upon assessment of qualifying property at its present-use value represent the second largest category of excluded property—measured by dollars of untaxed value—after the exclusion for property owned by the federal, state, and local government.[140]

The statutes classifying and providing for a present-use assessment standard for qualifying agricultural, horticultural, and forest property are codified at G.S. 105-277.2 through 105-277.7. The statutory scheme is undoubtedly the most complicated of any in the Machinery Act. This section discusses the various requirements in detail.[141]

The 1973 act defined *present-use value* as "the price estimated in terms of money at which the property would change hands between a willing and financially able buyer and a willing seller, neither being under any compulsion to buy or to sell, *assuming that both of them have reasonable knowledge of the capability of the property to produce income in its present use and that the present use of the property is its highest and best use.*"[142] Thus the standard for appraising property based upon its present use was, from the outset, significantly narrower than the standard for appraising other property, pursuant to which the hypothetical buyer and seller were presumed to have reasonable knowledge of *all* uses to which the property was adapted.[143] What was unclear for a number of years was whether a property's present-use value could be determined by comparing sales of similar property purchased for continuing nondevelopmental uses or, instead, only by ascertaining the income producing potential of the property.[144] The North Carolina Supreme Court held in *In re McElwee*[145] that sales of comparable land could be used to appraise property based upon present-use value if the county demonstrated "that the buyers and sellers involved in the comparable sales transactions had knowledge of the property's capability to produce income in its present use, that the present use is the highest and best use and that the purchaser intended to continue to use the property in its present use." Methods for valuing property based upon its present use continued to vary from county to county. In 1985 the General Assembly amended the definition of *present-use value* to require that property in the present use program be appraised "solely on its ability to produce income and assuming an average level of management." Property in the present-use program thus must be valued using an income approach. For agricultural and horticultural property, the assessor must first determine the rate at which such land could be rented (the property's ability to produce income). The assessor must then apply a capitalization rate to the net income from the property. Improvements located on qualifying land must be appraised according to the schedules and standards used in apprising other similar improvements in the county.[146]

A county must adopt, before January 1 in a reappraisal year, a schedule of values governing the appraisal of property taxed, based upon the property's value in present use.[147] This schedule may be adopted separately or in conjunction with the schedule of values for other real property.[148]

To assist county assessors in developing values, standards, and rules for appraising property at present-use value, the Department of Revenue is required to prepare and distribute annually a manual prepared by the Use-Value Advisory Board that establishes cash rental rates for agricultural lands and horticultural lands and the net income ranges for forestland.[149] The department must conduct studies on cash rents for agricultural and horticultural lands on a county or regional basis and must furnish those results to the Use-Value Advisory Board,[150] which operates under the supervision of the Agricultural Extension Service of North Carolina State University. The use-value manual developed by the board must base cash rental rates for agricultural and horticultural land on the various classes of soils in the state. The rental rates must recognize the productivity levels by class of soil or geographic area and the crop as either agricultural or horticultural.[151]

While the use-value manual prepared and distributed by the Department of Revenue is advisory, the capitalization rates set by the use-value advisory board for agricultural and horticultural land are mandatory.[152] The capitalization rate for agricultural land and horticultural land must be no less than 6 percent and no more than 7 percent.[153] The Machinery Act requires that a rate of 9 percent be used to capitalize the expected net income of forestland.[154]

7.7.1 Application Requirement

A property owner must apply for taxation at present use-value during the regular listing period of the year for which the benefit of the classification is first claimed or within thirty days of the date shown on a notice of change in value made pursuant to a reappraisal or a change in value made in a nonreappraisal year as permitted under G.S. 105-287. A new application is not required unless the property is transferred or becomes ineligible for use-value appraisal because of a change in use or acreage. An application due to transfer of the property must be submitted within sixty days of the date of the property's transfer. A late-filed application may be approved by the board of equalization and review or the board of county commissioners upon a showing of good cause by an applicant for failure to timely apply. An untimely application so approved applies only to property taxes levied by the county or municipality in the calendar year in which the untimely application is filed. Decisions regarding late applications may be appealed to the Property Tax Commission.

An application for taxation of property based upon its present-use value must show that the property falls within one of the classes eligible for the special treatment and must contain any relevant information required by the assessor to appraise the property at its present-use value.

7.7.2 Appeal Process

A property owner may appeal an assessor's decision regarding the qualification of property for taxation in the present-use program or the appraisal of property in the program to the county board of equalization and review.[155] If that board is not in session, the property owner may appeal to the board of county commissioners. An appeal must be made within sixty days of the date of the assessor's decision. If an owner submits additional information to the assessor pursuant to the assessor's review of property already enrolled in the program, as provided in G.S. 105-296(j), the owner must file any appeal within sixty days of the assessor's decision based on the additional information. Decisions of the board of equalization and review or the board of county commissioners may be appealed to the Property Tax Commission.

7.7.3 Classes of Property Eligible for Present-Use Taxation

There are five classes of eligible property: agricultural land, horticultural land, forestland, wildlife conservation land, and working waterfront property. Because the wildlife conservation land and working waterfront qualification requirements differ significantly from the first three classifications, they will be discussed at the end of this section.

Agricultural land is defined as "[l]and that is a part of a farm unit that is actively engaged in the commercial production or growing of crops, plants, or animals under a sound management program."[156] A farm unit may consist of more than one tract of agricultural land owned by the same person or entity, but at least one of the tracts must consist of at least ten acres and must have produced an average gross income of at least $1,000 for the three years preceding January 1 of the year for which present-use value is claimed. Each tract must be under a *sound management program*, which is a program of production designed to obtain the greatest net return from the land consistent with its conservation and long-term improvement.[157] If agricultural tracts are located in different counties, qualifying tracts must be within fifty miles of the tract meeting the acreage and income requirements.[158]

Agricultural land includes woodland and wasteland that is a part of the farm unit, but woodland and wasteland must be appraised under the use-value schedules as woodland or wasteland. If the agricultural land includes less than twenty acres of woodland, then the woodland portion is not required to be under a sound management program. Woodland also is not required to be under a sound management program if its highest and best use is to diminish wind erosion of adjacent agricultural land, protect water quality of adjacent agricultural land, or serve as a buffer for adjacent livestock or poultry operations.

There are exceptions to the actual production and gross income requirements for agricultural property used for turkey growing within the two preceding years that qualified for present-use value while used for such production but was taken out of production due to the presence of Poult Enteritis Mortality Syndrome among turkeys in the same county or a neighboring county.[159] If the land is otherwise eligible for the present-use value program, it continues to qualify for present-use taxation, notwithstanding the interruption in production and income.

Farms for aquatic species[160] consisting of five acres in actual production *or* producing at least 20,000 pounds of aquatic species for commercial sale annually (regardless of acreage) also are classified as agricultural property eligible for taxation based upon present-use value if the gross income and ownership requirements are satisfied.

Horticultural land is "[l]and that is a part of a horticultural unit that is actively engaged in the commercial production or growing of fruits or vegetables or nursery or floral products under a sound management program." A horticultural unit may consist of more than one tract of horticultural land owned by the same person or entity, but at least one of the tracts must consist of at least five acres in actual production and for the previous three years must have produced an average gross income of at least $1,000. An exception to the gross income requirement applies to property used to grow Christmas trees, which are considered a horticultural crop.[161] Because it takes several years for evergreens used as Christmas trees to mature, the Department of Revenue promulgates requirements for Christmas tree farms that substitute for the gross income requirement in the years before the trees can be harvested and establishes a separate gross income requirement in the year of the harvest.[162] As with agricultural property, if horticultural tracts are located in different counties, each qualifying tract must be within fifty miles of the tract meeting the acreage and income requirements.

Land used to grow horticultural and agricultural crops on a rotating basis or where the horticultural crop is set out or planted and harvested within one growing season may be treated as agricultural land when there is no significant difference in the cash rental rates for the land. If the horticultural land includes less than twenty acres of woodland, the woodland portion is not required to be under a sound management program. Woodland also is not required to be under a sound management program if it is determined that the highest and best use of the woodland is to diminish wind erosion or protect water quality of adjacent horticultural land. Horticultural land includes woodland and wasteland that is a part of the horticultural unit, but the woodland and wasteland included in the unit must be appraised under the use-value schedules as woodland or wasteland.

Forestland is defined as "[l]and that is a part of a forest unit that is actively engaged in the commercial growing of trees under a sound management program." A forest unit may consist of more than one tract of forestland, but each tract must be owned by the same person or entity and must be under a sound management program. In addition, at least one tract must consist of twenty acres that are in actual production and are not included in a farm unit. If the tracts are located in different counties, they must be within fifty miles of the tract meeting the acreage and other requirements.

Forestland includes wasteland that is a part of the forest unit, but the wasteland included in the unit must be appraised under the use-value schedules as wasteland. There is no income requirement for forestland.

7.7.3.1 Sound Management Program. As mentioned above, each qualifying tract of agricultural and horticultural land must be operated under a sound management program. An owner of property may establish that property is operated under a sound management program by showing any of the following:

1. Enrollment in and compliance with an agency-administered-and-approved farm management plan
2. Compliance with a set of best management practices
3. Compliance with a minimum gross income per acre test
4. Evidence of net income from the farm operation
5. Evidence that farming is the farm operator's principal source of income

6. Certification by a recognized agricultural or horticultural agency within the county that the land is operated under a sound management program[163]

A property owner may also demonstrate sound management by evidence of other similar factors.[164] The failure of a property owner to receive income or rent from a farm operator does not negate the existence of a sound management program.

Forestland is operated under a sound management program when the operation is pursuant to a written sound forest management plan for the production and sale of forest products.[165]

7.7.3.2 Gross Income Requirement for Agricultural and Horticultural Property. To qualify for the present-use program, the entire farm unit used to produce agricultural and horticultural products must have produced an average gross income of at least $1,000 for the three years before the benefit of present-use taxation is claimed.[166] Gross income includes income from the sale of the agricultural or horticultural products produced from the land, any payments received under a governmental soil conservation or land retirement program, and the amount paid to the taxpayer pursuant to the Fair and Equitable Tobacco Reform Act of 2004.[167] There is no requirement that a profit be realized from the farming of the land.

The gross income requirements for Christmas trees differ depending upon where the property is located. For property located in the state's mountain region, the gross income requirement for horticultural land used to grow Christmas trees is $2,000 per acre.[168] For all other areas, the gross income requirement is $1,500 per acre. Note that these are *per acre* requirements, as contrasted with the general income requirements that apply per farm unit. The Use-Value Advisory Board and Department of Revenue explain that the trade-off for the immediate qualification of Christmas tree farms for use-value taxation "is a different gross income requirement in recognition of the potential for greater income than would normally be associated with other horticultural and agricultural commodities."[169]

Because gross income is calculated based upon a three year average, forestland that is cleared and converted to agricultural and horticultural use must wait a minimum of three years before it qualifies for present-use taxation in its new use. A three year waiting, or cultivation, period also applies to land converted from agricultural to horticultural use and vice versa. However, because there is no gross income requirement for forestland, property converted to forestland can, if it meets all other requirements, immediately qualify for the present-use program.

7.7.3.3 Land Held for Conservation. Land enrolled in the federal conservation reserve program authorized by 16 U.S.C. Chapter 58 is considered to be in actual production. Income derived from participation in the federal program may be used to meet the gross income requirements separately or in combination with income from actual production. Land enrolled in the federal conservation reserve program must be assessed as agricultural land if planted in vegetation other than trees or as forestland if planted in trees.

The owner of property that is taxed based upon its present-use value may donate a portion of the owner's interest in property to a qualified conservation organization without triggering a disqualification or a rollback of deferred taxes.[170] Such property may remain in the present-use program regardless of whether it continues to be used for actual production or produces income if it is subject to an enforceable conservation easement that would qualify for a state income tax credit[171] and the owner received no more than 75 percent of the fair market value of the donated property interest in compensation for the granting of the easement.[172]

7.7.3.4 Eligible Owners. The Machinery Act permits only individually owned agricultural, horticultural, and forestland to qualify for the present-use program.[173] While the term *individually owned* is defined to encompass some types of ownership by business entities and trusts as well as individuals, the limitations placed upon entity ownership evidence the General Assembly's desire to make the benefits of the program available only for property owned by individual landowners, family members entitled to beneficial ownership under trusts created for estate-planning purposes, and certain family-owned business entities.[174]

Not surprisingly, qualifying property owned by individuals is eligible for present-use taxation.[175] In addition, qualifying property owned by a business entity is eligible for taxation at present-use value under the following conditions. First, the principal business of the entity must be farming agricultural land, horticultural land, or forestland.[176] Second, all of the entity's members[177] must be, directly or indirectly, individuals who are actively engaged in the business or a relative of a member who is actively engaged in the business.[178] An individual is indirectly a member of a business entity that owns the land if the individual is a member of a business entity or a beneficiary of a trust that is a part of the ownership structure of the business entity that owns the land.[179] For example, land owned by a limited liability company may qualify as individually owned if one of its members is a trust with a beneficiary who is actively engaged in the farming business or a relative of a member actively engaged in the business. In such a case, the trust beneficiary is indirectly a member of the limited liability company. Likewise, if the land is owned by a limited liability company that has as a member another limited liability company, the land may qualify as individually owned so long as all the members of both limited liability companies are either actively engaged in the farming business or are relatives of a member actively engaged in the business. Land is not eligible for taxation based upon its present-use value if it is owned directly or indirectly by a corporation whose shares are publicly traded.[180] A business entity whose members are all individuals and relatives may lease land to be farmed and thereby satisfy the principal business and actively engaged requirements.[181]

Relatives are defined as (1) a spouse or the spouse's lineal ancestor or descendant, (2) a lineal ancestor or a lineal descendant, (3) a brother or sister or the lineal descendant of a brother or sister (including stepsiblings and their lineal descendants), (4) an aunt or uncle, or (5) a spouse of any of the aforementioned persons.[182]

Adopted relatives are included within these definitions, as are the surviving spouses of relatives by blood or adoption.[183]

Land held in a trust that was created by an individual who transferred the land to the trust also may be eligible for taxation at present-use value.[184] To qualify, each beneficiary of the trust must be, directly or indirectly, the creator of the trust or a relative of the creator.[185] An individual is indirectly a beneficiary of a trust that owns the land if the individual is a beneficiary of another trust or a member of a business entity that has a beneficial interest in the trust that owns the land.[186]

Land held in testamentary trusts may qualify as individually owned if (1) the trust was created by an individual who transferred land to the trust that qualified for present-use taxation while owned by the individual; (2) when the creator died, he or she had no relatives; and (3) the trust income, less reasonable administrative expenses, is used exclusively for educational, scientific, literary, cultural, charitable, or religious purposes as defined in G.S. 105-278.3(d).[187]

Land owned by tenants in common is considered individually owned if each tenant would qualify as an owner if that tenant were the sole owner.[188] Tenants in common may elect to treat their individual shares as individually owned; they then must meet the additional terms of ownership requirements set forth for individuals, business entities, or trusts, as appropriate.[189]

7.7.3.5 Term of Ownership Requirements. In addition to meeting size, use, and individual ownership requirements, to be eligible for taxation at present-use value, land owned by an individual must satisfy one of the following conditions: (1) it is the owner's place of residence; (2) it has been owned by the current owner or a relative of the current owner for the four years preceding January 1 of the year for which the benefit is claimed; or (3) at the time of transfer to the current owner, it qualified for classification in the hands of a business entity or trust that transferred the land to the current owner who was a member of the business entity or a beneficiary of the trust.[190]

Land owned by a qualifying business entity or trust must have been owned by the business entity or trust or one of its members or creators for the four years preceding January 1 of the year for which the benefit of taxation based upon present-use is claimed.[191]

Land transferred to a new owner may immediately qualify for taxation based upon its present-use value, notwithstanding the aforementioned term of ownership requirements, if the owner meets certain conditions and assumes liability for any deferred taxes or if, by acquiring the property, the new owner expands an existing unit of land in the present-use program.[192]

The first exception to the ownership requirements applies to property appraised at present-use value at the time title passed to the new owner.[193] Such property may immediately qualify for continued taxation at present-use value under the new ownership if the new owner meets the following conditions:

1. the new owner acquires and continues to use the land for the purposes for which it was classified for present use taxation under previous ownership,
2. the new owner files an application for taxation at present use value within sixty days of the date of the transfer, and
3. the new owner has certified that the new owner accepts liability for any deferred taxes and intends to continue the present use of the land.[194]

In addition, if these requirements are satisfied, there is no rollback of deferred taxes on the property.[195]

The second exception to the ownership requirements applies to property not appraised at its present-use value that is transferred to an owner who already owns land classified for taxation at its present-use value. Such land may immediately qualify for present-use taxation under the new ownership without having to meet the residence or four-year ownership requirements if the following conditions are met:

1. before the transfer, the land was being used for the same purpose (by the former owner) as other land already owned by the new owner and classified for present-use taxation, and
2. the land was eligible for appraisal at its present-use value under the same classification as other land already owned by the new owner.

The determination of whether the land "was eligible for appraisal at its present use value" is based upon the property's eligibility for such classification under the new ownership, rather than the old ownership.[196] To satisfy this condition, the new owner must demonstrate that the property was in active production and under a sound management program.[197]

7.7.3.6 Assessment of Deferred Taxes. Deferred taxes become due and payable when the land fails to meet any condition or requirement for classification, including the owner's failure to have an application approved.[198] The tax for the fiscal year that opens in the calendar year in which deferred taxes become due is computed as if the land had not been classified for that year, and taxes for the preceding three fiscal years that have been deferred are immediately payable, along with accrued interest from the date taxes for each fiscal year would have become delinquent. Assessors refer to the assessment and billing of deferred taxes as a *rollback*. The following example illustrates the taxes due upon disqualification and the applicable interest rate. Suppose Joe Brown, who has fifteen acres of land taxed at present-use value, sells all fifteen acres to a developer, We Build 'Em, Inc., on September 15, 2008. Taxes for the 2008–09 fiscal year will be reassessed based upon the property's market value.[199] Deferred taxes for the 2007–08, 2006–07, and 2005–06 fiscal years are immediately due and payable. The interest rate applicable to the 2007–08 deferred taxes is 8 percent (2 percent for January 2008 and 0.75 percent for each month thereafter, including September 2008). The interest rate applicable to the 2006–07 deferred taxes is 17 percent (10.25 percent for the 2007 calendar year and 6.75 percent for January through September 2008). The interest rate applicable to the 2005–06 deferred taxes is 26 percent (10.25 for the 2006 calendar year, 9 percent for the 2007 calendar year, and 6.75 percent for January through September 2008).

If only part of the qualifying tract of land fails to meet a condition or requirement for classification, the assessor must determine the amount of deferred taxes applicable to that part and that amount becomes payable with interest as provided above. Once deferred taxes are paid for the three years immediately preceding the year of disqualification, all liens arising from those deferred taxes are extinguished.

The payment of deferred taxes, by itself, does not render a qualifying tract of land ineligible for deferred status.

There are three ways in which property can lose its eligibility for deferred status without triggering an obligation to pay deferred taxes. Indeed, if property is rendered ineligible for any of the following reasons, the lien for deferred taxes is extinguished:

1. There is a change in income caused by the enrollment of the property in the federal conservation reserve program established under 16 U.S.C. Chapter 58.
2. The property is conveyed by gift to a nonprofit organization and qualifies for exclusion from the tax base pursuant to G.S. 105-275(12) (protected natural area) or G.S. 105-275(29) (historic preservation property).
3. The property is conveyed by gift to the state, a political subdivision of the state, or the United States.[200]

7.7.3.7 Wildlife Conservation. Beginning in 2010, qualifying wildlife conservation land may be taxed based upon its present-use value as though it was agricultural land.[201] Wildlife conservation land must be at least twenty contiguous acres; must be owned by an individual, a family business entity, or a family trust; and, with limited exceptions, must have been owned by the same owner for the previous five years.[202] Wildlife conservation land owned by a *family business entity*, defined as a business entity whose members are, directly or indirectly, individuals and are relatives,[203] may qualify for present-use taxation even if the business entity did not own the land for the previous five years if the land was owned by one or more members of the family business entity for the required time.[204] Wildlife conservation land owned by a *family trust*, which is a trust created by an individual whose beneficiaries are, directly or indirectly, the creator of the trust or a relative of the creator,[205] meets the five-year ownership requirements if the land was owned by one or more beneficiaries of the family trust for the required time.[206] In the final exception to the five-year ownership rule, wildlife conservation land may remain in the present-use program if it is acquired by a new owner who continues to use it as wildlife conservation land and, within sixty days of acquiring the property, files an application for tax relief and signs the wildlife habitat conservation agreement in effect for the property.[207]

Wildlife conservation land must be managed under a written wildlife habitat conservation agreement with the North Carolina Wildlife Resources Commission that is in effect as of January 1 of the year for which the benefit of taxation based upon present-use value is claimed.[208] The agreement must require the owner either to protect an animal species that lives on the land and is on a North Carolina protected-animal list or to conserve a longleaf pine forest, early successional habitat, small wetland community, stream and riparian zone, rock outcrop, or bat cave.[209] Wildlife conservation land must have been classified as agricultural, horticultural, or forestland under G.S. 105-277.3 when the conservation agreement was signed or the owner must demonstrate to the Wildlife Resources Commission and the assessor that the owner used the land for a purpose specified in the wildlife conservation agreement for three years preceding January 1 of the year for which present-use taxation is claimed.[210]

Certain restrictions apply. No more than one hundred acres of an owner's land in a county may be classified for present-use taxation.[211] Land owned directly or indirectly by a publicly traded corporation is ineligible for the benefit.[212]

As with other property in the present-use program, the difference between the taxes assessed on wildlife conservation property based upon its value in present use as agricultural land and those that would be due if the property were assessed at market value are carried forward as deferred taxes. When the land no longer qualifies as wildlife conservation land, the land loses its eligibility for deferral and taxes for the three previous years are due and payable. If wildlife conservation land previously classified as agricultural, horticultural, or forestland reverts to its previous use and satisfies the requirements of G.S. 105-277.3, no deferred taxes are payable.[213] Wildlife conservation land remains eligible for taxation based upon its present-use value, notwithstanding its transfer to a new owner, if the new owner signs the wildlife habitat conservation agreement in effect for the land at the time of the transfer.[214] If classified wildlife conservation land becomes ineligible for present-use taxation solely due to either its transfer by gift to a nonprofit organization, which renders it nontaxable under G.S. 105-275(12) or G.S. 105-275(9), or its conveyance by gift to the state, to one of the state's political subdivisions, or to the United States, no deferred taxes are due and the lien for deferred taxes is extinguished.[215]

7.7.3.8 Working Waterfronts. Land used as a working waterfront is the last category of property eligible for taxation at its present-use value.[216] The classification is effective beginning with the 2009 tax year. Working waterfront property must have produced an average gross income for the past three years of at least $1,000 and may consist of (1) a pier that extends into coastal fishing waters and can be accessed only by those who pay a fee; or (2) real property that is adjacent to coastal fishing waters and is primarily used for a commercial fishing operation or fish processing, including adjacent land being improved and used for one of these purposes. There are no restrictions on the ownership of property that meets these requirements.

The owner of working waterfront property must apply for the benefit of taxation based upon its value in present use. An initial application must be filed in the year for which the benefit is first claimed or within thirty days of a change in valuation. A new application is not required to be submitted unless the property is transferred or becomes ineligible for classification.

The difference between the taxes that are due on working waterfront property taxed at its present-use value and the taxes that would be due if the property were taxed at true value are a lien on the property and are carried forward in the records of the taxing unit as deferred taxes. When the property no longer qualifies as working waterfront property, the tax for the fiscal year that opens in the calendar year in which deferred taxes become due is based upon the property's true value and deferred taxes for the preceding three fiscal years are immediately payable, with interest calculated from the date the taxes originally would have been delinquent.

Notes

1. N.C. GEN. STAT. § 105-278.2 (hereinafter G.S.) (providing for exemption of certain burial property and special tax treatment of other property).

2. G.S. 105-278.6A actually is an exercise of the General Assembly's authority to exclude property from taxation.

3. 300 N.C. 563, 268 S.E.2d 472 (1980).

4. *Id.* at 577, 268 S.E.2d at 481.

5. 165 N.C. App. 379, 598 S.E.2d 701 (2004), *cert. denied*, 359 N.C. 68, 604 S.E.2d 307 (2004).

6. All real and personal property owned by Appalachian State University is owned by the State of North Carolina and thus exempt from taxation. *See* N.C. CONST. art. V, § 2(3); G.S. 105-278.1.

7. An active trust is a trust that requires the trustee to perform a duty with respect to the trust property or for the beneficiaries.

8. *In re* Forestry Foundation, Inc., 296 NC 330, 250 S.E.2d 236 (1979).

9. Letter from Reginald L. Watkins, Senior Deputy Attorney General, and George W. Boylan, Special Deputy Attorney General, to Huey Marshall, County Attorney (March 28, 2000), *available at* 2000 WL 33311502 .

10. ___ N.C. App. ___, 668 S.E.2d 354 (2008).

11. *Id.* at ___, 668 S.E.2d at 355.

12. *Id.*

13. *Id.* at ___, 668 S.E.2d at 356.

14. *Id.* at ___, 668 S.E.2d at 356.

15. *Id.* at ___, 668 S.E.2d at 356.

16. ___ N.C. App.___, ___ 668 S.E.2d 354, 356 (2008).

17. *Id.* at ___, 668 S.E.2d at 357.

18. *Id.*

19. U.S. Const. art. VI, c1.2.

20. Surplus Trading Co. v. Cook, 281 U.S. 647 (1930); Kohl v. United States, 91 U.S. 367 (1876); Ft. Leavenworth R.R. Co. v. Lowe, 114 U.S. 525, 531 (1885).

21. United States v. Gliatta, 580 F.2d 156, 158 & n.6 (5th Cir. 1978).

22. Paul v. United States, 371 U.S. 245, 263 (1963); State v. Smith, 328 N.C. 161, 165, 400 S.E.2d 405, 407 (1991).

23. *See* ROBERT L. FARB, ARREST, SEARCH, AND INVESTIGATION IN NORTH CAROLINA 48–49 n. 60 (3d ed. 2003).

24. Pub. Laws of 1887, Ch. 136.

25. State v. De Berry, 224 N.C. 834, 32 S.E.2d 617 (1945).

26. *Cf.* Surplus Trading Co. v. Cook, 281 U.S. 647 (1930) (interpreting state jurisdiction to exist only as specifically set forth in saving clause or proviso).

27. 224 N.C. 834, 32 S.E.2d 617.

28. De Berry was prosecuted for allegedly assaulting a woman in a federal post office building in the City of Winston-Salem. The United States had acquired the property

where the alleged assault occurred in 1899 with the state's consent as expressed in the 1887 act. As previously noted, the court interpreted the 1887 to cede exclusive jurisdiction to the federal government for purchases of property under the enclaves clause. Thus, the court determined that the state lacked jurisdiction to prosecute De Berry for an alleged assault that occurred on property under exclusive federal jurisdiction.

29. *See* Offutt Hous. Co. v. County of Sarpy, 351 U.S. 253 (1956).

30. United States v. Markham, 215 F.2d 56, 57 (4th Cir. 1954).

31. 40 U.S.C. § 3112(c).

32. State v. Burrell, 256 N.C. 288, 123 S.E.2d 795 (1962).

33. Atl. Marine Corps Communities, LLC v. Onslow County, 497 F. Supp. 2d 743, 755 (E.D.N.C. 2007).

34. *Id.* (citing Fort Leavenworth R.R. Co. v. Lowe, 114 U.S. 525, 542 (1885)).

35. *See Offutt Hous. Co.*, 351 U.S. 253 (determining that Nebraska county was authorized by Military Leasing Act of 1947 and Wherry Military Housing Act of 1949 to tax property of private lessee on Offutt Air Force Base, an area of exclusive federal jurisdiction).

36. General Services Administration, Inventory Report on Jurisdictional Status of Federal Areas within the States (June 30, 1962) (on file with author).

37. E. Band of Cherokee Indians v. Lynch, 632 F.2d 373 (4th Cir. 1980) (holding that lack of congressional consent barred North Carolina from imposing income tax on member of Eastern Band who derived income from activities on the reservation and barred Swain County from taxing personal property possessed by members of the Eastern Band on the reservation); *see also* Mescalaro Apache Tribe v. Jones, 411 U.S. 145, 148 (1973) ("[I]n the special area of state taxation, absent cession of jurisdiction or other federal statutes permitting it, there has been no satisfactory authority to taxing Indian reservation lands or Indian income from activities carried on within the boundaries of the reservation.").

38. E. Band of Cherokee Indians v. Lynch, 632 F.2d 373 (4th Cir. 1980); Moe v. Salish & Kootenai, 425 U.S. 463, 481 (holding that Montana's assessment and collection of personal property taxes on motor vehicles owned by tribal members residing on the reservation was unconstitutional under the supremacy clause).

39. *See, e.g.*, *Moe*, 425 U.S. 463 (upholding Montana's imposition of sales tax on-reservation sales of cigarettes to non-Indians).

40. *See, e.g.*, E. Band of Cherokee Indians v. N.C. Wildlife Res. Comm'n, 588 F.2d 75, 78 (4th Cir. 1978) (striking North Carolina's imposition of fishing license requirement upon non-Indian fishermen on the tribe's reservation as preempted by federal law).

41. Letter from Russell E. Dickenson, Director of the National Park Service, to Governor James B. Hunt, Jr. (July 27, 1984) (on file with author).

42. Atl. Marine Corps Communities, LLC v. Onslow County, 497 F. Supp. 2d 743, 747 (E.D.N.C. 2007) (determining that federal government had exclusive jurisdiction over Marine Corps training areas in Onslow and Craven counties based upon federal government's acceptance of jurisdiction and noting that since dates of acceptance, counties had not on lands at issue conducted health inspections of private food vendors, conducted

building inspections under county building code; provided waste removal services; attempted to enforce criminal laws (with one exception, *State v. Smith*, 328 N.C. 161, 400 S.E.2d 405 (1991)); provided police and fire protection, except by interlocal agreement with the United States; or attempted to tax real and personal property of nongovernmental entities, except where authorized by federal statute.); Op. Att'y Gen., 1997 WL 612858 (Feb. 4, 1997) (opining that state fisheries officers do not have jurisdiction to enforce state fisheries laws on Camp Lejeune, based on finding that the United States accepted jurisdiction of the federal military reservation of Camp Lejeune); *Smith*, 328 N.C. 161, 400 S.E.2d 405 (1991) (holding that the Superior Court, Onslow County, lacked jurisdiction to try the defendant as an adult for crimes he allegedly committed as a juvenile on the Camp Lejeune military reservation); State v. De Berry, 224 N.C. 834, 32 S.E.2d 617 (1945); State v. Burrell, 256 N.C. 288, 123 S.E.2d 795 (1962); State v. Graham, 47 N.C. App. 303, 267 S.E.2d 56 (1980); United States v. Raffield, 82 F.3d 611 (1996).

43. *In re Worley*, 93 N.C. App. 191, 195, 377 S.E.2d 270, 273 (1989).

44. *Id.*

45. Harrison v. Guilford County, 218 N.C. 718, 721, 12 S.E.2d 269, 272 (1940); *In re Worley*, 93 N.C. App. at 195, 377 S.E.2d at 273.

46. *Harrison*, 218 N.C. at 722, 12 S.E.2d at 272; *In re Worley*, 93 N.C. App. at 195, 377 S.E.2d at 273.

47. *Harrison*, 218 N.C. at 722, 12 S.E.2d at 272.

48. *In re Worley*, 93 N.C. App. at 195, 377 S.E.2d at 273.

49. *In re* Lee Memory Gardens, 110 N.C. App. 541, 546–47, 430 S.E.2d 451, 454 (1993) (citing Over-look Cemetery, Inc. v. Rockingham County, 273 N.C. 467, 470, 160 S.E.2d 293, 295 (1968)).

50. *Id.*

51. To qualify for exemption pursuant to G.S. 105-278.3, property must be owned by a qualifying entity—that is, a congregation, parish, mission, or similar local unit of a church or religious body; or a conference, association, presbytery, diocese, district, synod, or similar unit comprising local units of a church or religious body. Buildings, the land they occupy, and additional adjacent land reasonably necessary for the convenient use of any such building are exempted from taxation if wholly owned by a qualifying entity and (1) wholly and exclusively used by the owner for religious purposes or (2) occupied gratuitously by someone other than the owner and wholly and exclusively used by the occupant for religious, charitable, or nonprofit educational, literary, scientific, or cultural purposes. Personal property, likewise, is exempt if wholly owned by a qualifying agency and wholly and exclusively used by its owner for religious purposes or gratuitously made available to one other than the owner and wholly and exclusively used by the possessor for religious, charitable, or nonprofit educational, literary, scientific, or cultural purposes.

52. *In re Worley*, 93 N.C. App. at 195.

53. *Id.*

54. 219 N.C. 342, 13 S.E.2d 618 (1941).

55. *Id.* at 346, 13 S.E.2d at 621.

56. *Id.*

57. *Id.* at 346–47, 13 S.E.2d at 621.

58. 296 N.C. 330, 337, 250 S.E.2d 236, 241 (1979).

59. Indeed, one provision of the contract between the foundation and the paper company stated that "study groups or students will do nothing whatsoever to interfere with any program undertaken or in progress by the paper company in or on Hofmann Forest." *Id.* at 332, 250 S.E.2d at 238.

60. *In re* Worley, 93 N.C. App. 191, 377 S.E.2d 270 (1989); *In re* Southeastern Baptist Theol. Seminary, Inc., 135 N.C. App. 247, 520 S.E.2d 302 (1999).

61. *In re* Worley, 93 N.C. App. at 196–97; 377 S.E.2d at 273–74.

62. *Id.* at 197, 377 S.E.2d at 274.

63. *Id.*

64. 135 N.C. App. 247, 520 S.E.2d 302 (1999).

65. *Id.* at 257, 520 S.E.2d at 308.

66. 152 N.C. App. 640, 568 S.E.2d 208 (2002).

67. 152 N.C. App. at 648, 568 S.E.2d at 213.

68. *Id.* at 649, 568 S.E.2d at214.

69. G.S. 105-278.3(3); 105-278.4(c); 105-278.5(b); 105-278.8(b); 105-278.7(d); 105-278.8(b).

70. G.S. 105-278.3(f), 105-278.4(d), 105-278.5(c), 105-278.6(c), 105-278.7(e).

71. In a 2004 order, the Property Tax Commission determined that the New Bern Shrine Club's rental of its meeting building to nonmembers on more occasions than its members used the building in a given year did not result in a material amount of business or patronage by the general public. *In re* New Bern Shrine Club, 04 P.T.C. 21 (May 20, 2005); Order on Final Prehearing Conference (March 4, 2005) (establishing that shrine club rented its building thirty-three times in 2004 and had approximately twenty-five meetings and five social events for members that same year).

72. 273 N.C. 343, 347, 160 S.E.2d 62, 65 (1968).

73. *Id.* at 347, 160 S.E.2d at 347.

74. *In re* Taxable Status of Property, 45 N.C. App. 632, 636–37, 263 S.E.2d 838, 841 (1980).

75. G.S. 105-278.3(a), 105-278.4(a), 105-278.7(a).

76. *Id.*

77. G.S. 105-278.5(a).

78. *See In re* Church of Yashua, 160 N.C. App. 236, 584 S.E.2d 827 (2003) (denying exemption for fifty-acre tract owned by church on which no buildings were situated).

79. *Id.* at 238, 587 S.E.2d at 829.

80. 218 N.C. 718, 12 S.E.2d 269 (1940).

81. *See also In re* Worley, 93 N.C. App. 191, 377 S.E.2d 270 (1989) (five-acre parcel of vacant land adjacent to sanctuary building, education building, and parking lot acquired for future expansion held exempt); *In re* Temple Beth El, Inc., P.T.C. (Aug. 4, 1978) (twenty-four-acre parcel located five miles from existing building deemed adjacent and exempt).

82. G.S. 105-278.3(d)(1).

83. *Id.*

84. *Id.*

85. G.S. 105-278.3(d)(2); 105-278.6(b); 105-278.7(f)(4).

86. *Id.*

87. G.S. 105-278.3(d)(3); 105-278.4(f)(2); 105-278.7(f)(1); *see also In re* Maharishi Spiritual Ctr., 357 N.C. 152, 579 S.E.2d 249 (2003) (finding sufficient evidence to support property tax commission's conclusion that property was not wholly and exclusively used for an educational purpose based on expert testimony that while teaching of a meditation technique over a short period was an educational activity, the practice of meditation eight hours a day was not a learning activity); *In re* University for the Study of Human Goodness and Creative Group Work, 159 N.C. App. 85, 582 S.E.2d 645 (2003) (affirming property tax commission's conclusion that restaurant owned by a nonprofit corporation and used as a learning laboratory was not wholly and exclusively used for an educational purpose); *In re* Chapel Hill Day Care Ctr., Inc., 144 N.C. App. 649, 551 S.E.2d 172 (2001) (educational activities at day care center did not qualify center for an educational exemption given the center's primary purpose of providing custodial care for children as young as six weeks old).

88. G.S. 105-278.4(f)(2).

89. G.S. 105-278.3(d)(4); 105-278.7(f)(3).

90. G.S. 105-278.3(d)(5); 105-278.7(f)(5).

91. G.S. 105-278.3(d)(6); 105-278.7(f)(2).

92. G.S. 105-278.3(c)(1),(2).

93. G.S. 116-22 defines *institution* as "an educational institution with a main permanent campus located in this State that is not owned or operated by the State of North Carolina or by an agency or political subdivision of the State or by any combination thereof that satisfies all of the following:

a. Is accredited by the Southern Association of Colleges and Schools under the standards of the College Delegate Assembly of the Association or by the New England Association of Schools and Colleges through its Commission on Institutions of Higher Education.
b. Awards a postsecondary degree as defined in N.C. GEN. STAT. 116-15.
c. Is not a seminary, Bible school, Bible college or similar religious institution."

94. G.S. 105-278.4 was amended in 2004 to explicitly provide for the exemption from taxation of educational property owned by a nonprofit entity "for the sole benefit of" a University of North Carolina-affiliated institution, a North Carolina community college, or any institutions as defined in G.S. 116-22. S.L. 2004-173. These amendments arose out of Watauga County's denial of a property tax exemption for an apartment complex owned by the nonprofit Appalachian Student Housing Corporation, which was designed and built to supplement student housing at Appalachian State University (ASU). As discussed earlier, subsequent to the statutory amendment, the state court of appeals held that ASU's equitable interest in the property as beneficiary of the trust rendered the apartment complex state-owned property exempt from taxation pursuant to G.S. 105-278.1(b). *In re* Appalachian Student Hous. Corp., 165 N.C. App. 379, 598 S.E.2d 701 (2004). The court's finding of state ownership mooted the inquiry into whether operation of the facility qualified as an educational purpose under G.S. 105-278.4, but the court nonetheless responded to the Property Tax Commission's determination that student housing was not

an activity naturally and properly incident to the operation of an educational institution. The court described student housing as "one of the more traditional accoutrements of an educational facility" and opined that it "should be considered incidental to the educational institution." *In re Appalachian Student Hous.*, 165 N.C. App at 389, 598 S.E.2d at 707. Being of like mind on this point, the General Assembly added the operation of student housing and dining facilities to the list of specific educational purposes.

The court of appeals' statements regarding the integral relationship between student housing and an institution's educational mission indicated that even before G.S. 105-278.4 was amended, a student housing facility owned by a nonprofit entity and held in trust for a public or private institution of higher education should be exempt from taxation, because such a facility presumably would be considered "owned" by the institution and "naturally and properly incident to [its] operation." G.S. 105-278.4(b). Thus, by requiring only that the nonprofit entity's educational property be owned "for the sole benefit of" an educational institution rather than requiring the specific trust arrangement present in *Appalachian Student Housing Corp.*, the amendments only minimally expand the scope of the G.S. 105-278.4 exemption.

95. G.S. 105-278.4(a)(2); *see also In re* Univ. for the Study of Human Goodness and Creative Group Work, 159 N.C. App. 85, 582 S.E.2d 645 (2003) (citing favorably expert witness testimony that restaurant was not part of an educational institution as there was no evidence of a curriculum, learning outcomes, or measurement of outcomes).

96. 112 N.C. App. 1, 434 S.E.2d 865 (1993).

97. *Id.* at 9, 434 S.E.2d at 870.

98. *Id.* at 10–11, 434 S.E.2d at 870–71.

99. 180 N.C. App. 160, 636 S.E.2d 292 (2006).

100. Beginning in 2008, it the homestead exclusion is the greater of $25,000 or 50 percent of the value.

101. A person is totally and permanently disabled if the person has a physical or mental impairment that substantially precludes him or her from obtaining gainful employment and that impairment appears reasonably certain to continue throughout the individual's life. G.S. 105-277.1(b)(4).

102. Amendments to the definition of *income* effective for the 2008–09 tax year eliminated the reference contained in earlier versions of the statute to *adjusted gross income* as defined by the Internal Revenue Code. S.L. 2007-497.

103. *Id.*

104. As a practical matter, most assessors do not list interests of tenants in common on separate abstracts or apportion property values among tenants in common. Likewise, the general practice is to send one bill to the tenants in common, without apportioning tax liability. So, in all likelihood, the apportionment issue here is an issue between Maude and Clementine, which does not affect the tax office. The assessed value for tax purposes does not change upon Maude's qualification.

105. G.S. 105-277.1B. This type of property tax relief program is "called a 'circuit breaker' because it protects taxpayers from a property tax 'overload' just like an electric circuit breaker; when a property tax bill exceeds a certain percentage of a taxpayer's income, the circuit breaker reduces property taxes in excess of this 'overload' level." INSTITUTE ON

Taxation and Economic Policy, Property Tax Circuit Breakers, Talking Taxes, Policy Brief #10 (2005), *available at* www.itepnet.org.

106. All of the definitions that apply to the traditional homestead exclusion under G.S. 105-277.1 apply to the circuit breaker benefit.

107. G.S. 105-277.1B(d).

108. The maximum amount owed consists of all property taxes levied on the property, including city, county, and special district taxes.

109. Memorandum from David D. Duty, Property Tax Division, North Carolina Department of Revenue, to County Assessors (July 1, 2008) (setting forth income eligibility limits for the 2009 homestead exclusion and circuit breaker benefit).

110. G.S. 105-277.1B(e).

111. G.S. 105-277.1(h).

112. G.S. 105-309(f).

113. G.S. 105-277.1C.

114. S.L. 2008-107, sec. 28.11.

115. G.S. 105-277.1(b)(1).

116. G.S. 105-277.1C(d).

117. G.S. 105-277.1C(e).

118. *Id.*

119. *Id.*

120. *Id.*

121. G.S. 105-277.1C(f).

122. *Id.*

123. G.S. 105-282.1(a).

124. *Id.*

125. G.S. 105-282.1(a)(2).

126. G.S. 105-282.1(c).

127. *See In re* K-Mart Corp., 319 N.C. 378, 354 S.E.2d 468 (1987) (determining that property was exempt in 1978 and 1979, two of the years included in the tax assessor's 1983 discovery).

128. G.S. 105-282.1(a1); *see also In re* Wesleyan Educ. Ctr., 68 N.C. App. 742, 316 S.E.2d 87 (1984).

129. *See In re Wesleyan Educ. Ctr.*, 68 N.C. App. at 745, 316 S.E.2d at 89 (employing this rationale to justify former Machinery Act provisions that did not allow late-filed applications for exemption).

130. *Id.*

131. G.S. 105-330.3(b).

132. G.S. 105-330.3(c).

133. G.S. 105-296(l); *see also* G.S. 105-282.1(e).

134. G.S. 105-296(l).

135. *Id.*

136. G.S. 105-282.1(d).

137. *Id.*

138. *Id.*

139. The provisions of the 1973 act were codified at G.S. 105-277.2 through 105-277.7.

140. These numbers are based upon calculations from 2005–06 AV-50 forms submitted by counties and tabulated by the Property Tax Division of the Department of Revenue. In 2005–06 taxes on a value of $16,598,438,636 were deferred statewide for property in the present-use program. Property owned by the federal, state, and local governments valued at $41,497,268,961 statewide was exempted from property taxation. *Id.*

141. For detailed explanations and sample application of the laws governing the present-use program, see North Carolina Department of Revenue, Property Tax Division, Present-Use Value Program (1st ed. April 2, 2007), *available at* www.dornc.com/publications/puv_manual_1st_2007.pdf.

142. G.S. 105-277.2(5) (emphasis added).

143. *In re* McElwee, 304 N.C. 68, 283 S.E.2d 115 (1981).

144. *Id.*

145. *In re McElwee,* 304 N.C. 68, 283 S.E.2d 115.

146. G.S. 105-277.4(b).

147. G.S. 105-317(c).

148. *Id.*

149. G.S. 105-289(a)(5).

150. G.S. 105-289(a)(7). The Use-Value Advisory Board is chaired by the Director of the Agricultural Extension Service of North Carolina State University and includes representatives of the Department of Agriculture and Consumer Services, the Forest Resources Division, and the Agricultural Extension Service of North Carolina Agricultural and Technical State University. G.S. 105-277.7(a).

151. G.S. 105-277.7(c)(1).

152. G.S. 105-277.2(5) (providing that the capitalization rate for agricultural land and horticultural land is to be determined by the Use-Value Advisory Board as provided in G.S. 105-277.7).

153. G.S. 105-277.7(c)(3).

154. G.S. 105-277.2(5).

155. G.S. 105-277.4(b1).

156. G.S. 105-277.2(1).

157. G.S. 105-277.2(1), (6).

158. G.S. 105-277.2(7).

159. G.S. 105-277.3(e)(2).

160. *Aquatic species* is defined in G.S. 106-758(3) as "any species of finfish, mollusk, crustacean, or other aquatic invertebrate, amphibian, reptile, or aquatic plant, and including, but not limited to, 'fish' and 'fishes' as defined in N.C. Gen. Stat. 113-129(7)."

161. G.S. 105-277.3(a)(2); G.S. 105-289(a)(6).

162. North Carolina Use-Value Advisory Board & North Carolina Department of Revenue, 2008 Use-Value Manual for Agricultural, Horticultural, and Forest Land, 22–23 (May 2007) (hereinafter 2008 Use-Value Manual), *available at* www.dor.state.nc.us (requiring sound management

practices in lieu of income for acreage in production for Christmas trees but not yet undergoing harvest).

163. G.S. 105-277.3(f).

164. *Id.*

165. G.S. 105-277.3(g).

166. G.S. 105-277.3(a)(1), (2); *In re* Briarfield Farms, 147 N.C. App. 208, 555 S.E.2d 621 (2001) (holding that income requirement applies to entire farm unit rather than to each ten-acre portion of farmland).

167. G.S. 105-277.3(a)(1).

168. 2008 Use-Value Manual at 20.

169. 2008 Use-Value Manual at 21.

170. G.S. 105-277.3(d1).

171. *See* G.S. 105-130.34 (providing tax credit for qualified donations by corporations) and G.S. 105-151.12 (providing tax credit for qualified donations by individuals and pass-through entities).

172. G.S. 105-277.3(d1).

173. G.S. 105-277.2(4).

174. *Id.*

175. G.S. 105-277.2(4).

176. G.S. 105-277.2(4)(b).

177. The term *member* is defined as "[a] shareholder of a corporation, a partner of a general or limited partnership, or a member of a limited liability company." G.S. 105-277.2(4a).

178. G.S. 105-277.2(4)(b)(2).

179. *Id.*

180. *Id.*

181. G.S. 105-277.2(4)(b)(4).

182. G.S. 105-277.2(5).

183. *Id.*

184. G.S. 105-277.2(4)(c).

185. G.S. 105-277.2(4)(c)(2).

186. *Id.*

187. G.S. 105-277.2(4)(d).

188. G.S. 105-277.2(4)(e).

189. *Id.*

190. G.S. 105-277.3(b).

191. G.S. 105-277.3(b1).

192. G.S. 105-277.3(b2).

193. G.S. 105-277.3(b2)(1).

194. *Id.*

195. *Id.*

196. G.S. 105-277.3(b2)(2); *In re* Davis, 113 N.C. App. 743, 749, 440 S.E.2d 307, 311 (1994).

197. *See Davis*, 113 N.C. App. at 749, 440 S.E.2d at 311; *see also* North Carolina Department of Revenue, Property Tax Division, Present-Use Value Program, 19–20 (1st ed. April 2, 2007), *available at* www.dornc.com/publications/puv_manual_1st_2007.pdf (concluding that eligibility of transferred land for appraisal at present-use value depends upon the land's satisfaction of production and sound management requirements, but not size requirements).

198. G.S. 105-277.4(c).

199. These taxes are referred to as reassessed because Joe Brown will already have been billed for 2008–09 taxes based upon the property's initial assessment at present-use value.

200. G.S. 105-277.4(d)(3).

201. S.L. 2008-171 (H 1889) (enacting new G.S. 105-277.15).

202. G.S. 105-277.15(c).

203. G.S. 105-277.15(a)(2) provides that "[a]n individual is indirectly a member of a business entity if the individual is a member of a business entity or a beneficiary of a trust that is part of the ownership structure of the business entity.

204. G.S. 105-277.15(c)(2)(a).

205. G.S. 105-277.15(a)(3).

206. G.S. 105-277.15(c)(2)(b).

207. G.S. 105-277.15(c)(2)(c).

208. G.S. 105-277.15(c)(3).

209. *Id.*

210. G.S. 105-277.15(c)(3)(b).

211. G.S. 105-277.15(d)(1).

212. G.S. 105-277.15(d)(2).

213. G.S. 105-277.15(f)(1).

214. G.S. 105-277.15(f)(2).

215. G.S. 105-277.15(g).

216. G.S. 105-277.14.

8 Release and Refund

8.1 **Action by the Governing Board** 227

8.1.1 Definition of Clerical Error 228

8.1.2 What Is an Illegal Tax? 230

8.1.3 When a Tax Is Imposed for an Illegal Purpose 230

8.2 **Procedures for Requesting a Refund or Release** 231

8 Release and Refund

The subject of refunds and releases is typically considered the concern of the tax collector rather than the assessor. Nonetheless, the assessor frequently must address the issue of whether a taxpayer is entitled to a refund or release when appraisal errors are discovered. While Section 105-325 of the North Carolina General Statutes (hereinafter G.S.) permits the governing body of the taxing unit and the assessor to correct clerical and appraisal errors affecting taxes for the current year, and any resulting refund or release may be issued without further action on the part of the taxpayer,[1] a taxpayer's ability to obtain a refund or release in circumstances outside the scope of G.S. 105-325 is quite limited.

8.1 Action by the Governing Board

Neither the tax collector nor the assessor is authorized to reduce, refund, or release taxes, including accrued interest, penalties, and costs. To the extent that there is any authority to release taxes, it rests with the governing body. A strong public policy supports the stability of sources of government revenue. As previously noted, property taxes are the largest source of revenue for counties and are second only to utility revenue for cities. For this reason, governing bodies are given only limited authority to release or refund property taxes and are strictly prohibited from compromising taxes for any reason not expressly authorized.[2] Lest any governing body ignore this admonition, the Machinery Act provides that any member of a governing body who votes for the unlawful release, refund, or compromise of taxes may be held personally liable for the amount of the taxes forgiven.[3]

There are three permissible bases for releasing or refunding taxes. The governing body of a taxing unit may release or refund a tax that was (1) imposed through a clerical error, (2) illegal, or (3) levied for an illegal purpose.

8.1.1 Definition of Clerical Error

Just what sorts of errors are clerical? The North Carolina Court of Appeals provided some guidance on that point in *Ammons v. Wake County*.[4] Justus Ammons and his wife, Jo Ellen Ammons, acquired forestland in 1991 from Ammons Land Company, a corporation owned by members of the Ammons family. In 1993 Mr. Ammons asked the Wake County Tax Assessor whether this forestland would qualify for reduced taxation based upon present-use value. The assessor told Mr. Ammons that the property would not qualify for taxation based on present-use value because the property would not meet the ownership requirements of G.S. 105-277.3(b). Mr. Ammons followed the assessor's advice and did not apply for present-use taxation. The next year, notwithstanding the assessor's previous advice, the taxpayer applied for taxation at present-use value based upon the property's status as forestland. The assessor denied present-use classification to the property. The taxpayer appealed to the board of equalization and review, which determined that the property was eligible for present-use taxation. The state court of appeals had recently decided *In re Davis*,[5] in which it determined that a property's eligibility for present-use taxation upon transfer depended upon whether the property was eligible for appraisal in the hands of the grantee rather than the grantor. The taxpayer then requested a refund from the board of county commissioners for three years during which the property was taxed at market, rather than present-use, value. The board denied the taxpayer's request for refund, and the taxpayer filed suit in superior court. The court concluded that the taxes were not "imposed through clerical error" as the term was defined under G.S. 105-381(a) and that the taxpayer was not entitled to a refund. The court of appeals agreed that the error was not clerical within the meaning of G.S. 105-381 and held that the term *clerical error* applied only to transcription errors; that is, mistakes in writing or copying, that were ordinarily apparent on the face of the document. The court noted that the error in *Ammons* was not apparent on the face of the assessor's statement in 1993 but only by reference to the court's subsequent decision in *Davis*. Moreover, the court noted that a clerical error must be unintended and that the assessor in *Ammons* fully intended that Mr. Ammons accept his interpretation that the property did not qualify for present-use value taxation. The court stated that "[m]istake of judgment or law" is not a defense set forth in G.S. 105-381. *Ammons* makes clear that mistakes in judgment may not serve as the basis for a taxpayer's claim for refund pursuant to G.S. 105-381.

Errors resulting from typographical errors in the transfer of information from source appraisal documents to computerized databases certainly are clerical in nature, as are errors made in mathematical computations. Thus, if the amount of tax has been erroneously computed at a figure higher than is proper due to such an error, a governing body is within its authority to order a release or refund of taxes. Yet it is not always easy to distinguish a clerical error from an error in judgment. Suppose the appraiser who visits the residence mistakenly concludes, based on viewing the home from the outside, that the home has one and one-half stories when, in fact, it is a one-story house with cathedral ceilings. Is this sort of data error a judgment error or an appraisal error? The *Ammons* case involved a mistaken judgment about whether the determination of transferred property's eligibility to immediately qualify for the present-use program was based upon the ownership characteristics of the grantor or grantee—not an error about the raw data characteristics pursuant to which property is appraised. May the latter type of error serve as the lawful basis for a release or refund of taxes? Some assessors have concluded that it may. Suppose instead that the assessor misjudged the quality of construction on the home based on viewing the outside of the structure and assigned a Grade A construction to the home. Upon the taxpayer's request that the assessor view the inside of the home three years later, the assessor notes several items, present since the time of the last reappraisal, that warrant a reduction to Grade C. Is the taxpayer entitled to a refund or release of the additional taxes attributable to this overstatement of value in earlier years? Most assessors would conclude that the taxpayer is not entitled to a refund or release in such a circumstance. Is there a meaningful distinction between the two situations just described and one in which a clerical assistant entering handwritten data from a field appraiser transposes numbers; for example, by entering 4,200 square feet instead of 2,400 square feet? The analysis is further muddied by the fact that entering one and one-half stories for a one-story house may, through operation of appraisal software, result in the same overstatement of square footage, and thus the same increase in tax, that resulted from the clerical assistant's transposition of numbers. Yet the typographical error is clearly clerical in nature, while the error regarding the number of stories appears to be an error in judgment. Assessors have taken different stances on the circumstances that warrant a refund or release, and the courts have not decided any cases post-*Ammons* to clarify the distinction between clerical errors and errors in judgment. Given the *Ammons* court's strict definition of clerical error, the author's view is that a refund or release maybe granted in only one circumstance described above; that is, the typographical error resulting in taxation of the property based upon 4,200 square feet rather than 2,400 square feet.

8.1.2 What Is an Illegal Tax?

Taxpayers occasionally contend that any appraisal error—including the miscalculation of acreage, mistaken assumptions about the condition of or amenities in the interior of a structure, and the listing of property in the wrong name—renders the resulting tax imposed upon property illegal and thus eligible for a refund or release pursuant to G.S. 105-381. Yet, if this were the case, there would be little reason for the Machinery Act to require counties to have boards of equalization and review that must meet during designated times each year to consider taxpayer appeals from decisions and assessments made by the county assessor.[6] The ability to appeal any perceived overassessment to the board of commissioners would diminish the effectiveness of the relatively expedient appeal process set forth in the Machinery Act that provides taxpayers an opportunity to challenge the assessment of their property during certain times in the current fiscal year before boards sitting especially for that purpose. Moreover, the ability to challenge assessments years after the fact also would undermine the stability in the tax base that results from it being relatively insulated from challenge after a certain time.

Thus the term *illegal tax* in G.S. 105-381 must mean something other than any tax that results from a mistake or error. The North Carolina Supreme Court has explained that "[a]n illegal or invalid tax results when the taxing body seeks to impose a tax without authority."[7] This can occur if the rate is unconstitutional, the property is exempt from taxation, or the taxing unit lacks authority to impose the tax because the property's tax situs is in another jurisdiction.[8] Discriminatory assessment among taxpayers who own the same class of property also results in an illegal tax.[9] Likewise, a taxing unit's failure to reduce the assessed valuation of property upon being ordered to do so by the board of equalization and review, the Property Tax Commission, or a court also would result in the imposition of an illegal tax.

8.1.3 When a Tax Is Imposed for an Illegal Purpose

A tax refund or release is warranted pursuant to the illegal purpose defense if the tax is levied for something other than a "public purpose" or a purpose permitted by statute,[10] without a vote of the people in a situation in which such a vote is required by law, or for an amount greater than that authorized by the state constitution, statutes, or a vote of the people.

8.2 Procedures for Requesting a Refund or Release

To claim a right to release or refund of taxes, the taxpayer must submit a written statement of his or her demand to the governing body of the taxing unit. A request for release of taxes not yet paid may be made at any time. A taxpayer may only request a refund, however, within five years after the tax became due or within six months from the date the tax was paid, whichever is later.[11] Upon receiving the taxpayer's request, the governing board must decide within ninety days whether legal grounds for the release or refund exist.

If the board fails to grant the relief requested by the taxpayer or takes no action on the taxpayer's request within ninety days of receiving the request, the taxpayer must, if he or she has not already done so, pay the tax. The taxpayer may then within three years bring a civil action against the taxing unit for the amount claimed. If the initial request was a request for release, the taxpayer may file the civil action within three years from the date of payment of the tax. If the initial request was a request for a refund, the taxpayer may bring the civil action within three years of the expiration of the period in which the governing body is required to act.[12] If the court determines that the tax or any part of it was illegal or levied for an illegal purpose or that the tax was excessive as the result of a clerical error, the court must enter a judgment in favor of the taxpayer.[13] The judgment must provide for interest at the rate of 6 percent per annum, plus costs.

The board of county commissioners may delegate authority to make refunds and releases of less than $100 to the county attorney, finance officer, or manager. The officer to whom this authority is delegated must make a monthly report to the board of all releases and refunds granted.

As previously noted, special refund procedures apply when the property owner has appealed the value to the Property Tax Commission and paid the tax and after payment the commission orders a reduction in the value. In this case, the county may be required to pay interest on the amount refunded.[14] The rate of interest to be paid is the rate set by the North Carolina Secretary of Revenue under G.S. 105-241.1(i), which is the interest to be paid on delinquent state taxes. This rate may not be higher than 16 percent a year or lower than 5 percent a year.

Notes

1. William A. Campbell, Property Tax Collection in North Carolina 107 (4th ed. 1998) (noting that if the tax has already been paid when the correction is made, the assessor or board of county commissioners should direct the finance officer to make a refund if the amount of the tax has been reduced.)

2. N.C. Gen. Stat. § 105-380 (hereinafter G.S.).

3. *Id.*

4. 127 N.C. App. 426, 490 S.E.2d 569 (1997).

5. 113 N.C. App. 743, 440 S.E.2d 307 (1994).

6. *Cf.* Gwinnett County, Ga. v. Gwinnett I Ltd. Partnership, 458 S.E.2d 632, 634 (Ga. 1995) (discussing similar dual mechanism for appeal under Georgia law and concluding that "to suppose that the two very different procedures are available in every case without regard to the underlying basis of the taxpayer's challenge would render the [valuation] appeal process[,] . . . with its short time periods, meaningless.")

7. Redevelopment Comm'n of High Point v. Guilford County, 274 N.C. 585, 164 S.E.2d 476 (1968).

8. *Id.*

9. Edward Valves, Inc. v. Wake County, 117 N.C. App. 484, 451 S.E.2d 641 (1995), *affirmed as modified and remanded*, 343 N.C. 426, 471 S.E.2d 342 (1996).

10. *See* G.S. 153A-149 (setting forth authorized purposes for which counties may levy property taxes); G.S. 160A-209 (setting forth authorized purposes for which cities may levy property taxes).

11. G.S. 105-381(a)(3).

12. G.S. 105-381(c).

13. G.S. 105-381(d).

14. G.S. 105-290(b)(4).

Appendix An Outline of Property Tax Exemptions and Exclusions

Antique Airplanes 237

Antique Automobiles 237

Arts Objects 238

Bill and Hold Goods 238

Brownfields Improvements 238

Burial Property 239

Cargo Containers 239

Charitable Purposes 239

Computer Software 240

Continuing Care Retirement Homes 240

Cotton Dust Emission Control Equipment 241

Development Rights That Are Severable 242

Disabled Veterans—Specially Equipped Motor Vehicles 242

Domestic Property Held in Foreign Trade Zone 243

Educational Institutions 243

Educational, Scientific, Literary, and Charitable Property 244

Elderly or Disabled Individuals' Residential Property 245

Farm Products Held by Cooperatives 247

Federal Government Property 247

Fertilizer 247

Flight Equipment of Air Couriers 248

Fraternal and Civic Orders 248

Global Transpark Authority Property 249

Goodwill Industries 249

Hazardous Waste Management Commission 249

Health Care Facilities Financed by Medical Care Commission 250

Heavy Equipment Rental 250

Historic Landmark Sites 250

Historic Preservation Property 251

Historic Property 251

Homeowners Association Property 251

Hospital Authority Property 252

Hospitals, Charitable 252

Housing Authority Property 253

Imported into Foreign Trade Zone 253

Imported through a North Carolina Seaport Terminal 253

Industrial and Pollution Control Facilities 254

Intangible Personal Property 254

Inventory of Contractors 254

Inventory of Manufacturers 254

Inventory of Retail and Wholesale Merchants 255

Leased to Local Governments 255

Leased School Facilities 255

Leasehold Interest in Exempt Property Used for Affordable Housing 256

Low-Income Housing 256

Masonic Orders 256

Motor Vehicle Chassis 257

Non-Business Personal Property 257

Nuclear Materials 257

Pollution Abatement Property 258

Poultry and Livestock 259

Precious Metals 259

Prescription Drug Samples 259

Protected Natural Areas 260

Public Parks and Drives 260

Radioactive Waste Disposal Authority 260

Recycling Facilities 260

Recycling and Resource Recovery 261

Regional Sports Authority Property 262

Religious Educational Assemblies 262

Religious Property 263

Repaired Personal Property 264

Roadway Corridors 264

Short-Term Rental Vehicles 265

Solar Energy Electric Systems 265

Solar Energy Systems 265

Standing Timber 266

State and Local Government Property 266

Turnpike Authority Property 266

Use-Value Appraisal 267

Veterans Organizations 271

Water Companies, Private 272

Water and Sewer Associations, Nonprofit 272

Wildlife Conservation Land 272

Working Waterfront Property 273

Appendix
An Outline of Property Tax Exemptions and Exclusions

Antique Airplanes

Citation: G.S. 105-277.12
Qualifying property: Airplanes that are registered with the FAA and are model year 1954 or older
Qualified owner: Individual persons
Qualifying use: Maintained primarily for use in exhibitions, club activities, air shows, and other public interest functions, are used only occasionally for other purposes, and are not used for production of income or in connection with a business
Application procedure: Annual
Relief granted: Assessed at the lower of true value or $5,000

Antique Automobiles

Citation: G.S. 105-330.9
Qualifying property: An automobile that is registered and has a historic vehicle special license plate
Qualified owner: Individual person
Qualifying use: Maintained primarily for use in exhibitions, club activities, parades, and other public interest functions and only occasionally for other purposes and is used by the owner for purposes other than production of income and not in connection with a business
Application procedure: One-time
Relief granted: Is assessed at the lower of market value or $500

Arts Objects

Citation: G.S. 105-275(41)
Qualifying property: Objects of art
Qualified owner: North Carolina State Art Society, Inc.
Qualifying use: None specified
Application procedure: One-time
Relief granted: Exempt

Bill and Hold Goods

Citation: G.S. 105-275(26)
Qualifying property: Tangible personal property manufactured in North Carolina "for the account" of a qualifying owner
Qualified owner: A nonresident customer of a North Carolina manufacturer
Qualifying use: Held by the manufacturer for shipment (to a destination either in-state or out-of-state)
Special provisions: Effective for the tax year immediately following transfer of title to the goods from the manufacturer to the buyer
Application procedure: None required
Relief granted: Exempt

Brownfields Improvements

Citation: G.S. 105-277.13
Qualifying property: Improvements made to real property that is subject to a brownfields agreement between the owner and the Department of Environment and Natural Resources pursuant to G.S. 130A-310.32
Qualified owner: None specified
Qualifying use: None specified
Application procedure: One-time
Relief granted: Assessed by excluding a portion of the value from assessment for the first five years after completion as follows: Year 1–90%; Year 2–75%; Year 3–50%; Year 4–30%; Year 5–10%

Burial Property

Citation: G.S. 105-278.2
Qualifying property: Real property *set apart* for qualifying use
Qualified owner: None specified
Qualifying use: Burial purposes, but *not* held for purposes of (1) sale or rental or (2) sale of burial rights
Application procedure: None required
Relief granted: Exempt

Cargo Containers

Citation: G.S. 105-275(24)
Qualifying property: Cargo containers and chassis, defined as nonadjustable receptacles of a permanent character, strong enough for repeated use, specially designed to facilitate the carriage of goods by one or more modes of transport (one of which must be by ocean vessel) without intermediate reloadings and fitted with devices permitting ready handling, particularly in the transfer from one transport mode to another
Qualified owner: Any person, firm, or corporation
Qualifying use: Transportation of cargo by vessels in ocean commerce
Application procedure: Annual
Relief granted: Exempt

Charitable Purposes

Citation: G.S. 105-278.6
Qualifying property: Real and personal property owned by a qualified owner
Qualified owner: The following agencies, as long as they are not organized or operated for profit:

1. YMCA or similar organization
2. Home for the aged, sick, or infirm
3. Orphanage or similar home
4. SPCA
5. Reformatory or correctional institution
6. Monastery, convent, or nunnery

7. Nonprofit, lifesaving, first aid, or rescue squad organization
8. Nonprofit corporation providing housing for individuals or families with low or moderate income

Qualifying use: (1) As to real property actually and exclusively occupied and used for charitable purposes; (2) as to personal property, entirely and completely used for charitable purposes; (3) incidental use for other purposes does not defeat exemption; exemption prorated upon partial use for nonexempt purpose. G.S. 14-309.7(d) provides that conduct of bingo or raffles on property belonging to an organization eligible for a bingo license does not affect eligibility of the property for exemption or classification under the Machinery Act.

Definitions: *Charitable purpose*

Special provisions: Property held by an organization providing housing for low- or moderate-income individuals as a future site for such housing qualifies for exemption, subject to a lien for deferred taxes. If housing units are constructed on the property within five years, the lien is extinguished; otherwise after five years the deferred taxes become due and payable with interest from the original due date.

Application procedure: One-time

Relief granted: Exempt

Computer Software

Citation: G.S. 105-275(40)

Qualifying property: Computer software and related documentation

Qualified owner: None specified

Qualifying use: No use requirement imposed

Special provisions: The exclusion does not apply to (1) embedded software or (2) software acquired from a person unrelated to the taxpayer and capitalized on taxpayer's books.

Application procedure: None required

Relief granted: Exempt

Continuing Care Retirement Homes

Citation: G.S. 105-278.6A

Qualifying property: Real and personal property owned by a qualified retirement facility

Qualified owner: A community that meets all of the following criteria and conditions:

1. Is licensed under G.S. Ch. 58, Art. 64
2. Is designed for elderly residents
3. Includes independent-living units for elderly residents
4. Includes a skilled nursing facility or an adult care facility

Qualifying use: Use in the operation of a qualified retirement facility
Application procedure: Annual
Relief granted: Total exclusion if the property meets all of the following criteria:

1. Exempt from North Carolina income tax and private shareholders do not benefit from its operations
2. All net revenue applied to providing uncompensated goods and services to the elderly and local community or applied to endowment or reserve for those purposes
3. Charter provides that upon dissolution all assets will revert to an organization exempt from federal income tax under Int. Rev. Code sec. 501(c)(3)
4. Has an active program to generate funds to assist serving persons who might not be able to reside in the facility without financial aid
5. Serves all residents without regard to ability to pay or devotes at least 5 percent of resident revenue to charity care for its residents

Partial exclusion is allowed if the facility meets criteria 1–4, above, and devotes at least 1 percent but less than 5 percent of resident revenue to charity care for its residents. The amount of exclusion varies on a sliding scale from 20 percent to 80 percent depending on the percentage of resident revenue devoted to charity care.

Cotton Dust Emission Control Equipment

Citation: G.S. 105-275(8)c.
Qualifying property: Tangible personal property
Qualified owner: Any person, firm, or corporation
Qualifying use: Exclusively used or to be used to prevent or reduce cotton dust inside a textile plant, in accordance with the Occupational Safety and Health Act (G.S. Ch. 95, Art. 16). All parts of a ventilation or air

conditioning system that are integrated into a system used to prevent or reduce cotton dust emissions, except chillers and cooling towers, qualify for exemption.

Special provisions: The Department of Revenue is directed to adopt guidelines to aid in administering the exclusion

Application procedure: One-time

Relief granted: Exempt

Development Rights That Are Severable

Citation: G.S. 105-275(35)

Qualifying property: Severable development rights, as defined in G.S. 136-66.11(a)

Qualified owner: None specified

Qualifying use: None specified

Application procedure: One-time

Relief granted: Exempt

Disabled Veterans—Specially Equipped Motor Vehicles

Citation: G.S. 105-275(5) and (5a)

Qualifying property: (1) Motor vehicle given to qualified owner by United States government on account of disabilities suffered in World War II, the Korean Conflict, or the Viet Nam Era, or (2) motor vehicle altered with special equipment to accommodate a service-connected disability

Qualified owner: As to category (1), disabled veteran of World War II, the Korean Conflict, or the Viet Nam Era receiving gift of qualifying property, or a person entitled to receive gift of qualifying property under 38 U.S.C. § 252. As to category (2), disabled veteran, as defined by 38 U.S.C. § 101(2), who is entitled to special automotive equipment for service-connected disability, as provided by 38 U.S.C. § 3901.

Application procedure: Single application required

Relief granted: Exempt

Domestic Property Held in Foreign Trade Zone

Citation: G.S. 105-275(23)
Qualifying property: Tangible personal property produced in the United States and held in a Foreign Trade Zone either in its original form or as altered by manufacture, processing, assembly, grading, cleaning, or mixing
Qualified owner: None specified
Qualifying use: Held for export
Application procedure: Annual
Relief granted: Exempt

Educational Institutions

Citation: G.S. 105-278.4
Qualifying property:

1. Buildings, the land they actually occupy, and additional adjacent land reasonably necessary to the convenient use of any such building
2. Land (exclusive of improvements), improvements other than buildings, land actually occupied by improvements, and additional adjacent land reasonably necessary to the convenient use of any such improvements
3. As to both buildings and land, of a kind commonly employed in the performance of activities naturally and properly incident to the operation of an educational institution such as the owner
4. Personal property

Qualified owner:

1. As to buildings, above, nonprofit educational institutions or a nonprofit entity for sole benefit of qualifying post-secondary educational institution
2. As to land, nonprofit educational institutions owning qualified buildings
3. As to personal property, a church or religious body or a nonprofit educational institution owning qualified buildings and land

Qualifying use:

1. As to land and buildings,
   A. Wholly and exclusively used by the owner for educational purposes, *or*
   B. Occupied gratuitously by another nonprofit educational institution

and wholly and exclusively used by the occupant for nonprofit educational purposes

2. As to personal property,
   A. Wholly and exclusively used by the owner for educational purposes *or*
   B. Held gratuitously by a church, religious body, or nonprofit educational institution and exclusively used for nonprofit educational purposes by the possessor
3. Incidental use for other purposes does not defeat exemption; exemption prorated upon partial use for nonexempt purpose
4. Operation of golf course, tennis court, sports area, or similar facilities is deemed an educational purpose regardless of the extent to which such facilities may be used by the general public
5. G.S. 14-309.7(d) provides that conduct of bingo or raffles on property belonging to an organization eligible for a bingo license does not affect eligibility of the property for exemption or classification under the Machinery Act

Definitions: *Educational purpose, illustrative list of educational institutions*
Application procedure: One-time
Relief granted: Exempt

Educational, Scientific, Literary, and Charitable Property

Citation: G.S. 105-278.7
Qualifying property: Buildings, the land they actually occupy, and additional adjacent land reasonably necessary for the convenient use of any such building and personal property wholly owned by a qualified owner
Qualified owner: One of the following agencies:

1. Charitable association or institution
2. Historical association or institution
3. Veterans' organization or association
4. Scientific association or institution
5. Literary association or institution
6. Benevolent association or institution
7. Nonprofit community or neighborhood organization

Qualifying use: Wholly and exclusively used by its owner for nonprofit educational, scientific, literary, charitable, or cultural purposes *or* gratuitously occupied by or made available to one who would be a qualified owner and wholly and exclusively used by the occupant for nonprofit educational, scientific, literary, charitable, or cultural purposes; incidental use for other purposes does not defeat exemption; exemption prorated upon partial use for nonexempt purpose. G.S. 14-309.7(d) provides that conduct of bingo or raffles on property belonging to an organization eligible for a bingo license does not affect eligibility of the property for exemption or classification under the Machinery Act.

Definitions: *Educational purpose, scientific purpose, literary purpose, charitable purpose*

Application procedure: One-time

Relief granted: Exempt

Elderly or Disabled Individuals' Residential Property

Citation: G.S. 105-277.1 (Homestead Exclusion)

Qualifying property: The greater of $25,000 (beginning in 2008) or 50 percent of the appraised value of residential real property or a manufactured home

Qualified owner: North Carolina resident individual either sixty-five years of age or older or totally and permanent disabled who meets the income limit. For 2008, the income limit is $25,000. For future years, the income limit will be adjusted by the same cost-of-living adjustment made to Social Security benefits for the preceding calendar year, rounded to the nearest $100.

Qualifying use: Occupied by owner as permanent residence

Definitions: *Owner, income, permanent residence, totally and permanently disabled*

Special provisions: Makes special provision for (1) temporary absence because of illness, (2) computing disposable income for married individuals living with spouse,(3) limiting to $25,000 or 50 percent of appraised value the total exclusion applicable to any one residence.

Application procedure: One-time application. Special notice and application form to be printed on abstract or furnished separately. Disabled applicants required to furnish medical certification at time of first application. Special application deadline of June 1 for eligibility in the upcoming tax year.

Citation: G.S. 105-277.1B (Circuit Breaker) (effective for 2009 and subsequent years)

Qualifying property: Residential real property or a manufactured home

Qualified owner: North Carolina resident individual either sixty-five years of age or older or totally and permanent disabled whose income is no more than 150 percent of the income eligibility limit for the homestead exclusion. If owned by two or more persons who are not married, all of the owners must qualify and must elect circuit breaker.

Qualifying use: Occupied by owner as permanent residence for at least five years

Special provisions: Makes special provision for temporary absence because of illness

Application procedure: Annual application. Special notice and application form to be printed on abstract or furnished separately. Disabled applicants required to furnish medical certification at time of first application. Special application deadline of June 1 for eligibility in the upcoming tax year.

Relief granted: Deferral of a portion of property taxes assessed on permanent residence to extent taxes exceed 4 percent of income if total income is at or below the income eligibility limit for the homestead exclusion, or 5 percent of the owner's income if the income is over, but no more than 150 percent of, the income eligibility limit for the homestead exclusion. Deferred taxes for three previous years due upon disqualifying event (which occurs when the property is transferred, the owner dies, or the property is no longer used as the owner's permanent residence) and payable within nine months. Gaps in deferral do not trigger an obligation to pay deferred taxes, but deferred taxes are carried forward until a disqualifying event occurs.

Citation: G.S. 105-277.1C (Disabled Veterans' Exclusion) (effective for 2009 and subsequent years)

Qualifying property: First $45,000 in assessed value of permanent residence

Qualified owner: Honorably discharged disabled veteran who receives benefits under 38 U.S.C. § 2101 or has a veteran's disability certification, or the unmarried surviving spouse of such a veteran

Qualifying use: Owned and used as a residence

Special provisions: Makes special provision for temporary absence because of illness. Provides for claiming of exclusion by co-owners of residences.

Application procedure: One-time
Relief granted: First $45,000 in assessed value is exempt

Farm Products Held by Cooperatives

Citation: G.S. 105-277.01
Qualifying property: Farm products (including crops but excluding poultry and other livestock) held by or for qualified owner
Qualified owner: Cooperative stabilization or marketing association or corporation
Qualifying use: Delivered, conveyed, or assigned to qualified owner by original producer for purposes of sale
Application procedure: Annual
Relief granted: To be assessed at appraised value less amount of any unpaid loan or advance made or granted thereon by the United States government or agency thereof or by a cooperative stabilization or marketing association or corporation

Federal Government Property

Citation: G.S. 105-278.1(a)
Qualifying property: Real and personal property owned by qualified owner
Qualified owner: United States of America and all departments, institutions, and agencies thereof
Qualifying use: No restrictions
Special provisions: Only federally owned property not subject to state and local taxes "by virtue of federal law" included in the class
Application procedure: None required
Relief granted: Exempt

Fertilizer

Citation: G.S. 105-277(d)
Qualifying property: Fertilizer and fertilizer materials
Qualified owner: Any person, firm, association, or corporation owing debt to another as principal debtor for purchase of qualifying property
Qualifying use: Held for qualified owner's own use in agriculture during current year

Application procedure: Annual
Relief granted: Amount of bona fide indebtedness incurred by qualified owner in purchase of qualifying property deducted from appraised value

Flight Equipment of Air Couriers

Citation: G.S. 105-275(24a)
Qualifying property: Aircraft owned by or leased to an interstate air courier and apportioned under G.S. 105-227 to the owner's hub in North Carolina
Qualified owner: An air courier with a hub in North Carolina that meets all of the following criteria:

1. The hub has allocated to it under G.S. 105-338 more than 60 percent of the aircraft value apportioned to North Carolina
2. The primary function of the hub is to sort and distribute letters and packages received from multiple consolidation locations
3. The courier's primary function at the hub is not to consolidate letters and packages and deliver them to another airport for sorting and distribution

Qualifying use: Used in the air courier's operations in North Carolina
Application procedure: Annual
Relief granted: Exempt

Fraternal and Civic Orders

Citation: G.S. 105-275(19)
Qualifying property: Real and personal property belonging to a qualified owner and additional adjacent real property necessary for the convenient, normal use of buildings on qualified property
Qualified owner: Loyal Order of Moose, Benevolent and Protective Order of Elks, Knights of Pythias, Odd Fellows, Woodmen of the World, and similar fraternal and civic orders and organizations (other than social fraternities and sororities and similar college, university, or high school organizations) operated for nonprofit benevolent, patriotic, historical, charitable, or civic purposes
Qualifying use: Exclusively for meeting or lodge purposes by qualified owner; incidental use for other purposes does not defeat exemption; exemption

prorated upon partial use for nonexempt purposes. G.S. 14-309.7(d) provides that conduct of bingo with a license does not affect eligibility of the property for exemption or classification under the Machinery Act
Application procedure: One-time
Relief granted: Exempt

Global Transpark Authority Property

Citation: G.S. 63A-5
Qualifying property: Property owned by the authority
Qualified owner: North Carolina Global Transpark Authority
Qualifying use: None required
Application procedure: None required
Relief granted: Exempt

Goodwill Industries

Citation: G.S. 105-275(20)
Qualifying property: Real and personal property belonging to qualified owner
Qualified owner: Goodwill Industries and other charitable organizations organized for training and rehabilitation of disabled persons
Qualifying use: Exclusively for training and rehabilitation, including commercial activities directly related to such training and rehabilitation
Application procedure: One-time
Relief granted: Exempt

Hazardous Waste Management Commission

Citation: G.S. 105-275(38)
Qualifying property: All real and personal property belonging to the qualified owner
Qualified owner: North Carolina Hazardous Waste Management Authority
Qualifying use: None specified
Application procedure: One-time
Relief granted: Exempt

Health Care Facilities Financed by Medical Care Commission

Citation: G.S. 131A-21
Qualifying property: Health care facilities financed by bonds or notes issued by the North Carolina Medical Care Commission
Qualified owner: None specified
Qualifying use: None specified
Application procedure: One-time
Relief granted: Exemption of the lesser of the original principal amount of the bonds or notes or the assessed value of the facility. Exemption applies only to that portion of the facility financed by Medical Care Commission bonds.

Heavy Equipment Rental

Citation: G.S. 105-275(42a) (effective for 2009 and subsequent years)
Qualifying property: Heavy equipment on which a gross receipts tax may be imposed under G.S. 153A-156.1 and G.S. 160A-215.2, which permit counties and cities to tax gross receipts from the short-term lease or rental of heavy equipment by a person whose principal business is the short-term lease or rental of heavy equipment at retail
Qualified owner: Person whose principal business is the short-term lease or rental of heavy equipment at retail
Qualifying use: None specified
Application procedure: None required
Relief granted: Exempt

Historic Landmark Sites

Citation: G.S. 105-275(29a)
Qualifying property: Land within an historic district
Qualified owner: A nonprofit corporation organized for historic preservation purposes
Qualifying use: Held by owner for use as future site for an historic structure to be moved to the site from another location
Special provisions: Taxes that would have been otherwise due on the property are carried forward as deferred taxes for up to five years; if property becomes ineligible, deferred taxes for current and prior five years become due.

Application procedure: Annual
Relief granted: Exclusion from the tax base for up to five years pending moving of an historic structure to the site

Historic Preservation Property

Citation: G.S. 105-275(29)
Qualifying property: Real property and easements
Qualified owner: Any nonprofit historical association or institution or any nonprofit corporation organized for historic preservation purposes
Qualifying use: Exclusively held and used for nonprofit historic preservation purposes or exclusively held for sale under an historic preservation agreement prepared and recorded pursuant to the Conservation and Historic Preservation Agreements Act (G.S. Ch. 121, Art. 4)
Application procedure: Annual
Relief granted: Exempt

Historic Property

Citation: G.S. 105-278
Qualifying property: Real property designated as an historic structure or site by a local ordinance adopted pursuant to G.S. 160A-399.4 or as an historic landmark by a local ordinance adopted pursuant to G.S. 160A-400.6
Qualified owner: None specified
Qualifying use: None specified
Application procedure: One-time
Relief granted: Assessment at 50 percent of appraised value. Taxes due under full-value assessment are computed but deferred while property remains eligible. Upon losing eligibility for reason other than damage or destruction by fire or other natural disaster, deferred taxes for three prior years (including interest) become due and payable.

Homeowners Association Property

Citation: G.S. 105-277.8
Qualifying property: Any real and personal property

Qualified owner: Any nonprofit homeowners association, as defined by Section 528(c) of the Internal Revenue Code

Qualifying use: Use of the property meets all of the following criteria:

1. All property owned by the association is held for the use, benefit, and enjoyment of all its members equally
2. Each member has an irrevocable right to use and enjoy, on an equal basis, all of the association's property
3. Each such right is appurtenant to taxable real property owned by a member of the association

Application procedure: One-time

Relief granted: Value of the property is to be included in appraisals of property owned by members of the association and not assessed to the association; the assessor may allocate the value of the property among the association's members on any fair and reasonable basis

Hospital Authority Property

Citation: G.S. 131E-28

Qualifying property: Hospital authority property used for public purposes

Qualified owner: Hospital authority

Qualifying use: Public purpose

Application procedure: None required

Relief granted: Exemption from all local and municipal taxes

Hospitals, Charitable

Citation: G.S. 105-278.8

Qualifying property: Real and personal property held for or owned by qualified owner

Qualified owner: Hospital organized and operated as a nonstock, nonprofit, charitable institution (without profit to members or their successors)

Qualifying use: Actually and exclusively used for charitable hospital purposes; exemption prorated upon partial use for nonexempt purpose

Definitions: *Charitable hospital purpose*

Special provisions: Fact that qualifying hospital charges patients who are able to pay for services rendered does not defeat exemption.

Application procedure: One-time
Relief granted: Exempt

Housing Authority Property

Citation: G.S. 157-26
Qualifying property: Property owned by a housing authority and bonds and other obligations issued by an authority or its corporate agent
Qualified owner: Housing authority
Qualifying Use: None specified
Application procedure: None required
Relief granted: Exempt

Imported into Foreign Trade Zone

Citation: G.S. 105-275(23)
Qualifying property: Tangible personal property imported from outside the United States and held in a foreign trade zone
Qualified owner: None specified
Qualifying use: Held for purpose of sale, manufacture, processing, assembly, grading, cleaning, mixing, or display
Application procedure: Annual
Relief granted: Exempt

Imported through a North Carolina Seaport Terminal

Citation: G.S. 105-275(2)
Qualifying property: Tangible personal property imported from a foreign country through a North Carolina seaport terminal
Qualified owner: None specified
Qualifying use: Stored at the North Carolina seaport terminal through which imported for not more than twelve months following importation
Application procedure: Annual
Relief granted: Exempt

Industrial and Pollution Control Facilities

Citation: G.S. 159C-14
Qualifying property: Any project or property owned by a county industrial facility and pollution control financing authority
Qualified owner: A county industrial facilities and pollution control financing authority
Qualifying use: None specified
Application procedure: None required
Relief granted: Exempt

Intangible Personal Property

Citation: G.S. 105-275(31)
Qualifying property: Intangible personal property other than leasehold interest in exempt real property
Qualified owner: None specified
Qualifying use: None specified
Application procedure: None required
Relief granted: Exempt

Inventory of Contractors

Citation: G.S. 105-275(32a)
Qualifying property: Inventories, as defined in G.S. 105-273(8a)
Qualified owner: Contractors, as defined in G.S. 105-273(5a)
Qualifying use: None specified
Application procedure: None required
Relief granted: Exempt

Inventory of Manufacturers

Citation: G.S. 105-275(33)
Qualifying property: Inventories, as defined in G.S. 105-273(8a)
Qualified owner: Merchants, manufacturers, and contractors, as defined in G.S. 105-273
Qualifying use: None specified
Application procedure: None required
Relief granted: Exempt

Inventory of Retail and Wholesale Merchants

Citation: G.S. 105-275(34)
Qualifying property: Inventories, as defined in G.S. 105-273(8a)
Qualified owner: Retail merchants, as defined in G.S. 105-273(13a), and wholesale merchants, as defined in G.S. 105-273(19)
Qualifying use: None specified
Application procedure: None required
Relief granted: Exempt

Leased to Local Governments

Citation: G.S. 105-275(39)
Qualifying property: All real and personal property belonging to qualified owner that (1) is leased to a unit of local government and (2) meets the qualifying use test
Qualified owner: A nonprofit corporation organized upon the request of a unit of local government for the sole purpose of financing projects for public use
Qualifying use: Used wholly or partially for a public purpose by the lessee unit of local government
Special provisions: Proration required if only part of the property is used for public purposes. Exclusion does not apply if any dividends or other distributions are paid to any members, officers, or directors of the owning corporation.
Application procedure: One-time
Relief granted: Exempt

Leased School Facilities

Citation: G.S. 105-275(43)
Qualifying property: Real and tangible personal property subject to a capital lease under G.S. 115C-531, which permits local boards of education to enter into capital leases of real or personal property for use as school buildings or facilities
Qualified owner: None specified
Qualifying use: None specified
Application procedure: Annual
Relief granted: Exempt

Leasehold Interest in Exempt Property Used for Affordable Housing

Citation: G.S. 105-275(31e)

Qualifying property: Leasehold interest in real property exempt under G.S. 105-278.1 and used to provide affordable housing for employees of the unit of local government that owns the property

Qualified owner: None specified

Qualifying use: Affordable housing for employees of the unit of government that owns the property

Application procedure: One-time

Relief granted: Exempt

Low-Income Housing

Citation: G.S. 105-277.15 (effective for 2009 and subsequent years)

Qualifying property: A North Carolina low-income housing development to which the North Carolina Housing Finance Agency allocated a federal tax credit

Qualified owner: None specified

Qualifying use: Low-income housing

Application procedure: None required

Relief granted: Requires assessor to use the income approach to appraise property and to consider rent restrictions in determining income. Prohibits the assessor from considering income tax credits in determining income.

Masonic Orders

Citation: G.S. 105-275(18)

Qualifying property: Real and personal property belonging to a qualified owner and additional adjacent real property necessary for the convenient, normal use of buildings on qualified property

Qualified owner: Grand Lodge of Ancient Free and Accepted Masons of North Carolina; Price Hall Masonic Grand Lodge of North Carolina; subordinate lodges and appendant bodies including Ancient and Arabic Order Nobles of the Mystic Shrine and Ancient Egyptian Order Nobles of the Mystic Shrine

Qualifying use: Exclusively for meeting or lodge purposes by qualifying owner; incidental use for other purposes does not defeat exemption; exemption prorated upon partial use for nonexempt purpose. G.S. 14-309.7(d) provides that conduct of bingo or raffles on property belonging to an organization eligible for a bingo license does not affect eligibility of the property for exemption or classification under the Machinery Act.
Application procedure: One-time
Relief granted: Exempt

Motor Vehicle Chassis

Citation: G.S. 105-275(14)
Qualifying property: Motor vehicle chassis belonging to qualified owner
Qualified owner: Any nonresident individual or corporation
Qualifying use: Temporarily in North Carolina for purpose of having body mounted thereon
Application procedure: Annual
Relief granted: Exempt

Non-Business Personal Property

Citation: G.S. 105-275(16)
Qualifying property: Personal property other than motor vehicles, watercraft, motors for watercraft, or aircraft
Qualified owner: Individual persons
Qualifying use: Personal use and not otherwise used in connection with a business, trade, or profession for the production of income
Application procedure: None required
Relief granted: Exempt

Nuclear Materials

Citation: G.S. 105-275(6)
Qualifying property: Special nuclear fuels, excluding source materials
Qualified owner: None specified
Qualifying use: Held by the manufacturer or processor of the materials (whether or not the owner) for the purpose of manufacture, processing, or delivery, but *not* for the use of the materials as fuel

Definitions: *Special nuclear materials, source materials*
Special provisions: Property may become disqualified if the manufacturer fails to observe applicable health and safety standards and procedures.
Application procedure: Annual
Relief granted: Exempt

Pollution Abatement Property

Citation: G.S. 105-275(8)a
Qualifying property: Category 1: any real or personal property; Category 2: waste lagoons and facilities
Qualified owner: Category 1: any person, firm, or corporation; Category 2: public or private utilities
Qualifying use: Category 1: property used or to be used exclusively for air cleaning or waste disposal, or to abate, reduce, or prevent the pollution of air or water; Category 2: facilities built and installed primarily to provide sewer service to areas that are predominantly residential in character or lie outside a territory that already has sewer service
Special provisions: Contingent on a certificate from the Environmental Management Commission (EMC) or a certified local air pollution control program that:

1. The property has been or will be constructed
2. The property complies with EMC requirements
3. The property will operate under an EMC permit
4. The primary purpose of the property is pollution abatement

Real and personal property constituting an animal waste management system qualifies for exclusion only if EMC determines that the facility will:

1. Eliminate the discharge of animal waste to surface waters and groundwater through direct discharge, seepage, or runoff
2. Substantially eliminate atmospheric emissions of ammonia
3. Substantially eliminate odor detectable beyond the boundaries of the parcel or tract of land on which the farm is located
4. Substantially eliminate release of disease-transmitting vectors and airborne pathogens
5. Substantially eliminate nutrient and heavy metal contamination of soil and groundwater

Application procedure: One-time
Relief granted: Exempt

Poultry and Livestock

Citation: G.S. 105-275(37)
Qualifying property: Poultry, livestock, and feed
Qualified owner: None specified
Qualifying use: With respect to poultry and livestock, no restrictions. With respect to feed, must be used in production of poultry and livestock.
Application requirements: None required
Relief granted: Exempt

Precious Metals

Citation: G.S. 105-277.10
Qualifying property: Precious metals, including rhodium and platinum
Qualified owner: Manufacturer
Qualifying use: Held for use directly in manufacturing or processing
Special provisions: One-time application required; approved application covers after-acquired property as well.
Application procedure: One-time
Relief granted: Special appraisal instructions

Prescription Drug Samples

Citation: G.S. 105-275(44)
Qualifying property: Free samples of drugs that are required by federal law to be dispensed only by prescription
Qualified owner: Physicians and other medical practitioners
Qualifying use: Given to physicians and other medical practitioners to dispense at no charge
Application procedure: None required
Relief granted: Exempt

Protected Natural Areas

Citation: G.S. 105-275(12)
Qualifying property: Real property owned by qualified owner
Qualified owner: Nonprofit corporation or association
Qualifying use: Exclusively held and used by owner for educational and scientific purposes as a protected natural area
Definitions: *Protected natural area*
Application procedure: One-time
Relief granted: Exempt

Public Parks and Drives

Citation: G.S. 105-275(7)
Qualifying property: All real and personal property owned by qualified owner
Qualified owner: (1) Nonprofit corporation formed under G.S. Ch. 55A or (2) bona fide charitable organization
Qualifying use: Operated by owner or leased to another who would be a qualified owner and appropriated exclusively for public parks and drives
Application procedure: One-time
Relief granted: Exempt

Radioactive Waste Disposal Authority

Citation: G.S. 105-275(36)
Qualifying property: All real and personal property belonging to qualified owner
Qualified owner: North Carolina Low-Level Radioactive Waste Management Authority
Qualifying use: None specified.
Application procedure: One-time
Relief granted: Exempt

Recycling Facilities

Citation: G.S. 105-275(8)d.

Qualifying property: Any real or personal property located at or on land in the same county and reasonably near the plant site, including utility infrastructure and transportation infrastructure

Qualified owner: Any person, firm, or corporation that operates a manufacturing plant meeting the following criteria: (1) at least 75 percent of whose products are made of at least 50 percent post-consumer waste material measured by weight or volume; (2) at the time construction began, the facility was located in an enterprise tier one area as defined in G.S. 105-129.3; (3) the Secretary of Commerce has certified that by the end of the second year after construction begins, the owner will have invested at least $300 million in the facility and will have created at least 250 new full-time jobs at the facility; and (4) the jobs will meet the wage standard in effect pursuant to G.S. 105-129.4(b) as of the date construction begins.

Qualifying use: Used by a qualified owner (or if under construction, to be used) predominantly for recycling or resource recovering of or from solid waste in a recycling facility and used to perform business functions related to the recycling facility or to transport materials and products to or from the plant

Special provisions: The Department of Environment and Natural Resources must furnish a certificate to the county assessor stating that the department has found that the described property complies with the department's rules and that it has or will have as a purpose recycling or recourse recovery of or from solid waste.

Application procedure: One-time

Relief granted: Exempt

Recycling and Resource Recovery

Citation: G.S. 105-275(8)b.

Qualifying property: Any real and personal property used for qualifying use

Qualified owner: None specified

Qualifying use: Used or to be used exclusively for recycling or resource recovering of or from solid waste

Special provisions: Contingent on certificate of Department of Human Resources (DHR) that property has been or will be constructed, complies with regulations of DHR, and has as its primary purpose recycling or recourse recovering of or from solid waste

Application procedure: One-time
Relief granted: Exempt

Regional Sports Authority Property

Citation: G.S. 160A-479.14
Qualifying property: Real and personal property owned by the authority
Qualified owner: A regional sports authority
Qualifying use: None specified
Special provisions: If regional sports authority property is leased to a private party, the exemption does not apply to the value of the leasehold interest.
Application procedure: None required
Relief granted: Exempt

Religious Educational Assemblies

Citation: G.S. 105-278.5
Qualifying property: Buildings, the land they actually occupy, and additional adjacent land reasonably necessary for the convenient use of any such building, of a kind commonly employed in those activities naturally and property incident to the operation of a religious educational assembly such as the owner, and personal property
Qualified owner: Religious educational assembly, retreat, or similar organizations, no officer, shareholder, member, or employee of which or any other person entitled to receive pecuniary profit from owner's operations except reasonable compensation for services
Qualifying use: As to real property, wholly and exclusively used for religious worship or purposes of instruction in religious education; as to personal property, exclusively maintained and used in connection with qualifying real property; incidental use for other purposes does not defeat exemption; exemption prorated upon partial use for nonexempt purpose. G.S. 14-309.7(d) provides that conduct of bingo or raffles on property belonging to an organization eligible for a bingo license does not affect eligibility of the property for exemption or classification under the Machinery Act.
Application procedure: One-time
Relief granted: Exempt

Religious Property

Citation: G.S. 105-278.3

Qualifying property: Buildings, the land they actually occupy, and additional adjacent land reasonably necessary for the convenient use of any such building and personal property wholly owned by a qualified owner

Qualified owner: (1) A congregation, parish, mission, or similar local unit of a church or religious body or (2) a conference, association, presbytery, diocese, district, synod, or similar unit comprising local units of a church or religious body

Qualifying use:

1. Wholly and exclusively used by the owner for religious purposes, i.e.,
   A. Any purpose pertaining to practicing, teaching, and setting forth a religion
   B. Worship
   C. Activities that demonstrate and further the benefits and objectives of a given church or religious body
   D. As to qualified owners in category 2, above, maintenance of general or promotional office or headquarters
   E. Residences for clergy, rabbis, priests or nuns assigned to or serving a qualified owner but *specifically not including* maintenance of residences for other employees
   F. Residences for clergy on furlough or unassigned
2. Use of portion of otherwise qualifying property as residence for individual who
   A. Provides guardian, janitorial, or custodial services for the property *or*
   B. Oversees and supervises qualifying activities upon and in connection with the property
3. Parking, when the total revenue from such use does not exceed the portion of maintenance expenses reasonably estimated to be attributable to such use
4. Gratuitously occupied by or made available to an occupant or possessor other than the owner who uses the property wholly and exclusively for religious, charitable, or nonprofit educational, literary, scientific, or charitable purposes

5. Incidental use for other purposes does not defeat exemption; exemption prorated upon partial use for nonexempt purpose
6. G.S. 14-309.7(d) provides that conduct of bingo or raffles on property belonging to an organization eligible for a bingo license does not affect eligibility of the property for exemption or classification under the Machinery Act

Definitions: *Religious purpose, charitable purpose, educational purpose, literary purpose, cultural purpose, scientific purpose*
Application procedure: One-time
Relief granted: Exempt

Repaired Personal Property

Citation: G.S. 105-275(25)
Qualifying property: Tangible personal property shipped into North Carolina from another state or nation
Qualified owner: Any nonresident of North Carolina
Qualifying use: Held in North Carolina for the purpose of repair, alteration, maintenance, or servicing and eventual reshipment to the owner at a point outside North Carolina
Special provisions: Does not include raw materials, supplies, or goods in process of manufacture
Application procedure: Annual
Relief granted: Exempt

Roadway Corridors

Citation: G.S. 105-277.9
Qualifying property: Real property lying within a roadway corridor marked on an official map filed under G.S. Ch. 136, Art. 2E
Qualified owner: None specified
Qualifying use: No building or other structure located on the property and the property has not been subdivided since it was included in the corridor
Application procedure: Annual
Relief granted: Taxation at 20 percent of the rate applicable to property generally

Short-Term Rental Vehicles

Citation: G.S. 105-275(42)
Qualifying property: Vehicles offered at retail for short-term rental or lease
Qualified owner: Entities in the business of short-term vehicle rental
Qualifying use: None specified
Application procedure: None required
Relief granted: Exempt

Solar Energy Electric Systems

Citation: G.S. 105-275(45)
Qualifying property: 80 percent of the appraised value of a solar energy electric system, which includes all equipment used directly and exclusively to convert solar energy to electricity
Qualified owner: None specified
Qualifying use: Conversion of solar energy to electricity
Application procedure: None required
Relief granted: Exempt

Solar Energy Systems

Citation: G.S. 105-277(g)
Qualifying property: Buildings equipped with a solar energy heating or cooling system, or both
Qualified owner: None specified
Definitions: *System*
Application procedure: None required
Relief granted: Assessed in accordance with county's schedules of value for buildings equipped with conventional heating or cooling systems, with no additional value assigned for the difference in cost between solar energy heating or cooling system and conventional system typically found in the county

Standing Timber

Citation: G.S. 105-275(15)
Qualifying property: Standing timber, pulpwood, seedlings, saplings, and other forest growth
Qualified owner: Any person, firm, or corporation
Application procedure: None required
Relief granted: Exempt

State and Local Government Property

Citation: G.S. 105-278.1(b)
Qualifying property: All real and personal property of qualified owner
Qualified owner:

1. State of North Carolina
2. A county of this state
3. A municipality of this state

Qualifying use: No restrictions
Application procedure: None required
Relief granted: Exempt

Turnpike Authority Property

Citation: G.S. 136-89.185
Qualifying property: Turnpike authority property
Qualified owner: Turnpike Authority
Qualifying use: None required.
Application procedure: None required
Relief granted: Exempt

Use-Value Appraisal

Citation: G.S. 105-277.2–277.4.
Qualifying property:

1. Agricultural land: farm units consisting of one or more tracts, one of which has at least ten acres of land in actual production, including woodland and wasteland that is part of the unit and land under improvements, but not including buildings. Farms for aquatic species must consist of five acres in actual production or must produce 20,000 pounds of aquatic species for commercial sale annually.
2. Horticultural land: horticultural units consisting of one or more tracts, one of which has at least five acres of land in actual production, including woodland and wasteland that is part of the unit and land under improvements, but not including buildings.
3. Forestland: forestland consisting of one or more tracts, one of which consists of at least twenty acres in actual production, including wasteland that is part of the unit, excluding land that is part of a farm (or horticultural) unit.

Qualified owner: An individual or business entity falling within one or more of the following categories:

1. Individuals who meet one of the following criteria:
   A. The owner resides on the property
   B. The owner has owned the property for the previous four years as of January 1 of the first year for which eligibility is claimed
   C. The owner acquired the property from a relative, and the property has been owned by the current owner or a relative for the previous four years as of January 1 of the first year for which eligibility is claimed
   D. The owner expands an existing unit by acquiring land not appraised at present-use value but used for the same purpose and eligible for appraisal at its present-use value as other land already owned by the new owner and classified for present-use taxation
   E. The owner acquires land already classified as agricultural, horticultural, or forestland; continues to use it for the classified purpose; and accepts liability for any deferred taxes

2. A business entity that meets all of the following criteria:

A. The principal business of the entity is farming agricultural land, horticultural land, or forestland

B. All of the members of the business entity are, directly or indirectly,

(1) Individuals who are actively engaged in the business of the entity

or

(2) Relatives of an individual who is actively engaged in the business

C. The property for which eligibility is sought either

(1) Has been owned for the four previous years by the business itself or by one or more of its members, or

(2) Was eligible for use-value appraisal in the hands of the former owner at the time it was acquired by the entity and the entity acquires the land, continues to use it for the same purpose, and accepts liability for any deferred taxes, or

(3) The entity expands an existing unit by acquiring land not appraised at present-use value but used for the same purpose and eligible for appraisal at its present-use value as other land already owned by the entity and classified for present-use taxation

3. A trust that meets all of the following criteria:

A. The trust was created by an individual who transferred land to the trust and the beneficiaries are, directly or indirectly, the creator of the trust or a relative of the creator

B. The property for which eligibility is sought

(1) Has been owned for the four previous years by the trust or one or more of its creators, or

(2) Was eligible for use-value appraisal in the hands of the former owner at the time it was acquired by the trust and the trust acquires the land, continues to use it for the same purpose, and accepts liability for any deferred taxes, or

(3) The trust expands an existing unit by acquiring land not appraised at present-use value but used for the same purpose and eligible for appraisal at its present-use value as other land already owned by the trust and classified for present-use taxation

4. A testamentary trust that meets all of the following criteria:

A. The trust was created by an individual who transferred land qualified in that individual's hands for classification under G.S. 105-277.3, and

(1) The creator of the trust had no relatives at the time of death, and

(2) The trust income (less administrative expenses) is used exclusively for educational, scientific, literary, cultural, charitable, or religious purposes

B. The property for which eligibility is sought has been owned for the four previous years by the trust or one or more of its creators

5. Tenants in Common, if each tenant would qualify as an owner if that tenant were the sole owner

Qualifying use:

1. Agricultural units meeting all of the following criteria:
   A. Actively engaged in commercial production of growing crops, plants, or animals or used as farms for aquatic species
   B. Gross income from sale of agricultural products produced thereon (including government payments for soil conservation, land retirement, or tobacco buyout payments) averaging $1,000 per year over the three prior years
   C. Managed under a program of production designed to obtain the greatest net return from the land consistent with conservation and long-term development (sound management program)
2. Horticultural units meeting all of the following criteria:
   A. Actively engaged in commercial production of fruits, vegetables, or nursery or floral products
   B. Gross income from sale of horticultural products produced thereon (including government payments for soil conservation or land retirement) averaging $1,000 per year over the three prior years
   C. Managed under a program of production designed to obtain the greatest net return from the land consistent with conservation and long-term development (sound management program)
3. Forestland meeting all of the following criteria:
   A. Actively engaged in the commercial growing of trees
   B. Managed under a program of production designed to obtain the greatest net return from the land consistent with conservation and long-term development (sound management program)

Definitions:

1. *Relative* is defined to include the following persons:
   A. A spouse or a spouse's lineal ancestor or descendant
   B. A lineal ancestor or descendant

C. A brother or sister or the lineal descendant of a brother or sister (including stepbrothers and stepsisters)
D. An aunt or an uncle (but not lineal descendants of aunts or uncles)
E. A spouse of any of the above (but not lineal descendants of spouses other than the owner's own spouse)

2. *Business entity* is defined to include corporations, general partnerships, limited partnerships, and limited liability companies.

Special Provisions:

1. Enrollment in federal Conservation Reserve Program (CRP) does not disqualify otherwise eligible land solely on grounds that land is not in actual production; income from CRP may be used in meeting income requirements; CRP land is to be treated as agricultural land if planted in vegetation other than trees or as forestland if planted in trees; disqualification of CRP land due to failure to meet income requirement does not trigger deferred tax provisions.
2. Property appraised at present-use value is not disqualified based on failure to meet actual production or income requirements if an enforceable conservation easement that would qualify for the conservation tax credit is placed on the property. Subsequent transfer of such property does not eliminate present-use appraisal so long as enforceable conservation easement remains in effect.
3. Special rules apply to gross income requirement applicable to horticultural land used to produce Christmas trees.
4. A special rule applies to agricultural land out of production due to Poult Entertis Mortality Syndrome among turkeys (G.S. 105-277.3(e))

Application procedure: One-time application is required. Assessor is required to audit one-eighth of eligible units annually to verify continued eligibility. Eligibility review is based on average of preceding three years' data. If property is transferred, the new owner must apply for use-value appraisal within sixty days of the transfer.

Relief granted: Qualifying property is assessed for taxation at use-value rather than market value. The difference between taxes due under market value appraisal and those assessed under use value appraisal is deferred so long as the property remains eligible for use-value appraisal. When eligibility is lost, deferred taxes for the three prior years (including interest) become due and payable and taxes for the current year are due on the market-value appraisal.

Deferred taxes are extinguished when use-value land is conveyed by gift to (1) a governmental entity or (2) nonprofit corporation qualified for exclusion of its real property under G.S. 105-275(12) (protected natural areas) or G.S. 105-275(29) (historic preservation).

Veterans Organizations

Citation: G.S. 105-275(17)
Qualifying property: Real and personal property belonging to a qualified owner and additional adjacent real property necessary for the convenient, normal use of buildings on qualified property
Qualified owner:

1. American Legion, Veterans of Foreign Wars, Disabled American Veterans
2. Similar veterans organizations
   A. Chartered by Congress or
   B. Organized and operated on a statewide or nationwide basis
3. Any post or local organization of a qualifying veterans organization

Qualifying use: Exclusively for meeting or lodge purposes by the qualified owner; incidental use for other purposes does not defeat exemption; exemption prorated upon partial use for nonexempt purpose. G.S. 14-309.7(d) provides that conduct of bingo or raffles on property belonging to an organization eligible for a bingo license does not affect eligibility of the property for exemption or classification under the Machinery Act.
Application procedure: One-time
Relief granted: Exempt

Water Companies, Private

Citation: G.S. 105-277(h)
Qualifying property: All real and personal property of qualified owner
Qualified owner: Privately owned water companies
Qualifying use: None specified
Application procedure: One-time
Relief granted: In appraising qualified property, the portion of the capital investment of the company represented by contributions in aid of construction and acquisition adjustment shall be excluded.

Water and Sewer Associations, Nonprofit

Citation: G.S. 105-275(3)
Qualifying property: All real and personal property owned by qualified owner
Qualified owner: Nonprofit water or nonprofit sewer associations or corporations
Qualifying use: None specified
Application procedure: One-time
Relief granted: Exempt

Wildlife Conservation Land

Citation: G.S. 105-277.15 (effective for 2010 and subsequent years)
Qualifying property: Twenty contiguous acres managed under a written wildlife habitat conservation agreement with the North Carolina Wildlife Resources Commission that is in effect as of January 1 of the year for which the benefit of taxation based upon present-use value is claimed
Qualified owner: Individual, family business entity, or family trust and, with limited exceptions, must have been owned by the same owner for the previous five years
Definitions: Incorporates definitions of *business entity*, *member*, and *relative* from G.S. 105-277.2.
Special provisions: No more than one hundred acres of an owner's land in a county may be classified as wildlife conservation property eligible for use-value taxation under this section.

Application procedure: One-time application is required. If property is transferred, the new owner must apply for use-value appraisal within sixty days of the transfer.

Relief granted: Taxed upon present-use value as agricultural property rather than market value. Difference carried forward as deferred taxes. Upon disqualification, taxes for fiscal year that opens in calendar year in which disqualification occurred are assessed at market value. Deferred taxes for three previous years are due.

Working Waterfront Property

Citation: G.S. 105-277.14 (effective for 2009 and subsequent years)

Qualifying property: (1) A pier that extends into coastal fishing waters and that can be accessed only by those who pay a fee or (2) real property that is adjacent to coastal fishing waters and that is primarily used for a commercial fishing operation or fish processing, including adjacent land being improved and used for one of these purposes, and land necessary for convenient use of property

Qualified owner: None specified

Qualifying use: Average gross income for past three years of $1,000

Application procedure: One-time application is required. Must file during listing period or within thirty days of notice of a change in value.

Relief granted: Taxed at present-use, rather than market, value. Difference carried forward as deferred taxes. Upon disqualification, taxes for fiscal year that opens in calendar year in which disqualification occurred are assessed at market value. Deferred taxes for three previous years are due.

Index

Page numbers in *italics* indicate tabulated material.

A

abstracts, 25, 41
  contents, 52–54
  filing, 59–61
  personal property, 41, 47, 52–54
  real property, property record cards for, 41, 42, 47, 52–54
  signatures, 53–54
actual versus effective rates of tax, 28–29
Address Confidentiality Program, 77
administration of property tax, 21–33
  amount of tax due per property, computing, 26
  appointment of officers, 21–22, 32n1–4
  calendar for, 24–27
  city tax collector, 21
  county tax assessor, 21–24
  Department of Revenue, 21–22
  Machinery Act provisions. *See* Machinery Act
  Property Tax Commission, 21–22
  rates of tax, setting, 27–30, *31*
affordable housing, leasehold interests in exempted real property used for, 256
agricultural property
  cooperatives, farm products held by, 247
  cotton dust emission control equipment, 241–42
  fertilizer, 247–48
  land assessed at present-use value. *See under* present-use value assessments
  poultry and livestock, 259

aircraft. *See also* motor vehicles
antique, 237
flight equipment of air couriers, 248
airline company property, 100–104, *105,* 109n79
American Indian lands, 174–76, 215n37–40
annexations, 26–27
antique motor vehicles, 158, 237
appeal and review, 113–43, 114–35
board of commissioners, post-adjournment changes by, 117–19
board of equalization and review proceedings, 26, 114–20, 137
Court of Appeals proceedings, 133–35
deadlines for, 25
discovery appeals, 69–70
exemptions and exclusions, 84–85n141, 113
failure to assess, back taxes later assessed following, 129–32
informal process, 114
motor vehicles, 151
nonreappraisal years, changes to value of real property in, 136–37
present-use value assessments, 203
by Property Tax Commission. *See under* Property Tax Commission
representation of parties, 139n24
settlement of appeals, 132–33
standard of review
Court of Appeals proceedings, 134–35
Property Tax Commission proceedings, 123–27
standing to appeal, 119–21, 138–39n15
applications for exemptions and exclusions, 194–97
annual application requirement, 197
appeals, 84–85n141, 113
calendar, 66–67, 197
late applications, 197
listing rules, 66–67
no application requirement, 194–95
notice as to decision regarding, 113
present-use value assessments, 202–3, 270
single application requirement, 195–96
applications for refunds and releases, 231

appraisal and assessment
- appealing. *See* appeal and review
- book value, 125–26
- calendar, 25, 91
  - motor vehicles, 106n9, 149, *150*
  - personal property, 91, 93, 98, 106n9
  - public service company property, 100
  - real property, 91, 92–95
- CAMA, 97
- cost approach, 96, 99
- failure to assess, back taxes later assessed following, 129–32
- income approach, 96, 99–100
- infrequent reassessment, bias associated with, 106n2
- Machinery Act requirements, 25, 43, 101, 136
- motor vehicles, 106n9, 149–51, *150*
- nonreappraisal years, changes to value of real property in, 29, 93, 136–37, 202
- notice of assessed value, 114
- obsolescence, as factor, 98, 107–8n50
- personal property, 98–100
- at present-use value rather than market value. *See* present-use value assessments
- public service company property (system property), 100–105, *105,* 109n74
- real property, 91, 92–95
- sales assessment ratios, 102–4
- sales comparison approach, 96, 99, 106n21
- schedule of values, standards, and rules, 96–98
- standards for valuation, 95–96, 98–100

appraisers, 23, 32n14
armed forces. *See* uniformed services
arts objects, 238
assessment. *See* appraisal and assessment
assessors, 21–24, 116, 227
associations, real property owned by, 44
athletic authorities, regional, 262
attorney-client privilege, documents falling within, 74
automobiles. *See* motor vehicles

B

bill and hold goods, 238
boards of county commissioners, 21, 24, 117–19
boards of equalization and review, county, 26, 114–20, 137
boats. *See* motor vehicles
book value, 125–26
brownfields improvements, 238
Budget and Fiscal Control Act, 27
building permits, review of, 56–57
burial property, exemption for, 176–77, 239
bus company property, 100–104, *105,* 109n79
business enterprises
  multicounty business reports, 55–56
  personal property associated with, situs of, 62–64, *65*
  personal property owned in connection with, 49–50
  present-use value assessments, eligibility for, 207–8, 209
  real property owned by or in connection with, 44
business factors in appraisal of public service company property, 101, 109n84

C

calendar
  abstracts, filing, 59–61
  administrative requirements, 24–27
  appraisal/reappraisal. *See under* appraisal and assessment
  boards of equalization and review, 114–15
  exemptions and exclusions, applications for, 66–67, 197
  listing period, 59–61
  motor vehicles. *See under* motor vehicles
  nonreappraisal years, changes to value of real property in, 136, 137
  timely deadlines, determining, 158
CAMA (computer assisted mass appraisal approach), 97
cargo containers, 239
cars. *See* motor vehicles
cemetery exemption, 176–77, 238
chain of title, 46–47
charitable organizations
  defined, 186–87, 239–40

exemption for. *See* subhead "qualifying property exemptions" under exemptions and exclusions

Christmas tree farms, 204, 206, 270

circuit breaker benefit, 191–92

cities and towns

- local government property, exemption from taxation, 168–70
- motor vehicle taxes, municipal, 151–54, 163n43
- separate city/town listings, 59, 83n99
- tax collector, city, 21

civic orders, property belonging to, 248–49. *See also* subhead "qualifying property exemptions" under exemptions and exclusions

Civil War, 4–5

classification of property for taxation, constitutional power of, 7, 9–10, 167–69

classified motor vehicles. *See* motor vehicles

clerical errors, refunds and releases due to, 228–30

collection of taxes

- enforced collection
  - motor vehicles, 155
  - stay during appeals, 133
- motor vehicles, 154–55
  - calendar, *152–53,* 154–55
  - enforced collection, 155
  - integration of registration and taxation process to improve, 159–61
- tax collectors, 21, 227

combined records, 26

commissioners, county boards of, 21, 24, 117–19

compromising discovered amounts, 69, 84n138

computer assisted mass appraisal approach (CAMA), 97

computer software, 40–41, 240

confidential information in public records, 73–77

conservation areas

- historic properties, 250–51
- present-use value assessment of, 203, 207, 211–13, 272–73
- protected natural areas, 260
- public parks and drives, 260

consolidated registration of multiple motor vehicles, 159

Constitution, state. *See* North Carolina Constitution

continuing care retirement homes, 240–41
contractor inventory, 254
cooperatives, farm products held by, 247
corporate powers of counties, 143n123
corporations, real property owned by, 44. *See also* business enterprises
cost approach to appraisal, 96, 99
cotton dust emission control equipment, 241–42
county boards of commissioners, 21, 24, 117–19
county boards of equalization and review, 26, 114–20, 137
county property, exemption from taxation, 168–70
county tax assessors, 21–24, 116, 227
Court of Appeals, 133–35
covenants of title, seisen, and warranty, 80n37
credits against motor vehicle taxes, 157–58

D

deadlines. *See* calendar
decedents, property of
  business enterprises, personal property owned in connection with, 50
  real property with deceased last known owner, listing, 44–45
  situs, 65
deeds of trust, real property subject to, 44
deeds, register of, 56
deferred tax provisions, present-use value assessments, 200, 210–11, 270–71
Department of Revenue
  administrative duties, 21–22
  courses and examinations for officials, 23–24
  listing information, obtaining, 55
development rights, severable, 242
development value exemptions. *See* present-use value assessments
disabled persons. *See* elderly and disabled
discovery of unlisted property, 67–70
  compromising discovered amounts, 69, 84n138
  exemptions and exclusions, property entitled to, 198
  immaterial irregularity provisions and, 131–32
  sample discovery calculation, *69*
  situs issues, 65–66

Division of Motor Vehicles (DMV). *See* motor vehicles
DMV (Division of Motor Vehicles). *See* motor vehicles
dominant tenement, 43
Driver's Privacy Protection Act (DPPA), 76–77
drugs, prescription, samples of, 259
due dates. *See* calendar
due process requirements, listing property for taxation, 57–58

E

easements, 43
Eastern Cherokee Indian Reservation (Qualla Boundary), 174–76, 215n37–40
education
  definition of educational institution, 218–19n93–95, 243–44
  exemption for educational property. *See* subhead "qualifying property exemptions" under exemptions and exclusions
  leased school facilities, 255
  religious educational assemblies, 262
  state financing of, 5, 7
effective versus actual rates of tax, 28–29
elderly and disabled, 245–47
  circuit breaker benefit, 191–92
  continuing care retirement homes, 240–41
  definition of disabled, 219n101
  disabled veterans
    motor vehicles, specially equipped, 242
    real property exclusion, 193
  homestead exclusion for, 188–91
electricity company property, appraisal and assessment of, 100–104, *105*
embedded software, 41
enforced collection
  motor vehicles, 155
  stay during appeals, 133
environmental issues
  brownfields improvements, 238
  conservation. *See* conservation areas
  development value exemptions. *See* present-use value assessments

forestlands. *See* forestlands
Hazardous Waste Management Commission, 249
pollution abatement property, 258–59
pollution control facilities, 254
equalization and review, county boards of, 26, 114–20, 137
estates in land, 42
exclusive use requirement, qualifying property exemptions, 177–82, 217n71, 218n87
exemptions and exclusions, 167–223
annual review of exempt or excluded property, 199–200
applications for. *See* applications for exemptions and exclusions
circuit breaker benefit, 191–92
constitutional power of, 7, 9–10, 167–69
deadlines for claiming, 25
disabled persons. *See* elderly and disabled
discovery of unlisted property entitled to, 198
elderly persons. *See* elderly and disabled
as exception rather than rule, 11
exclusion clause, 15n14, 167, 187–88
exemptions clause, 7, 9–10, 167–68
government property
Eastern Cherokee Indian Reservation (Qualla Boundary), 174–76, 215n37–40
federal property and property on federal lands, 170–76, *175*, 214–15n42, 247
power of local taxation over specified federal lands, 174–76, *175*
state and local government property, 168–70, 266
homestead exclusion, 188–91
leasehold interests in exempted real property, 40, 79n12, 83n100, 256
motor vehicles. *See under* motor vehicles
notice and appeal of decisions regarding, 113
present-use value. *See* present-use value assessments
qualifying property exemptions, 176–87, 244–45
burial property, 176–77, 239
charitable organizations, defining, 186–87, 239–40
educational institutions defined for purposes of, 218–19n93–95, 243–44

exclusive use requirement, 177–82, 217n71, 218n87
land required to be adjacent to building, 183–84
nature of entity owning property, 185–86, 216n51
property gratuitously made available to another, 182–83
purpose or use, defining, 184–85
real and personal property included in, 177
religious property, 263–64
roster of exempt or excluded property, 199–200
software, 40, 240
specific types of excluded property, 237–73

F

Fair and Equitable Tobacco Reform Act of 2004, 206
farm property. *See* agricultural property
federal property and property on federal lands, 170–76, *175*, 214–15n42, 247
fee simple absolute interest in property, 80n23
fertilizer, 247–48
fiduciaries, situs of property of, 65
fiscal year basis of property tax calendar, 24–25
fixtures, 38, 79n5
foreign trade zones, property held in or imported into, 243, 253
forestlands
present-use value assessment of
defined, 205, 267
eligibility for assessment, 200, 203
qualifying use requirements, 269
sound management program, 206
standing timber, 266
4-R Act (Railroad Revitalization and Regulatory Reform Act of 1976), 104–5
fraternal orders, property belonging to, 248–49. *See also* subhead “qualifying property exemptions” under exemptions and exclusions

G

gas company property, appraisal and assessment of, 100–104, *105*
geographic information system (GIS) databases, 72–73

GIS (geographic information system) databases, 72–73
Global Transpark Authority, 249
Goodwill Industries, 249. *See also* subhead "qualifying property exemptions" under exemptions and exclusions
government property exempt from taxation
  Eastern Cherokee Indian Reservation (Qualla Boundary), 174–76, 215n37–40
  federal property and property on federal lands, 170–76, *175,* 214–15n42, 247
  power of local taxation over specified federal lands, 174–76, *175*
  state and local government property, 168–70, 266
gross income requirement, present-use value assessments, 204, 206–7, 269

H

Hazardous Waste Management Commission, 249
health care
  hospitals, 252–53
  Medical Care Commission, health care facilities financed by, 250
  prescription drug samples, 259
heavy equipment rentals, 250
historic properties, 250–51
historical background to property tax in North Carolina, 3, 4–8
homeowners association property, 251–52
homestead exclusion, 188–91
horticultural land, present-use value assessment of. *See under* present-use value assessments
hospitals, 252–53
housing
  affordable housing, leasehold interests in exempted real property used for, 256
  low-income, 256
  property of housing authority, 253

I

identifying information, confidentiality of, 75–76
Identity Theft Protection Act of 2005, 75, 86n189
illegal purposes, taxes imposed for, 230–31

illegal taxes, 230
imported items, 253
improvements
  brownfields improvements, 238
  defined, 38
  listing, 82n82
  separate ownership of, 45
in rem versus *in personam* taxes, 3
income
  appraisal, income approach to, 96, 99–100
  confidentiality of income or receipts of taxpayers, 73–74, 86n178
  gross income requirement, present-use value assessments, 204, 206–7, 269
  low-income elderly and disabled. *See* elderly and disabled
  low-income housing, 256
Indian lands, 174–76, 215n37–40
industrial facilities, 254
intangible personal property, 39–40, 61, 254
International Association of Assessing Officers, 106n15, 107n50
International Registration Plan (IRP) for motor vehicles, 161, 164n73
inventory items, 254–55
IRP (International Registration Plan) for motor vehicles, 161, 164n73

J

joint ownership. *See* tenancy ownership

L

land. *See* real property
leasehold interests in exempted real property, 40, 79n12, 83n100, 256
leases. *See* rentals
life estate, real property subject to, 45
listing property for taxation, 37–87
  abstracts. *See* abstracts
  additional information, obtaining, 54–57, 74
  calendar for, 25–26
  discovery. *See* discovery of unlisted property
  division of property into real and personal, 37–41

due process requirements, 57–58
exemptions and exclusions, applications for, 66–67, 84–85n141
failure to list, 81n47
improvements, 82n82
location of listing, 61–66
motor vehicles, 51, 147, 149–50, *150*
permanent listing system for real property, 25, 41, 42, 57, 67, 69, 82n82, 132
personal property, 47–52
procedures for, 41
public records. *See* public records
real property, 42–47
separate city/town listings, 59, 83n99
situs, 61–66, *65*
subpoena powers, 54–55
literary property exemption. *See* subhead "qualifying property exemptions" under exemptions and exclusions
livestock, 259
local governments. *See also* cities and towns, and headings at county
exemption of property from taxation, 168–70, 266
power of taxation over specified federal lands, 174–76, *175*
property tax in North Carolina under control of, 6
location of property for tax purposes. *See* situs
low-income elderly and disabled. *See* elderly and disabled
low-income housing, 256
Low-Level Radioactive Waste Management Authority, 260

M

Machinery Act, 11–12, 21
on appeal and review, 114, 123
appraisal and assessment rules, 25, 43, 101, 136
on calendar deadlines, 25, 158
on county tax assessors, 21, 32n4
division of property into real and personal, 37–41
exemptions and exclusions. *See* exemptions and exclusions
immaterial irregularities rule, 127–28, 132
listing requirements. *See* listing of property for taxation

ownership of personal property under, 49
on public records, 71
recordkeeping requirements, 26
situs requirements, 61
uniform rule requirement, 10
manufactured homes
as fixtures, 38
as real property, 11, 39
relationship to mobile homes, 79n8
manufacturer inventory, 254
Masonic orders, property belonging to, 256–57. *See also* subhead "qualifying property exemptions" under exemptions and exclusions
medical property
health care facilities financed by Medical Care Commission, 250
hospitals, 252–53
prescription drug samples, 259
mileage factors in appraisal of public service company property, 101, 109n84
military. *See* uniformed services
mills, 33n26
mobile homes, 79n8. *See also* manufactured homes
mortgages, real property subject to, 44
motor freight carrier company property, 100–104, *105,* 109n79
motor vehicles, 147–64
antiques, 158, 237
appeal and review procedures, 151
appraisal and assessment, 106n9, 149–51, *150*
calendar
appraisal and assessment, 106n9, 149–51, *150, 152–53*
collection of taxes, *152–53,* 154–55
enforced collection, 155
listing, 149, *150*
registration and listing, 149, *150*
staggered versus annual systems, 149, *152–53,* 156, 163n50
tax year, 156–58
timely deadlines, determining, 158

collection of taxes, 154–55
calendar, *152–53,* 154–55
enforced collection, 155
integration of registration and taxation process to improve, 159–61
confidentiality of records pertaining to, 76–77
consolidated registration, 159
defined, 51, 148
enforced collection of taxes, 155
exemptions and exclusions, 154, 198–99
antiques, 158, 237
chassis temporarily in North Carolina to have body mounted, 257
disabled veterans, vehicles specially equipped for, 242
short-term rental vehicles, 265
integration of registration and taxation process, 159–61
IRP, 161, 164n73
listing, 51, 147, 149–50, *150*
municipal taxes, 151–54, 163n43
ownership issues, 51, 150
prorated taxes, credits, refunds, and releases, 156–58
registration, 147–50
antique vehicles, 158
consolidated, 159
integration of registration and taxation process, 159–61
IRP, 161, 164n73
staggered versus annual systems, 149, *152–53,* 156, 163n50
situs, 150–51
tax year, 156–58
transfers of, 156–57
unregistered, 147, 148, 149
multicounty business reports, 55–56
multiple motor vehicles, consolidated registration of, 159
multiple owners. *See* tenancy ownership
municipalities. *See* cities and towns

N

National Tax Association, 16n32
Native American lands, 174–76, 215n37–40

nature. *See* conservation areas; environmental issues
non-business personal property, 257
nonprofit water and sewer associations, 272
nonreappraisal years, changes to value of real property in, 29, 93, 136–37, 202
North Carolina Constitution, 8–11
  of 1776, 4
  of 1835, 4
  of 1868, 5, 7, 9, 167
  1961 and 1971 amendments, 7
  classification/exemption of property under, 7, 9–10, 167–69
  public purposes only clause, 8–9
  service districts, defining, 10–11
  tax rate limitations, 5–7
  uniform rule requirement, 10
North Carolina Seaport Terminal, items imported through, 253
North Carolina Tax Collectors' Association, 159
notice requirements
  appeal of assessment to Property Tax Commission, 121
  assessed value of property, 114
  exemption/exclusion applications, 113
  relief provisions, 54
nuclear materials, 257–58
nursing homes, 240–41

O

obsolescence of personal property, 98, 107–8n50
out-of-state residents with personal property in North Carolina, 61, 62–64
ownership of property
  deadline for determining, 25, 51–52
  fee simple absolute interest in property, 80n23
  joint owners. *See* tenancy ownership
  motor vehicles, 51, 150
  payment of taxes and, 80–81n42
  personal property, determining ownership of, 47–49
  present-use value assessments, 207–10

qualifying property exemptions
nature of entity owning property, 185–86, 216n51
property gratuitously made available to another, 182–83
real property, types of ownership interests in, 42–43
standing to appeal assessments, 119–20
transfer of ownership. *See* transfer of property

P

parks and drives, public, 260
partnerships, real property owned by, 44
penalties
Address Confidentiality Program, violations of, 77
discovery of unlisted property, 68–69, *69*
public records offenses, 71
permanent listing system for real property, 25, 41, 42, 57, 67, 69, 82n82, 132
personal property, 11, 39–41
abstracts, 47, 52–54
appraisal and assessment, 98–100
of business enterprises. *See under* business enterprises
defined, 39–40
exempt or excluded. *See* exemptions and exclusions
intangible, 39–40, 61, 254
leasehold interests in exempted real property, 40, 79n12, 83n100
listing, 47–52
motor vehicles. *See* motor vehicles
non-business, 257
obsolescence of, 98, 107–8n50
out-of-state residents, 61, 62–64
ownership issues, 47–48
on possession of others, 51–52
public service company property, appraisal and assessment of, 100–105
repairs, in North Carolina for, 264
situs rules. *See* situs
software, 40–41
tangible, 39–40, 61
temporary absence rule, 62–64
temporary or seasonal dwellings, associated with, 62, *65*
tenancy ownership, 50

time-sharing arrangements, 51
transfers. *See* transfers of property
types of, 47
unknown owners, 50
personnel records, confidentiality of, 74
place of property for tax purposes. *See* situs
poll taxes, 4–5
pollution abatement property, 258–59
pollution control facilities, 254
poultry, 259
precious metals, 259
prescription drug samples, 259
present-use value assessments, 200–213, 267–71
agricultural land
defined, 203–4, 267
eligibility for assessment, 200, 203
gross income requirement, 204, 206–7, 269
qualifying use of, 269
sound management program, 203, 205–6
appeal and review, 203
applications for, 202–3, 270
Christmas tree farms, 204, 206, 270
classes of property eligible for, 203–5
conservation/wildlife conservation land, 203, 207, 211–13, 272–73
deferred tax provisions, 200, 210–11, 270–71
forestlands
defined, 205, 267
eligibility for assessment, 200, 203
qualifying use requirements, 269
sound management program, 206
gross income requirement, 204, 206–7
horticultural land
defined, 204–5, 267
eligibility for assessment, 200, 203
gross income requirement, 204, 206–7, 269
qualifying use requirements, 269
sound management program, 205–6
owner eligibility for, 207–10, 267–69

sound management program, 205–6
working waterfront property, 203, 213, 273
Privacy Act, 75
privacy of information in public records, 73–77
private water companies, 272
progressive tax, 12–13, 16n31, 17n48
property factors in appraisal of public service company property, 101, 109n84
property record cards (abstracts), 25, 41, 42, 52–54
Property Tax Commission
administrative duties, 21–22
members, appointment of, 121
nonreappraisal years, changes to value of real property in, 137
review proceedings, 120–32
appeal to Court of Appeals from, 133–35
hearings, 121–23
immaterial irregularities rule, 127–32
notice of appeal to, 121
open meetings law, excepted from, 116
settlements, 132–33
standard of review, 123–27
standing to appeal to, 121, 138–39n15
stay of enforced collection during, 133
property tax in North Carolina, 3–17
administration of. *See* administration of property tax
appeals. *See* appeal and review
appraisal and assessment of. *See* appraisal and assessment
average tax rates, 12
calendar for. *See* calendar
constitutional provisions regarding. *See* North Carolina Constitution
exemptions and exclusions. *See* exemptions and exclusions
historical background, 3, 4–8
as *in rem* versus *in personam* taxes, 3
listing property. *See* listing property for taxation
local government control of, 6
motor vehicles. *See* motor vehicles
personal property. *See* personal property

popular and professional views of, 12–14, 91–92, 106n2
rates. *See* rates of tax
real property. *See* real property
relief. *See* refunds and releases; relief provisions
state powers regarding. *See* state powers
valuation of property. *See* appraisal and assessment
proportional tax, 12–13
prorated taxes, 26–27, 156–58
protected natural areas, 260
public employees, confidentiality of personnel records of, 74
public parks and drives, 260
public records, 70–78. *See also* records and recordkeeping
access to and copies of, 71–72, 85n159
confidential information, 73–77
custody of, 71
defined, 70
GIS databases, 72–73
retention of, 78
transfers of property, 46–47
public service company property, 100–105, *105,* 109n74

Q

qualifying property exemptions. *See under* exemptions and exclusions
Qualla Boundary (Eastern Cherokee Indian Reservation), 174–76, 215n37–40
quitclaim deeds, 46, 80n42

R

radioactive waste, 260
Railroad Revitalization and Regulatory Reform Act of 1976 (4-R Act), 104–5
railway property, appraisal and assessment of, 100–105, *105,* 110n111
rates of tax
actual versus effective rates, 28–29
average tax rates in North Carolina, 12
constitutional limitations on, 5–7
prorating, 26–27

revenue-neutral rates, 29–30, *31,* 33n27–30
setting, 27–30, *31*
real property, 11, 37–39
appraisal and assessment, 91, 92–95
corporation, partnership, or association, owned by, 44
deceased last known owner, 44–45
defined, 37–38
easements, 43
estates in land, 42
exempt or excluded. *See* exemptions and exclusions
fixtures, 38, 79n5
improvements. *See* improvements
leasehold interests in exempted real property, 40, 79n12, 83n100, 256
life estate, subject to, 45
listing procedures, 42–47
manufactured homes
as fixtures, 38
as real property, 11, 39
relationship to mobile homes, 79n8
mortgage or deed of trust, subject to, 44
nonreappraisal years, changes to value in, 136–37
ownership interests, types of, 42–43
permanent listing system for, 25, 41, 42, 57, 67, 69, 82n82, 132
property record cards (abstracts), 25, 41, 42, 52–54
public service company property, appraisal and assessment of, 100–105
rights and privileges, 38–39
roadway corridors, 264
sole proprietorship, ownership in connection to, 44
tenancy ownership, 42–43, 45. *See also* tenancy ownership
time shares, 46
transfers of. *See* transfers of property
unknown owners, 45–46
reappraisal. *See* appraisal and assessment
receipts or income of taxpayers, confidentiality of, 73–74, 86n178
records and recordkeeping
abstracts. *See* abstracts
administration of property taxes, 25–26

board of equalization and review statement, 117
exempt or excluded property, roster of, 199–200
listing real property, 41, 42
public records. *See* public records
transfers of property, 46–47
recycling facilities, 260–62
redaction of confidential information, 75, 76, 86n189
refunds and releases, 227–32
applications for, 231
clerical errors, 228–30
governing body's authority over, 227
illegal purposes, taxes imposed for, 230–31
illegal taxes, 230
motor vehicle taxes, 156–58
regional sports authority property, 262
register of deeds, 56
registration of motor vehicles. *See under* motor vehicles
regressive tax, 12–14, 16n29, 17n48
releases. *See* refunds and releases
relief provisions. *See also* exemptions and exclusions; refunds and releases
notice requirements, 54
public perception of property tax affected by, 13
religious educational assemblies, 262
religious property, 263–64. *See also* subhead "qualifying property exemptions" under exemptions and exclusions
rentals
educational facilities, 255
heavy equipment, 250
local governments, property leased to, 255
short-term rental vehicles, 265
repairs, personal property in North Carolina for, 264
representation of parties to appeal, 139n24
residence, determining, 61
resource recovery facilities, 261–62
retail inventory, 255
retirement homes, 240–41
Revaluation Act of 1919, 6

Revenue Act of 1784, 4
revenue-neutral rates of tax, 29–30, *31,* 33n27–30
review
  of appeals. *See* appeal and review
  exempt or excluded property, annual review of, 199–200
  by Property Tax Commission. *See under* Property Tax Commission
Revolutionary War, 4
rights and privileges pertaining to real property, 38–39
roadway corridors, 264

S

sales assessment ratios, 102–4
sales comparison approach to appraisal, 96, 99, 106n21
sales of property. *See* transfers of property
schools. *See* education
scientific property exemption. *See* subhead "qualifying property exemptions" under exemptions and exclusions
scroll, 26, 37
seasonal or temporary dwellings, personal property associated with, 62, *65*
security features of government information systems, 73
service districts, constitutional power to define, 10–11
Servicemembers Civil Relief Act, 66
settlements
  appeals, 132–33
  discovered amounts, compromising, 69, 84n138
severable development rights, 242
ships. *See* motor vehicles
situs, 25
  business enterprises, property associated with, 62–64, *65*
  decedents, property of, 65
  fiduciaries, property of, 65
  listing requirements, 61–66, *65*
  military services, property of persons serving in, 66
  motor vehicles, 150–51
  out-of-state residents, 61, 62–64
  residence, determining, 61
  tangible versus intangible property, 61

temporary absence rule, 62–64
temporary or seasonal dwellings, property associated with, 62, *65*
Social Security numbers, confidentiality of, 75–76
software, 40–41, 240
solar energy, 265
sole proprietorship, real property owned in connection to, 44
sound management program for present-use value assessments, 205–6
sports authorities, regional, 262
standard of review
Court of Appeals proceedings, 134–35
generally, 123–27
standing timber, 266
standing to appeal assessments, 119–21, 138–39n15
state Constitution. *See* North Carolina Constitution
state government property, exemption from taxation, 168–70, 266
state powers
centralized funding of schools, roads, and prisons, 6–7
classification of property for exclusion or reduced taxation, 7
property, right to tax (1776-1921), 4–6
voter approval for property tax levies, control of, 7
State Privacy Act, 75
stay of enforced collection during appeals, 133
subpoena powers to obtain listing information, 54–55
supplemental financial information, privacy of, 74
system property, appraisal and assessment of, 100–105, *105,* 109n74

T

tangible versus intangible personal property, 39–40, 61
tax assessors, 21–24, 116, 227
tax book, 26
tax collection. *See* collection of taxes
tax collectors, 21, 227
tax credits against motor vehicle taxes, 157–58
tax database, 26
tax identification numbers, confidentiality of, 75–76
tax rates. *See* rates of tax
tax records, 26

tax relief. *See also* exemptions and exclusions; refunds and releases
notice requirements, 54
public perception of property tax affected by, 13
taxability of property, deadline for determining, 25
taxpayers
confidential information, 73–77
defined, 138n2
income or receipts, 73–74, 86n178
telephone company property, appraisal and assessment of, 100–104, *105*
temporary absence rule, 62–64
temporary or seasonal dwellings, personal property associated with, 62, *65*
tenancy ownership
appeals to Property Tax Commission by, 121
joint tenancy, 42–43
of personal property, 50
present-value use assessment, eligibility for, 209
of real property, 42–43, 45
tenants by the entireties, 43, 45
tenants in common, 43, 45, 209, 219n104
tenants, rental. *See* rentals
timber, standing, 266
time-sharing arrangements
personal property, 51
real property, 46
timing. *See* calendar
towns. *See* cities and towns
transfers of property
means of transferring real property, 46–47
motor vehicles, 156–57
prorated taxes on, 26–27
public records evidencing, 46–47
transportation. *See also* motor vehicles
aircraft
antique, 237
flight equipment of air couriers, 248
appraisal and assessment of rail, air, bus, and motor carrier company property, 100–105, *105,* 110n111

roadway corridors, 264
Turnpike Authority property, 264
Turnpike Authority property, 264

U

undeveloped property, present-use value assessment of. *See* present-use value assessments
uniform rule requirement, 10
uniformed services
defined, 83n111
disabled veterans
motor vehicles, specially equipped, 242
real property exclusion, 193
situs rules, 66
veterans organizations, property of, 271. *See also* subhead "qualifying property exemptions" under exemptions and exclusions
unknown owners
of personal property, 50
of real property, 45–46
unlisted property, discovery of. *See* discovery of unlisted property
unregistered motor vehicles, 147, 148, 149
Use-Value Advisory Board, 202, 206, 221n150
use value assessments. *See* present-use value assessments
utilities property
nonprofit water and sewer associations, 272
private water companies, 272
public service company property, appraisal and assessment of, 100–105, *105*
solar energy, 265

V

vacation homes, personal property associated with, 62, *65*
valuation of property. *See* appraisal and assessment
vehicle identification numbers (VINs), 76
veterans. *See* uniformed services
VINs (vehicle identification numbers), 76

W

warranty deed, transfer of real property by, 46, 80n37
water and sewer associations, nonprofit, 272
water companies, private, 272
waterfront property, working, present-use value assessment of, 203, 213, 273
wholesale inventory, 255
wildlife conservation. *See* conservation areas
will, transfer of property by, 46, 47
woodlands. *See* forestlands
working waterfront property, present-use value assessment of, 203, 213, 273